THE LEGAL SCHOLAR'S
GUIDEBOOK

ASPEN COURSEBOOK SERIES

THE LEGAL SCHOLAR'S GUIDEBOOK

ELIZABETH E. BERENGUER
Associate Professor of Law and Director,
Upper Level Writing
Norman Adrian Wiggins School of Law
Campbell University

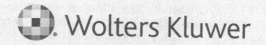

Wolters Kluwer

Published by Wolters Kluwer in New York.

Wolters Kluwer Legal & Regulatory U.S. serves customers worldwide with CCH, Aspen Publishers, and Kluwer Law International products. (www.WKLegaledu .com)

Cover Image: iStock.com/Misha Shutkevych

To contact Customer Service, e-mail customer.service@wolterskluwer.com, call 1-800-234-1660, fax 1-800-901-9075, or mail correspondence to:

Wolters Kluwer
Attn: Order Department
PO Box 990
Frederick, MD 21705

Printed in the United States of America.

1 2 3 4 5 6 7 8 9 0

ISBN 978-1-5438-1305-0

Library of Congress Cataloging-in-Publication Data

Names: Berenguer, Elizabeth E., author.
Title: The legal scholar's guidebook / Elizabeth E. Berenguer.
Description: First edition. | New York : Wolters Kluwer, 2020. | Includes index. | Summary: "This textbook will provide detailed guidance for individuals drafting scholarly legal writing including law review articles, casenotes, and seminar papers. It guides writers through topic selection, preemption checking, researching, evaluating sources, outlining, and drafting the scholarly article. It also teaches students the value of critical reading, critical thinking, and development of analytical frameworks"— Provided by publisher.
Identifiers: LCCN 2019046201 (print) | LCCN 2019046202 (ebook) | ISBN 9781543813050 (spiral bound) | ISBN 9781543820874 (ebook)
Subjects: LCSH: Legal composition. Classification: LCC KF250 .B47 2020 (print) | LCC KF250 (ebook) | DDC 808.06/634 —dc23 LC record available at https://lccn.loc.gov/2019046201 LC ebook record available at https://lccn.loc.gov/2019046202

About Wolters Kluwer Legal & Regulatory U.S.

Wolters Kluwer Legal & Regulatory U.S. delivers expert content and solutions in the areas of law, corporate compliance, health compliance, reimbursement, and legal education. Its practical solutions help customers successfully navigate the demands of a changing environment to drive their daily activities, enhance decision quality and inspire confident outcomes.

Serving customers worldwide, its legal and regulatory portfolio includes products under the Aspen Publishers, CCH Incorporated, Kluwer Law International, ftwilliam.com and MediRegs names. They are regarded as exceptional and trusted resources for general legal and practice-specific knowledge, compliance and risk management, dynamic workflow solutions, and expert commentary.

To all the voices longing to be heard.

SUMMARY OF CONTENTS

CONTENTS

Contents

Contents

PREFACE[1]

They say necessity is the mother of invention, and necessity is certainly what created this textbook. In Fall 2017, I began teaching a course called Foundations of Critical Legal Thought, Research and Scholarship, but I could not find a textbook to guide students through the process of scholarly writing. Over the course of a few semesters, I found myself creating volumes of material for the students enrolled in the course. I also saw these students successfully progress through their dissertation projects. I realized that by writing a textbook, I could make these materials more easily accessible to my own students as well as other burgeoning scholars.

The first question any reader of this book should ask is, "Why produce scholarship?" Scholarship may be written for the purpose of pursuing a degree, completing a seminar or other course, or achieving membership in a society or prestigious group, such as law review. Many professors initially begin producing scholarship for the purpose of achieving tenure. Tenure is a prestigious status that offers a sense of security to a professor; it is also a recognition of a certain level of achievement as an educator and scholar. In law school, students on law review produce scholarship, and they also review and edit scholarship written by other people. Law students produce scholarship nearly any time they enroll in a course that is assessed with a final paper as opposed to a final exam. Lawyers and judges may also produce scholarship for the purpose of advancing their careers or continuing their education through self-directed study.

When I first began teaching in 2008, I had no idea what my scholarly agenda would be. I was told, "You must write!" But I really had no idea how to go about writing scholarship. To make matters worse, I was a legal writing teacher — can you imagine my embarrassment at being a writing

---

1. A version of the thoughts and words in this Preface was previously published as *In Defense of Scholarship*, 27 The Second Draft: The Official Magazine of the Legal Writing Inst., no. 1, Summer 2013, at 4 (http://www.lwionline.org/uploads/FileUpload/LWISecondDraft_vol27no1b.pdf).

teacher yet not knowing how to write scholarship myself? I searched high and low for a book to guide me because I was truly afraid of asking advice. I was terrified of being exposed as an impostor. When I finally mustered the courage to ask for advice, I was told, "Writing scholarship is just like writing an appellate brief. You'll figure it out." Well, half of that was true—I did figure it out, but I learned that scholarly writing is nothing like appellate brief writing.

I stumbled through my first three articles before I found a generous mentor who began teaching me how to approach scholarship. Dr. Linda Coco showed me how to expand the scope of resources I was consulting. She introduced me to new thinkers—not just legal minds, but philosophers, sociologists, criminologists, and others. She exposed me to the concept of analytical frameworks and demonstrated how to critically analyze them in other scholars' work. We brainstormed ideas for scholarship. She helped me map out my articles on a white board. She also asked my advice on her articles, which furthered my development as a critical thinker and writer.

Over time, I found I had indeed become a scholar. And I felt proud of my work. The processes I have learned are laid out for you in this book. While I wish that a resource like this had existed when I first began writing, I am grateful for the opportunity to pay it forward.

For those pursuing a scholarly agenda, it becomes our responsibility to participate in a larger conversation, evolve our minds, and continually question our status quo for the benefit of those areas of society impacted by our scholarship. So often I have heard professors lament how they "have" to publish, how they "have" to get tenure, or how they "have" to check one more thing off their "list." Students express similar complaints when working on law review or completing a course or dissertation-based degree. I also hear people ask, "What is the purpose of this degree?" Or, "What do you expect to accomplish by writing this scholarship?"

This attitude is disheartening because writing is an opportunity for personal growth and edification, meaningful contribution to a community, and it can even be fun. Sure, writing can be difficult; if it were easy, everyone would be doing it. Most scholars possess some passion for learning, though, and engaging in research and scholarship teaches us in a way that is far more active, comprehensive, and meaningful than passive classroom learning could ever be. By participating in a larger scholarly conversation, we enrich our own understanding of the world around us, and once we begin understanding it, we can contribute to that conversation in a meaningful way. That is one way we can leave our mark on this world.

Scholarly research and writing also activates a healthy evolution of the mind. Scholars who do not challenge themselves through research and writing may find that they stagnate in their professions or become frustrated with problems and broken processes that seemingly have no solution. Not only do individual scholarly endeavors promote a healthy academic environment at educational institutions, they also promote better practice of law and a higher level of student engagement in the classroom.

The evolution of ideas inevitably leads to a questioning of the status quo, and this type of questioning serves to legitimize the very existence of societal institutions, especially educational and legal institutions. Critically assessing the foundation of ideas leads not only to a better understanding of those ideas, but it can also lead to new discoveries and ways of understanding them. Part of becoming and being a lawyer is learning how to engage in a professional and respectful pattern of questioning and investigation. Lawyers must critically assess evidence and witness statements, they must thoroughly consider and resolve weaknesses in their cases, and they must question the premises for their arguments to ensure they are invulnerable to attack. Scholars perform similar activities when we critically assess, consider, and resolve weaknesses in the law and theories. Questioning the law and theories ensures any assessments meaningfully contribute to the discourse. So, for anyone engaged in the scholarly process, these skills can be relevantly translated into the field of professor, lawyer, judge, or student.

Before embarking on your scholarly journey, I would like to share one more personal experience. On one of my editing days, I spent two hours working on one paragraph. Just one. But I did not feel the time at all. I distinctly recall seeing the clock at 1:18 p.m., and then again at 3:23 p.m. I peered back up and felt shocked that an entire two hours had passed by. The writing and thinking process held me in such a trance that time ceased to matter; I became one with the words on my page. A few days later, once I finished the final edits, I felt exhausted in that enormously proud way that you do when you have accomplished something truly meaningful. Although my family thought I was crazy to spend my Thanksgiving break working so hard, I felt more sane than ever. That compulsion to finish the article could not be hampered by their relentless pleas to join them. Studying, contemplating, and writing that article brought me alive, and once I finished and joined them, they shared in that vibrant energy created through my work. In the course of writing and answering one question, I also developed a long list of many more questions I now wish to study and explore. Every time I write an article, a list of so many other articles I am compelled to write awakens in me.

For me, I write because my mind needs to express the ideas it contains. Of course, it is a plus that my ideas can contribute to a larger discourse community and (hopefully) add value to the existing ideas. The goal of achieving tenure has been an added bonus, but I would still write even if I were not eligible for tenure. Researching, thinking, and writing help to create an enduring legacy. Scholarship helps me absorb the imprint of the world as I leave my own mark.

My hope for you is that you join me as a scholar in studying complex questions and wrestling with challenging problems. I look forward to hearing your voice and experiencing the mark you make.

Elizabeth Berenguer

ACKNOWLEDGEMENTS

This book would not have been possible without the support and understanding of my devoted husband, Paul, and my extraordinary children, Cydni, Jake, Mills, Nate, and Cate. Thank you for the boundless love, space to write, and encouragement to complete this project. I love you more than you know, and I hope I have made you proud.

I am indebted to the entire legal writing community for its generosity in sharing wisdom and support. I offer special thanks to Ellen Podgor who offered valuable insight and guidance early in my career to help me develop into the scholar I am today. I am also particularly grateful to my mentors and friends, Linda Coco, Teri McMurtry-Chubb, and Lucy Jewel. This project would not have been completed without your feedback and support. Thank you for giving me a place at your table. I am humbled to be a part of your conversation.

To my family, I appreciate you all more than you know. Thank you, Mama and Daddy, for teaching me that the limits my mind imposes are merely barriers calling to be broken. To Mo, thank you for sitting me down as a little girl and teaching me to write poetry and short stories. Those lessons taught me the discipline demanded of a writer. To Mami, thank you for always being unquestionably proud of me. I miss you every day.

Photo and image credits: Photos by Rich Burkhart (Chapter 5) and Eric Brehm, Court Atkins Group, Bluffton, SC (Chapter 6).

5.2. Universal Intellectual Standards. Adapted from "Universal Intellectual Standards," by Linda Elder & Richard Paul from The Foundation for Critical Thinking, http://www.critical thinking.org/pages/universal-intellectual-standards/527.

Introduction

This book is a guide for students, academics, and anyone who seeks to study and ponder complex questions. Because I am a lawyer and law professor, I refer to legal analysis and legal questions throughout the book. The processes described in this book, however, can be adapted to many other disciplines. This book is helpful for professors who wish to produce scholarship, students who wish to write for law review, students in seminar courses or dissertation-based advanced degree programs, or professionals who want to publish scholarship. The desired end-product of these processes is the production of scholarship.

Scholarship is the written analysis of a complex question or issue, and it can take a variety of forms, as will be more fully explained in Chapter 6. Just like a research paper written in secondary school is a natural progression from the five-paragraph essays written in primary school, scholarship is a natural progression from the research paper. A research paper generally reports information that the writer has learned from other sources, but it does not typically call for independent evaluation or additional input by the author regarding the author's inferences about the implications of the research. The research paper is more of a synthesized report or survey of information that already exists.

Like a research paper, scholarship depends on accurate reporting, but it also demands the author contribute something new, novel, and unique to the body of existing research. A scholar must have independent ideas and make inferences about the significance or meaning of the information. Most people reading this book will be familiar with how to write a research paper and may even possess some expertise related to drafting a research paper. This knowledge will be helpful in the initial stages of the scholarly project. What is likely new for most reading this book is the contribution of your own thoughts on the topic. Although scholarly authors often desire to be published, publication is not what makes a written analysis scholarship. Scholarship is created when a question

1

is deliberately and thoughtfully researched, pondered, and studied in written form.

Many scholars face impostor syndrome — "Who am I to say anything about anything?" This fear of being exposed as a fraud is natural, albeit unnerving. When you begin your project, you may have an idea of what you want to contribute to the body of research, or you might feel completely clueless. Either way, you must be open to being informed by the research. When I began my first two scholarly articles, I thought I clearly knew what I wanted to say. As I researched and wrote, however, I realized that my initial hypothesis was wrong. Ultimately, I changed my conclusion because the research demanded I change my mind. In more recent years, I often start with a question but no definitive answer to the question. The research tells me the answer. In fact, research is the *only* way to quiet the impostor voice. As long as you approach the research with an open mind, you, too, will figure out what it is you have to say, and it will be a valuable contribution to the world in which we live. At the end of each chapter, you will find two sections that can help you kill the impostor. The Never Forget, You **Can** Do This! section offers advice on what to expect at each stage of the process. It is helpful for reassuring yourself that what you are experiencing is a natural part of the process. The Squelch the Impostor section includes helpful tips for identifying the impostor and specific actions you can take to quiet the voice.

This book has been designed to make the scholarly writing process more accessible to nascent scholars. It offers a detailed process that is likely to lead a scholar to produce sound scholarship. Though the book lays out the process in a linear fashion, scholarly projects require a recursive process. So, most readers will find themselves revisiting earlier chapters even once they have progressed to a later phase of the project.

WHAT TO EXPECT IN EACH CHAPTER

Chapter 1 covers topic selection. Scholars who have a good idea of what they want to say will be able to use the processes explained in the chapter to further refine their topic to a manageable scope. Scholars who have yet to decide what they want to research will also find Chapter 1 helpful in learning how to identify topics to research and then refining those topics to a manageable scope.

Chapters 2, 3, and 4 provide detailed processes for developing strategies for identifying resources, conducting a preemption check, and managing relevant resources. If you have never written a scholarly article, you have limited experience (perhaps no experience) conducting the kind of research that is necessary to produce sound analysis. The process can be overwhelming. You may not know when to stop, you may not know where to start, or you may not understand how to process all the information that exists on your topic. Chapter 2 will guide you on choosing databases and other broad strategies for research. Chapter 3 will guide you on using research strategies to verify that your topic is unique. Chapter 4 will guide you on managing and organizing the volume of information.

Chapter 5 explains analytical frameworks and provides detailed instruction on how to identify, adopt, and adapt analytical frameworks to a given scholarly project. A strong analytical framework is one of the primary characteristics that legitimizes scholarship because it ensures you are employing a systematic method of inquiry. It offers a lens for scrutinizing a legal question. It is the key component that makes a paper full-fledged scholarly analysis rather than a mere research paper. Chapter 5 also explains Universal Intellectual Standards and will guide you in validating your research by questioning whether your sources meet those standards. Additionally, it provides strategies for ensuring the standards are met in your own work.

Finally, Chapter 6 provides information about the most common organizational paradigms and strategies for transforming your research into scholarship. This chapter guides you in creating structure for your final written project and provides strategies for adding your own ideas to the existing body of scholarly work on your topic. You will learn how to take the volumes of information you have researched and organize them into a coherent written document in support of your thesis.

The Appendixes offer various resources. Appendixes I through VIII provide sample assignments for each of the chapters to give you an idea of what your own assignment might look like. These sample assignments are related to the Megale article printed in Appendix IX so you can clearly see how the assignments move the project through the essential prewriting phases to ultimately produce a solid piece of scholarship.

The assignments are a critical component of your scholarly project. If you take the time to complete each assignment, you will see your scholarly project unfold in a timely and predictable way. You should also be willing to repeat some of the assignments. For example, your first topic selection essay will be too broad—everyone's is. As you work through the research strategies explained in Chapters 2, 3, and 4, you will gain knowledge that will cause you to refine your topic into a thesis. During this process, it would be helpful to revise your topic selection essay to capture this new knowledge. Do not see this revision as a waste of time; on the contrary, it is a critical part of the recursive process required for producing sound scholarship.

Appendix IX is comprised of two scholarly papers, Elizabeth Megale, *A Call for Change: A Contextual-Configurative Analysis of Florida's "Stand Your Ground" Laws*, 68 U. Miami L. Rev. 1052 (2014), and Anna Stearns, *Patch by Patch: North Carolina's Crazy Quilt of Campaign Finance Regulation*, 40 Campbell L. Rev. 669 (2018). They are both annotated in Appendix IX to highlight their analytical frameworks. Analytical frameworks are discussed in Chapter 4.

The Megale article is one I wrote in 2014 under my former married name. I have chosen this article because it is a detailed and explicit example of the concepts and strategies I describe. Any time you see a reference to work by Elizabeth Megale or Elizabeth Berenguer, I am referencing my own work. While there are many scholars who use the strategies I have described in this book, I have chosen to rely on my own work for a few reasons. First, I want you to see that I practice what I preach. By using my own work, you can see for yourself the end product of following the advice in this book. Second, I am intimately familiar with my own work, so I can offer you depth of insight into the processes that led to the production of the final paper. Third, most scholarly papers do not require such an explicit description of analytical framework as provided in the article reproduced in Appendix IX. Analytical frameworks are difficult to understand; it is perhaps the most complex topic covered in this book. Because it is so explicit, this article is particularly good as a teaching tool for this concept.

That said, your final product will probably not be nearly as complex as my article. For that reason, I have also included the Stearns comment in Appendix IX. This comment was written by a former Campbell Law student and is a good example of the type of final product you might expect from yourself. I supervised her writing of this paper and guided her through all of the strategies outlined in this book. I chose her comment because I am intimately familiar with the process she used to produce the final piece and can attest that she followed the strategies outlined in this book. You can see for yourself the quality of the final product. Because I worked directly with her, I can also offer you specific insights into the development of the analytical framework.

At the end of Appendix IX, I have included excerpted tables of contents from a few other scholarly works to demonstrate the organizational paradigms and different types of scholarly papers explained in Chapter 6. From the table of contents, you can easily see the broadscale organization of each one. I have chosen papers that cover the same general topic but utilize different organizational paradigms. In the interest of conserving space (and protecting your wallet), I have not reproduced them in their entirety, but I invite you to pull them and read them for yourself. They are all good examples of strong scholarly analysis.

Appendixes X and XI provide helpful editing information regarding citations, grammar, and punctuation. Appendix X on citations is not intended to be a replacement for a comprehensive citation guidebook, such as the *ALWD Guide to Legal Citation* or *The Bluebook: A Uniform System of Citation*. It is a helpful guide in the initial drafting stages and it will help you easily navigate your citation guidebook when you begin editing, proofreading, and polishing. Similarly, Appendix XI is not a comprehensive grammar, style, or usage manual. It emphasizes some of the most common issues you might expect to see in your own work, and it provides useful checklists as you work through the revision, editing, proofreading, and polishing stages of the project.

The chapters in this book are designed to be concise because scholars should focus their time reading the resources relevant to their projects. Where helpful, I have provided examples of the processes and concepts. Each chapter includes a Brainstorm at the beginning and an Assignment at the end. The Brainstorm questions should be answered before you read each chapter because they are designed to put you in the right frame of mind for that particular chapter. It may be that you cannot answer all the questions before reading the chapter, and you should ponder and attempt to answer them as you progress through the chapter.

The assignments at the end of each chapter will help you advance the scholarly project through all the essential pre-writing stages. If you are diligent in completing the assignments, the scholarly project should naturally unfold. The topic selection essay at the end of Chapter 1 will likely be a much broader topic than you ultimately choose, but this essay is the first step in identifying a topic and direction for the project. Throughout the research and preemption phases, you will continue to refine the topic and discover what else has been said about it. The working bibliography and research summary assignments are designed to help you track what has been done and stay focused on the narrow question the project is designed to explore. These assignments naturally lead to the annotated outline, which merges the working bibliography with the research summary and adds in your own thoughts, ideas, and intuitions on the thesis. This annotated outline is then converted into a scholarly article as you build a strong analytical framework around an appropriate organizational paradigm. These final assignments help you establish structure and produce scholarship that is understandable, coherent, organized, and obviously relevant to the field.

Since the process of creating scholarship is recursive, you may from time to time not only revisit earlier chapters, but also revise earlier assignments. As I mentioned earlier, if the research process has led you to want to explore a more refined question than originally identified in the topic selection essay, then it may be helpful to draft a new topic selection essay or modify your research plan. Writing the essay will help you find focus, and it will be a useful artifact to revisit in the research phase to stay on track. Similarly, as you begin to write the article, you may discover that some research is incomplete and that phase needs to be revisited, or you may determine that the chosen analytical framework is not working well for the development of the article and you need to choose a different one. Revisiting earlier stages and assignments is a natural part of the scholarly process that you must embrace.

IDENTIFYING A MENTOR AND SUPPORT COMMUNITY

It is important for you to identify a supportive community during the scholarly writing process. This community may be comprised of teachers, colleagues, or classmates. If you are a student writing for a seminar, your professor is likely your mentor. If you are writing for law review, you may have been assigned a mentor who is a student or a professor. If you are exploring scholarship on your own, your mentor may be a more experienced scholar in the field you wish to study.

As you work through each phase of the project, it is important to check in with your mentor and support community. Their input should challenge you, and if you have completed too much work without checking in, you might discover that you have to revisit or rework major parts of the project. It is incredibly frustrating to have to redo large chunks of work after you have already invested so much time in developing your thesis. Your supportive community can help you work through the frustration and exhaustion, and you can minimize frustration and exhaustion by checking in frequently.

As I mentioned before, impostor syndrome is bound to rear its ugly head. Your mentor and support community can help you conquer the impostor by reminding you that you are capable and your voice is valuable. You can also use the Never Forget, You **Can** Do This! and Squelch the Impostor sections of each chapter to reassure yourself, identify impostor syndrome, and quiet the voice. When you are feeling overwhelmed, visit these sections in the chapter that corresponds to the stage where you are in the process.

These projects can also seem interminable at times. If you follow the steps in this book and trust the process, you will produce scholarship in time. Each project has its own lifespan. Speaking from personal experience, I have written some articles in a weekend, and others have taken more than five years. With persistence and commitment, you can and will accomplish your goals of producing excellent scholarship.

HOW TO USE THIS BOOK

If this book has been assigned to you by a professor in association with a class, follow the syllabus or agenda provided by your professor. If you are working on your own or your professor has not provided a specific agenda, I suggest approaching the book as follows:

1. Lightly read Chapters 1-4. The first four chapters give you a broad overview of what you will be doing in the early stages of your project. You will probably spend most of your time researching and thinking; the writing probably will take less time than the researching and thinking.
2. Carefully read Chapter 1. If you have a good idea of what you want to say, go ahead and write your topic selection essay. If you do not have a good idea of what you want to say, move on to Chapter 2.
3. Carefully read Chapter 2. Begin gathering as much data as possible. If you have not yet written your topic selection essay, revisit Chapter 1 once you have an idea of what you want to say and complete your essay. Once your essay is written, move on to Chapter 3. You cannot conduct an effective preemption check until you know

what you want to say, so do not move on to Chapter 3 until your topic selection essay is complete.

4. Carefully read Chapter 3. Conduct your preemption check and take careful notes regarding any sources that are related to and similar to what you plan to say. It will be beneficial to revise your topic selection essay to account for any related scholarship that you plan to address in the final paper. Take copious notes about how you plan to distinguish yourself from any similar sources.

5. Lightly read Chapters 5 and 6, and carefully read Chapter 4. Through the preemption checking process, you should have organized and prioritized your materials. This is a good time to start conceptualizing how your research will become a final product. Chapters 4 and 5 will give you the information you need to start visualizing a final product. Chapter 4 will guide you as you carefully read your sources and begin drafting your research summary. Your notes should include details about the source and page number, the author's position, your impressions, and the significance of the source for your project. Revisit Chapters 1, 2, and 3 as necessary to continually refine your topic into an actual thesis and ensure your research is comprehensive and complete.

6. Carefully read Chapter 5. Dig even deeper into your resources and turn your research notes into a full-fledged research summary. Cross-reference throughout so you can begin to see themes, topics, and sub-topics emerge in anticipation of drafting your annotated outline, and ultimately your final product.

7. Carefully read Chapter 6. Begin to frame your thoughts around concepts instead of sources. Convert your research summary into an annotated outline. Settle in on the type of document you are drafting and choose an organizational paradigm. If you have been assigned a specific type of document, like a comment or note, study the conventions for that type of scholarly work. If you have not been assigned a specific type of document, decide what you want to write.

Because scholarly writing is recursive, you might feel like you are spinning your wheels from time to time. If you begin to feel this way, the following guide may help you figure out your next step.

Visit Chapter 1:

- Early in the process to choose your topic and begin refining it into a thesis

- Anytime you begin to feel overwhelmed with the research
- When the impostor voice tells you that you have nothing unique to say
- When you think you have been preempted
- When you have any revelations about further refining your topic into a thesis

Visit Chapter 2:

- Early in the process to create your research plan
- When you feel stuck in the research
- When you are struggling to find a source
- When you refine your topic into a more specific thesis

Visit Chapter 3:

- Once you have written your topic selection essay
- If you discover a source that is very similar to what you had planned to say
- When you refine your topic into a more specific thesis

Visit Chapter 4:

- Once you have written your topic selection essay
- When you are ready to begin careful study of your sources
- When your preemption check is mostly complete
- When you refine your topic into a more specific thesis
- When you feel stuck in the research process
- When you are trying to figure out the significance of a resource
- When you are trying to understand how your own thoughts fit into the broader conversation

Visit Chapter 5:

- Later in the process once you start carefully reading your sources
- When you are engaged in careful study of other sources
- When you verify your sources comport with Universal Intellectual Standards
- When you try to identify analytical frameworks in your sources
- When you try to develop your own analytical framework
- When you refine your topic into a more specific thesis
- When you create your research summary
- When you convert your research summary into an annotated outline

Visit Chapter 6:

- Later in the research process once you start carefully reading your sources
- After you have completed your research summary
- Once you have a clear idea of what you want to say
- After you refine your topic into a more specific thesis
- When you create your annotated outline

Never forget, you can do this!

CHAPTER **1**

What in the World Should I Write About?

Topic Brainstorm

What areas of the law are interesting to me?

Why did I come to law school?

Is there a social problem that might have a legal solution?

Is there a cultural problem that might have a legal solution?

Is there an economic problem that might have a legal solution?

Is there a case that seems unfair, discriminatory, ineffective, or wrong?

Is there a legal principle that seems unfair, discriminatory, ineffective, or wrong?

Is there a law that seems unfair, discriminatory, ineffective, or wrong?

Is there a gap in the law that needs to be filled in order to protect someone or a group, advance socially sound policies, or prevent social or cultural harm?

A good scholarly article makes a novel claim that is nonobvious, useful, and sound to both the writer and the reader.[1] In other words, it should be interesting, manageable, and significant to both you and the community at large, however you define community. This chapter will help you identify a broad topic, narrow it down, find focus, define a specific question, and determine the broad category that encompasses the legal question.

---

1. Eugene Volokh, *Academic Legal Writing: Law Review Articles, Student Notes, Seminar Papers, and Getting on Law Review* (5th ed. 2016); Elizabeth Fajans & Mary R. Falk, *Scholarly Writing for Law Students: Seminar Papers, Law Review Notes, and Law Review Competition Papers* (5th ed. 2017).

By the end of this chapter, you should be able to hypothesize a solution to a question of legal importance. A question is important when it identifies a law-related problem, reveals an injustice, highlights inconsistency in the law, or shows a gap in the law. As you will learn in this chapter, questions of legal importance may arise from myriad sources—proposed or recent legislation, recent court opinions, concurring or dissenting court opinions, or circuit splits, to name just a few. Important questions are also timely, meaning that they relate to a current legal issue, not necessarily a past or future problem unless the past or future issue is somehow related to present-day issues. For example, legal questions related to climate may address future problems or past causes, but they are simultaneously relevant today because solutions must be implemented now to prevent inevitable future harm. On the other hand, a legal issue regarding funding for military space forces to protect against space pirates is too futuristic to have much relevance in today's world. While it may be interesting, it is probably not the most important or timely topic about which a scholar might write.

As you consider a potential topic, you should gauge the depth and breadth of your interest in the general subject matter as well as the specific question you wish to answer. You should also consider how much you already know about the topic, how deeply entrenched your preexisting opinions about the topic might be, whether there are any other biases that may influence your ability to objectively research and analyze the issue, how much has already been written about the topic, and whether resources are readily available for you to research.

1.1 | IN THE BEGINNING

Chances are, if you are reading this book, you have some idea of a broad topic you are interested in exploring. But even if you do not have an idea for a topic yet, there is no need to worry. In fact, sometimes our preconceived notions rein us in too much and make it difficult to narrow the topic to a manageable legal question. The process of scholarly writing necessarily involves whittling a topic down to a precise question, so coming into this project with a blank slate and an open mind can be a liberating opportunity.

When you are choosing a topic, be careful not to get lost in a sea of abstraction. It can be tempting to choose a broad topic like the "Fourth

Amendment" or "free speech." Defining a topic as an entire doctrine is going to be unmanageable, and you will be able to do little more than describe the area of law; likely, you will not even be able to describe it completely or accurately. This type of topic is just too vast and nuanced to be tackled in a single project.

1.2 | BITE OFF WHAT YOU CAN CHEW

Notwithstanding the caution above, identifying an area of law that interests you is an important first step to focusing on a manageable topic. Narrowing down a discrete topical question can initially seem overwhelming. There are infinite questions and problems that could have a legal solution, and you have to live with this problem for several months (or even years), so you should choose a question that will maintain your interest. As you attempt to narrow your topic, continually ask yourself: "What single question continually piques my interest?"

As you work through identifying the discrete question, your initial thought process for narrowing down a topic like the "Fourth Amendment" to a manageable project might look something like this:

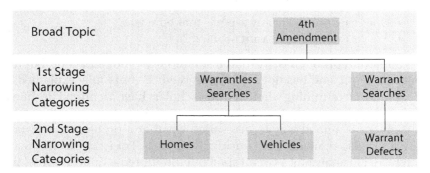

You would continue to narrow down in this fashion, perhaps eight or ten levels more, before identifying one single question to answer. As you move through the process, explore the law to uncover areas that have not been obviously addressed by existing doctrine. Identifying gaps in the law is a good way to find a question that is ripe for exploration.

Keep in mind that the topic you identify needs to be one you can concretely define in a way that conveys meaning to your audience. Identifying your audience is frequently easy. If you are writing a seminar paper, your most important audience is your professor. Similarly, if you are drafting a dissertation, your most important audience is your review panel. For scholars seeking general publication, however, audience might be difficult to ascertain. If you are entering a conversation, as more fully explained in section 1.4, your audience may be other scholars who are studying the same issues. If you are analyzing a circuit split, your audience may be the courts and other lawyers. Identifying potential audience is important because it helps you define the scope and breadth of your article.

Once you have determined who your audience is likely to be, you must figure out how your audience will understand the issue you have identified and how receptive your audience will be to your proposed solution. Your audience's understanding of the meaning will influence how much background you should include and how much attention you should give to counterarguments. It may even influence which counterarguments are relevant. If you relegate yourself to the sea of abstraction, not only will you have difficulty defining or describing the topic generally, but your audience will likely not understand the meaning and will lose interest in what you are saying.

As you continue to refine the topic, you will also want to keep these guidelines in mind:

- Is the topic interesting to you?
- Does the topic have any aspects that bore you?
- Are you solving a relevant problem?

A relevant problem is one that resonates with your audience, has not been resolved, and has not been preempted, as more fully explained in Chapter 3. Determining whether other scholars have identified the question or whether courts, lawyers, or legislatures have been wrestling with a problem is a good way to determine whether a problem is relevant. You must also remember to consider timeliness. For example, if you are interested in analyzing a circuit split, but the Supreme Court resolves the split before your article is published, your article is no longer timely and likely has lost relevance. Similarly, geographic scope should be a serious consideration. Sometimes, limiting your analysis to an issue arising in a single state narrows the potential audience too much and makes your article less relevant, generally speaking. On the other hand, if a particular jurisdiction is an outlier regarding a particular legal issue, it may be a worthy question to study. For example, when Colorado decriminalized marijuana, a study of the regulatory and statutory scheme would have been relevant in a broader geographic scope because other states were soon to move in the same direction and a national audience was interested in the issue.

1.3 | FIND FOCUS

Remember that you don't need to try to solve every aspect of every problem, and your thoughts do not have to be wholly unique and disconnected from anything else that has ever been studied. What is important is that you identify something that has not yet been said. You can bring a new and unique perspective

> As you contemplate your topic, persistently narrow it down. More often than not, a writer finds that the topic is too broad to thoroughly study and the project becomes overwhelming. Find one focus, one angle, and run with that.

to a topic even if it has been explored by other scholars. Though it may not seem logical at this stage of your project, you can in fact organize an entire article around a single unique perspective on a legal question. In fact, the best scholarly articles are those that narrow down to a single, salient idea and fully explore its implications.

When you choose a topic that other scholars have already been exploring, you are essentially entering into a conversation with these other authors. It is important that your article be more than just a rebuttal or sequel to something someone else has already written. Instead of focusing on writing responsively, focus on establishing your thesis and acknowledging how your position fits into the broader conversation. You must acknowledge others who are already in conversation and address how their positions are flawed, incomplete, or otherwise not as valid as the position you are advancing. As you take notes and digest the research, document your impressions so you can easily explain how your position fits into the existing discourse. Chapters 5 and 6 on developing analytical frameworks and organizing the final article provide more information about how to enter a conversation with other scholars.

1.4 | FIND IDEAS

Ideas for topics can come from a variety of sources. Perhaps you have taken a class that has piqued your curiosity about a particular area of the law. Maybe you came to law school to prepare yourself to fight against a great social injustice. It could be that you have become increasingly concerned about issues that you find repeatedly appearing on the news or at the Supreme Court. The law pervades all aspects of society, so your topic could derive from just about anywhere.

> A research agenda naturally evolves as you develop a scholarly project. Most scholars find they identify more questions than they answer. Tracking those additional questions creates a research agenda for future scholarly projects.

Case law is one place ripe for finding topics. The rationale of cases themselves often raise significant legal questions, particularly when it comes to applying precedent through *stare decisis*. Many times, the cases included in law school casebooks have already identified questions left unanswered by a case or a line of cases. If a specific case has captured your interest, these questions can provide a good start for narrowing down your topic. Additionally, dicta, concurring opinions, and dissenting opinions are ripe for mining topics. These areas of cases often reveal the competing policy interests related to a given area of law, and they can also help us predict how the law might evolve. As you read cases, look for phrases like "[w]ithout addressing the broad question"[2] or "the unanswerable questions."[3]

MINING A DISSENT FOR SCHOLARLY INQUIRY

In *Plessy v. Ferguson*, despite denigrating individuals of non-white races as inferior to those of the white race, Justice Harlan wrote a dissent challenging the doctrine of separate but equal. Yet, more than 50 years passed before the Supreme Court, in *Brown v. Board of Education*, accepted the argument that separate can never be equal. In the interim, this dissent could have served as excellent fodder for a scholarly article on a number of related questions, such as:

- Can separate ever be equal?
- Is separate but equal a legitimate legal dichotomy?
- Should racial "purity" matter in the eyes of the law?
- How can the myth of white as a superior race be effectively challenged?

What other scholarly questions come to your mind based on this single dissent?

---

2. *Pruett v. Commercial Bank of Ga.*, 211 Ga. App. 692, 693 (1994).
3. *Rucho v. Common Cause*, No. 18-422, slip op. at 28 (U.S. June 27, 2019).

The practice of law is another place where scholarly questions present themselves. If you have had the opportunity to work in a law firm, at legal aid, or with some other legal institution, you might have been exposed to questions that you are curious to answer. Speaking from personal experience, my practice greatly influenced my initial choices for scholarly research. Shortly before entering academia, I represented an individual accused of aggravated battery and we faced a question regarding whether Florida's recently passed Stand Your Ground law applied. When I began identifying topics for scholarly research, this case continued to haunt me, and I decided to explore the law in depth. That first article led to an entire research agenda on Florida's Stand Your Ground laws, and I have since written four scholarly articles on various aspects of the law. Who knew there was so much to say?

Similarly, news outlets, blogs, and social media provide many ideas for legal questions that have no clear answers. For example, questions regarding foreign policy and trade, immigration, separation of powers, gun regulation, environmental policy, and countless other areas of law frequently receive media attention. Social justice and special interest groups tend to have a social media presence where they bring attention to pressing legal issues. Even legislators and other political figures utilize social media to garner attention for the legal issues of our day. It does not require much digging to begin to identify where the murky areas of law exist. These questions are good places to begin identifying questions you want to explore for your project.

Finally, other scholars might be a source for your topic. Often, legal scholars identify questions or issues that are beyond the scope of a particular article. Such a question or issue is likely a good one to explore. You may find another scholar's research agenda and be inspired to pick up a topic. You may also find that a scholar has reached a conclusion with which you disagree. Perhaps you see the research as supporting a different resolution. In such a case, you might write an article arguing for a different conclusion. When you are responding to or taking inspiration from other scholars, you are entering into a conversation. It is important that you acknowledge the source of your inspiration. Additionally, if you disagree with another scholar's conclusion, you must explain why you disagree in a respectful and well-reasoned fashion. Finally, it would be prudent to reach out to the scholar and engage in an actual conversation so that you better understand that scholar's thesis. Most scholars are eager to discuss their work with others. It is important to preserve your credibility by demonstrating respect even if you argue for a different outcome.

1.5 | FIND THE CATEGORY

Identifying the category of the legal question you have chosen will be helpful as your scholarly project develops. The category will dictate how the scholarly project unfolds, and it will influence the organization of the final product. For example, empirical questions will require collection and study of data points, and you might even need specialized training in statistical analysis. If you are studying human subjects, you will be required to obtain the approval of an Institutional Review Board. This process is tedious and can present significant challenges to completing the project. Historical questions may present challenges in acquiring accurate historical documents; doctrinal and interdisciplinary topics may, at first glance, seem like they have no novel questions left to explore because so many scholars have been researching these topics for decades. No category is better than another, but the course of your research project will be governed by the category into which your topic falls.

Doctrinal
- Studies a particular area or doctrine of law
- Sometimes challenging to narrow down

Empirical
- Studies the impact of a law or doctrine in practice
- Challenging to collect and quantify data; may require specialized training in statistical analysis

Interdisciplinary
- Studies the intersection of the law and some other scholarly, though non-legal, area such as economics, philosophy, society, feminism, race and culture, or any number of others
- Challenging to maintain primary focus on the law

Historical
- Studies the evolution of a historical legal problem
- Sometimes challenging to identify relevance to modern society

Regarding organization of the final project, historical questions could lend themselves to a more descriptive approach, but they can also be used to provide insight into the "textual and structural premises of mainstream views."[4] That is, the author generally describes the issue or legal landscape relevant to the historical question. Depending on the scope of the study, empirical questions may similarly lend themselves to a descriptive article that explains the significance of existing data but may not be able to justify prescriptive solutions for the problems revealed by the data. On the other hand, doctrinal and interdisciplinary questions readily lend themselves to a prescriptive approach—one that identifies a problem and offers a solution to that problem. Chapter 5 provides examples of some of the more common analytical frameworks within each category and guidance on how to choose, adapt, or create an analytical framework for your thesis. Chapter 6 provides examples of the organizational paradigms most common to each category.

NEVER FORGET, YOU **CAN** DO THIS!

SQUELCH THE IMPOSTOR

The impostor voice may have you questioning:

- Who am I to say anything?
- How can I possibly narrow this idea down anymore?

Here is what you can do:

- Talk to your mentor
- Freewrite
- Read your research and take notes
- Write the topic selection essay
- Ask "why" and "how"
- Make a list of questions
- Be curious
- Avoid thinking about your grade or long-term impact of your scholarship

---

4. Markus D. Dubber, *Legal History as Legal Scholarship: Doctrinalism, Interdisciplinarity, and Critical Analysis of Law* (July 13, 2017). *Oxford Handbook of Historical Legal Research* (2016). Available at SSRN: https://ssrn.com/abstract=3002587.

As you narrow down your topic, make sure it is <u>interesting, manageable, significant, novel, useful, and sound</u>. If you aren't sure, ask someone; indeed, ask more than one person. It is true that seeking feedback makes you vulnerable to critique, but listening to others expands your perspective and guides you in developing your scholarly voice. External perspective is essential to understanding whether your topic is relevant. Critique will also reveal weaknesses in your position, gaps in your thinking, and assumptions you are making. Listening thoughtfully to others will help you develop a better scholarly question than you would be able to develop in a vacuum or entirely on your own. Finally, do you best to squelch feelings of frustration if you find yourself continuing to narrow your topic even after you have moved on into the research, or perhaps, drafting stages of your project. This entire process is recursive, and you may need to conduct significant research or begin drafting before you realize exactly the best way to define the scope of your thesis. It is normal to revisit early stages even after you have moved on.

ASSIGNMENT

Draft an essay (three to five paragraphs) explaining the topic/legal question you have selected. An example is provided in Appendix I. Use the guidelines below as you write your essay.

1. Describe the topic and state the thesis or specific legal question.
2. Explain why you chose the topic.
3. Explain what else has been written or said on the topic and by whom.
4. Explain any questions or problems you expect to resolve on the topic.
5. Explain the unique perspective you will offer on the topic.

This essay will help you establish a baseline for beginning your scholarly project, and you will continue to develop these initial ideas through the research and preemption phase, outlining phase, and final drafting phase. This document will also prove useful when your research begins to take you down rabbit holes—it will ground you in the original question and keep you focused on the single question you have decided to answer.

CHAPTER **2**

How Do I Find What Has Been Said and Who Has Said It?

Research Brainstorm

What do I already know about my topic?

What do I need or want to know about my topic?

Am I aware of any sources that may provide helpful information about my topic?

What have I read about my topic?

What organizations do I know that may have information relevant to my topic?

What time frame do I have to complete my research?

How much time do I expect to spend in the initial research phase?

Every scholarly writer will develop a personalized and unique research methodology. The information in this chapter is designed to give you guidance as you begin and to offer strategies for ensuring your research is complete.

Research can be simultaneously exhilarating and frustrating. There is no feeling comparable to the exhilaration of discovery. Learning something new about your topic or finding the answer to a question you have been tackling is pure elation. But sometimes answers are elusive, or the sheer volume of information is overwhelming. Sometimes it is difficult to know whether information is relevant and reliable. Developing a process and implementing the strategies described in this chapter will help you minimize frustration while maximizing positive results.

The techniques described in this chapter require you to organize and track lots of information. Before you dive into the deep end, it is helpful for you to consider the ways you prefer to handle information. Are you a pen and paper person? If so, you may need to collect several binders and notebooks to house all of the articles and track your notes about impressions. You should probably invest in a variety of colored pens, tabs, and highlighters to mark important information. Color-coding can help you track related concepts across sources. If color-coding does not work for you, use symbols or some other method for categorizing. Speaking from personal experience, my husband is color-blind, so none of my color-coding has ever worked for him. Instead, he uses a system of highlighting, underlining, circles, squares, and capitalization to organize and connect related ideas. You should work out a system that functions for you.

Tracking with pen and paper can be a challenge if you need to take your work with you. Many scholars work at home, in the office, and in the library. Carrying volumes of notebooks may not always be practical. In that case, you may choose to download sources and save them into file folders in the directory on your computer. You can use the comment and highlight feature to take notes on .pdf documents. Word processors also have commenting and highlighting features for taking notes and tracking your impressions. As you take notes on the source itself, it is helpful to make notes in a separate document so that your impressions are simultaneously collected in a centralized location for easy searching.

If you are more comfortable with technology, consider using a program like Zotero (www.zotero.org) or Juris-M[1] (https://juris-m.github.io/). As explained on its website, "Zotero is, at the most basic level, a reference manager. It is designed to store, manage, and cite bibliographic references, such as books and articles. In Zotero, each of these references constitutes an item. More broadly, Zotero is a powerful tool for collecting and organizing research information and sources."[2] Zotero offers a number of advantages for researchers beyond just collecting your sources in one place. It allows you to make notes about the resource within Zotero, and you can also create standalone notes. You can create tags for documents for tracking related information and easily searching for specific information later in the process. It integrates with Microsoft Word so you

---

1. As stated on its website, "Juris-M [is] a research environment that is based on, but separate from, the well-known Zotero reference manager. It adds support for legal materials, legal citation styles, and multilingual materials." https://juris-m.github.io/about/. Juris-M works substantially the same as Zotero, and Zotero also supports legal materials, including legal citation styles.

2. https://www.zotero.org/support/quick_start_guide.

can easily track and cite resources during the drafting phase. It offers a robust collection of citation formats, so you can easily adapt the citations in your bibliography and final product to meet the expectations of your publisher. It will even generate a bibliography for you. Zotero also permits you to share access to your collection with others. So, if you are co-authoring a piece or need to share your resources with a mentor or reviewer, Zotero makes that easy, too.

2.1 | PLANNING

There are four primary steps to planning the research phase:

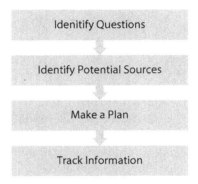

While you should generally follow these steps in order, the research process itself is not linear. That means you might find yourself identifying new questions as you locate sources, or you may need to modify your original plan as you begin to understand more about your topic. The beginning of your research project should set you on a course for continuing to refine your topic to a manageable thesis.

2.1.1 | Identifying Questions

To identify questions, you might want to begin with a freewriting or brainstorming session. Make sure to write down all the questions you think you need to answer. The topic selection essay you wrote in Chapter 1 likely prompted you to think of a number of questions that will require additional research for your project.

As you research, you will find that you need to update your list of questions. Depending on what you find, you may realize that you have been asking the wrong questions. You might eliminate a line of questions altogether or simply reframe them to capture the real issue. The process of researching provides the vocabulary you need to refine the questions you ask, and it also helps you to identify new questions you did not know to ask when you first began your project.

Early in a project, your questions will be broad. As you work through the research, your searches will naturally become more refined because your understanding of the terms of art, area of law, and precise questions you want to ask will improve.

For example, if you are researching a Fourth Amendment issue, you may not initially include terms like *"Terry* stop" or "stop and frisk." Your research, however, might reveal these terms of art, which might cause you to modify your searches. You may also read a case or an article that sparks a question you had not yet considered. For example, you might not have previously asked the question, "what is a consensual encounter?" But, when reading *Terry* cases and articles interpreting *Terry*, you realize that consensual encounters are routinely analyzed in the context of *Terry* stops to determine where the line is between a consensual encounter and a *Terry* stop. You may need to update your list of questions to include ones about consensual encounters so you have a comprehensive understanding of your issue.

As you progress through the questions, do not delete anything. In the future, you may need to circle back to a question that you once thought irrelevant. It will be helpful if you can track every question you have asked and the resolution you reached regarding that question. Instead of deleting a question, you can simply write *eliminate* beside it so you know not to invest energy in researching it for now.

2.1.2 | Identifying Potential Sources

Legal sources come in two basic forms: primary and secondary. A primary source is any source of actual law like statutes, constitutions, rules, regulations, treaties, and cases. A secondary source is a source that explains the law or helps you find primary sources. Secondary sources are things like treatises, hornbooks, law review articles, digests, and American Law Reports.

For scholarly writing, you will likely need to rely on non-legal sources, as well. Depending on your topic, you may need to rely on data collected by other agencies, such as the Department of Justice, the Department of Defense, or other governmental groups. You may rely on studies conducted by special interest groups like the NAACP or PETA. You may also rely on papers written by scholars in other fields such as criminology, history, sociology, psychology, philosophy, or anthropology, to name a few.

Always go to the original source! If you have read about the results of the study, look at the study itself to ensure you understand what exactly was being studied. Do not confuse correlation with causation. Make your own informed decisions about the implications and meaning of the data — do not blindly rely on someone else's conclusions about its significance. Pull the sources cited in footnotes of other articles to verify accuracy and interpret the meaning for yourself.

In scholarly writing, secondary and non-legal sources play a much bigger role than they do in practical legal writing. In practice, judges and attorneys are much more concerned with the law itself because the law is what will govern the outcome in a case. A secondary or non-legal source is only persuasive authority—it is powerless to mandate a particular outcome in a real case. That is why practitioners and judges emphasize the importance of primary sources.

On the other hand, in scholarly writing, the whole point is to think about why the law is what it is, how the law should be, why the law should or should not change, how the law impacts culture and society, and many other questions like these. Because of the nature of the inquiry, it is imperative to look at secondary and non-legal sources to find answers. It is important to figure out what others have said about the law, to study data about the impacts of the law, and to learn from other disciplines to accurately predict how changes in the law will likely unfold.

As with identifying questions, keep a list of potential sources and track whether you have been able to locate the source, whether the source was helpful, and what additional sources you want to find based on what you discovered. If a source was not helpful, make a note of that, but do not delete the source from your list. You may find that the source becomes relevant later in your project, and you want to keep a ready list of all the sources you have consulted throughout the project.

2.1.3 | Make a Plan

If you do not create a research plan, you will undoubtedly find yourself flailing in the sea of abstraction. The research plan needs to be sufficiently detailed to ensure you explore the questions and sources you have identified, while maintaining enough flexibility to be modified to account for new information, new questions, and new sources. At a minimum, the plan should prioritize the questions and sources you will consult. If you do not set these priorities in advance, you will find yourself wasting valuable time bouncing around your topic without being able to focus and drill down on the most important concepts.

> Treat researching like a job. Set a realistic schedule and manage your time.

One of the most critical aspects of a research plan is creating a schedule. If you do not plan your research time in advance, it will be very easy to let the time get away from you. Researching a scholarly project is not something that can generally be done in a weekend or compressed time frame just before the assignment is due. The research process can take weeks (sometimes months or even years) to complete. In fact, even once you begin writing, you may find that you need to refresh your research or find the answer to an unexpected question.

A good practice is to allot time in blocks, usually two to four hours, for research. Less than that, you probably will not have time to find enough helpful resources, which will require you to revisit the same research task at another time. Longer than that, you will likely hit a wall and become inefficient in your research process. Of course, the time you allot is not a hard and fast rule. On any given day, you may wrap up your research inquiry in less than two hours, or you might keep going a little longer than four to wrap up a thought.

The point here is not to create a draconian schedule, but rather to give you space to work on your project. The time you carve out in advance for research is sacred—do not schedule anything else during this time, and do not allow your time to be hijacked by others. Put your phone away and silence alerts on your computer. Treat researching like a job and report for duty as scheduled.

2.1.4 | Track Information

Tracking your research is a critical aspect of your scholarly research project. You will need to digest a massive amount of information to finalize your project, and very few people can keep that much information in brain storage. Most people need an easily accessible reference sheet to quickly recall the information, how it relates to the project, and how they intend to use the information.

Each researcher and project is unique, so there is no singular way to create a tracking chart. Some people integrate the research plan and tracking chart into one document and others track them separately. You may find that you like to organize around the questions you intend to ask. Others may prefer to organize around the sources. Depending on how much you know about your topic, you may have a well-formulated outline that you can use to create the research plan. At a minimum, your research plan should track:

Question Asked

Database Searched

Search Terms

Results

Date

2.1.4.1 | Sample Tracking Charts

If you are using Zotero, you can upload your research tracking chart to the folder you have created for your specific project, or you may choose to create the chart as a standalone note. If you prefer pen and paper, you may find comfort in printing out your chart and filling it in by hand. Consider developing shorthand symbols as you track your research to remind yourself of each source's substance and potential use. As more fully discussed in Chapter 4, you should take detailed notes on the source itself, in your research chart, and in a separate document for all critical resources. It is important to document your thought process as you read through the materials because you will not always accurately recall your impressions once you have moved on. By taking good notes, you will not have to re-familiarize yourself with sources later in the process.

SAMPLE TRACKING CHART 1

QUESTIONS	DATABASE SEARCHED	SEARCH TERMS USED	RESULTS
[INSERT QUESTION 1]	1. [INSERT DATE] [INSERT DATABASE SEARCHED] 2. [INSERT DATE] [INSERT ADDITIONAL DATABASE SEARCHED]	1. [INSERT SEARCH TERMS] 2. [INSERT SEARCH TERMS]	[LIST SOURCES/ INDICATE IF YOU PLAN TO USE EACH SOURCE AND HOW]
[INSERT QUESTION 2]	1. [INSERT DATE] [INSERT DATABASE SEARCHED] 2. [INSERT DATE] [INSERT ADDITIONAL DATABASE SEARCHED]	1. [INSERT SEARCH TERMS] 2. [INSERT SEARCH TERMS]	[LIST SOURCES/ INDICATE IF YOU PLAN TO USE EACH SOURCE AND HOW]

SAMPLE TRACKING CHART 2

[INSERT SOURCE 1]	[INSERT QUESTION(S) RELATED TO SOURCE]	[INSERT DATE, DATABASE, AND SEARCH TERMS THAT LED YOU TO SOURCE]	[EXPLAIN HOW THIS IMPACTS THESIS]	[STATE WHETHER YOU PLAN TO USE THE SOURCE]
[INSERT SOURCE 2]	[INSERT QUESTION(S) RELATED TO SOURCE]	[INSERT DATE, DATABASE, AND SEARCH TERMS THAT LED YOU TO SOURCE]	[EXPLAIN HOW THIS IMPACTS THESIS]	[STATE WHETHER YOU PLAN TO USE THE SOURCE]

29

The format of the tracking chart is not important—it is important for the chart to be helpful to you. You are the person most familiar with your project, so you must decide what is important to track. You must decide the format that will help you identify important information when you need it for drafting your final project.

In addition to the tracking chart, you should maintain a working bibliography, which can be a separate document or incorporated into the research chart itself. If you are using Zotero, you are automatically tracking your working bibliography. A working bibliography is a simple list of all the resources you intend to use, in alphabetical order and correct citation format. This list will be helpful during the writing stage so you can quickly access citation information to incorporate into your footnotes. Most people choose to maintain the working bibliography as a separate document so that the information is easily accessed during the writing stage.

2.2 | RESEARCHING

If you have made a research plan, you have already tackled some of the more challenging aspects of research: (1) knowing what to ask; and (2) knowing where to look. This section provides an overview of available databases and techniques for your scholarly project.

2.2.1 | Databases

The dilemma of the Information Age is an embarrassment of riches—it is not so much that information is not available; rather, there is so much information that it is difficult to figure out how to find what you need. Researching often feels like drinking from a firehose because there is just so much information out there. It can also be challenging to know when to stop researching. To handle these challenges, it is helpful to know a little bit about the most common databases available for scholarly research. The following list is comprehensive, but not exhaustive; depending on your project, you may need to consult databases that specialize in non-legal resources that do not necessarily appear on this list.

2.2.1.1 | The Big Three: Westlaw, Lexis, and Bloomberg

Westlaw, Lexis, and Bloomberg are the most commonly used electronic databases for primary sources of law. They each permit natural language and Boolean searching, and they all provide access to statutes, constitutions, regulations, and cases. Bloomberg has special databases related to business and bankruptcy law, so if your project involves a topic related to business or bankruptcy, Bloomberg is probably a good choice. These databases also have collections of secondary sources, but their secondary source libraries are not as robust as those found in other databases. In scholarly writing, it is typical to use a secondary source to identify primary sources and then consult one of the Big Three to locate the primary source. Keep in mind that the Big Three are subscription-based and cost money; students and academics generally have access through their academic institutions, but if you do not have access you may need to locate a free database like FastCase or a local law library to find primary sources.

2.2.1.2 | HEINOnline

HEINOnline is a repository of databases housing law review articles, international law sources, legislative history, and numerous other sources. This is a good place to find law review articles. It is also a good place to search for potential databases if you are not sure where to start your research. HEINOnline only utilizes Boolean searching, but it has advanced search features that guide the Boolean search to minimize errors. A Guide to Boolean Searching is available in section 2.3.3 of this chapter. Most law libraries offer access to this subscription-based service.

2.2.1.3 | SSRN (ssrn.com)

SSRN stands for the Social Science Research Network. It is a large repository that primarily provides access to law review articles. To access the full content, you will likely need to join SSRN, but the membership is free. This resource permits scholarly writers to upload their own work for others to read and cite. Some authors post both works in progress and published articles, so it is a source of timely information. For a work in progress, it is imperative you seek the author's permission to cite to it before relying on it in your project. Also, keep in mind that a work in progress is not yet fully fleshed out, so the conclusions could ultimately change. In other words, it may not be the most reliable source available to you. If you rely on a published work that you found on SSRN, use the official publication citation, not the SSRN citation. This database permits Boolean searching as well as browsing by topic and can be particularly helpful for preemption checking, which we will cover in more detail in Chapter 3. It can also help you choose a topic if you are still somewhat undecided, because scholars sometimes post scholarly agendas that can help you identify topics in a particular area that are worth exploring.

2.2.1.4 | LegalTrac

LegalTrac is an online database available through most law libraries. Because information is organized topically, this database of scholarly publications can help you identify relevant sources early in your research, and most of the sources are available by clicking on the hyperlink. If a source you want cannot be accessed via hyperlink, you can typically use the citation to locate it another way, like through SSRN, HEINOnline, or one of the Big Three.

2.2.1.5 | JSTOR

JSTOR is an online database that offers access to more than 28,000 academic titles from a variety of disciplines. It is available through most law libraries and university libraries. This resource is particularly valuable if you have chosen an interdisciplinary topic, because it will give you access to non-legal sources like criminology, sociology, economics, psychology, and the like. It also has collections of area studies such as African, Asian, African American, Jewish, Latin American, and Middle East. In addition to browsing the collections, you can conduct a search using keywords. The guided "advanced search" feature is particular helpful for searching JSTOR.

2.2.1.6 | ProQuest

ProQuest is an online database that offers access to congressional, legislative, and regulatory publications. This resource is invaluable if you are tracking the evolution of a law, attempting to identify policy concerns, or otherwise trying to understand the legislative history and process of a particular law or regulation. Most law libraries offer their students and faculty access to this database. Most legislatures also make this same information available through their own websites, so if you do not have access to ProQuest, you should try to locate the information by going directly to the legislature's website.

2.2.1.7 | govinfo (govinfo.gov)

Govinfo, the online service of the United States Government Publishing Office (GPO), provides free access to a database of U.S. government information. It is a good alternative to ProQuest if you do not have access to ProQuest. It houses official publications from all three branches of the federal government, including, but not limited to, presidential documents, legislative calendars, the congressional record, U.S. court opinions, the federal budget, and congressional hearings.

2.2.1.8 | Index to Legal Periodicals

The Index to Legal Periodicals online database provides citations to articles in law reviews, bar association journals, yearbooks, institutes, and government publications from August 1981 to the present. This database does not link directly to articles themselves; it only provides the citation. This resource, however, can be useful in the preemption process explained in Chapter 3. Using Boolean search terms, you can quickly identify articles with titles related to your area of inquiry. In the early phases of the research process, the Index is useful in making lists of sources to consult and understanding the scope and breadth of your project.

2.2.2 | Google Scholar (scholar.google.com)

Google Scholar permits natural language searching of scholarly resources. It functions much like a Google search does, but it confines the result to scholarly publications, including books and articles. This database also filters for caselaw and statutes. Often, the hyperlink will take you to a subscription-based source, so you may not be able to access the source in that way. You may have to make a note of the citation and get creative with how you access it. A research librarian will likely be able to help you locate a source you have trouble accessing.

2.2.3 | Libraries

Thought it may seem antiquated, researching in libraries remains one of the best ways to locate reliable, relevant sources for your project. In scholarly writing, it is common to rely on information published in books, not just law review articles. Reading books in print is far preferable to reading them online because the brain tends to process information in print better than it processes online information. This is because in print, we are forced to read left to right more carefully, whereas online, even when we try to read carefully, we tend to engage in active top-to-bottom scanning.

Another reason libraries are so useful is because they are staffed with reference librarians who are experts at finding relevant resources. Most libraries have relationships with other libraries, so they can usually obtain a source even if they do not stock it in house. Librarians are generally eager to help, and they can make the research process easier and less stressful. An added benefit is that you must be able to articulate your questions well in order to get their help. Thus, you may find that working with a research librarian will help you refine your thesis and focus your project.

2.3 | PROCESS

When you begin researching, you may initially feel overwhelmed at the volume of information available. Remember, you do not need to read in detail everything that is out there, especially at this stage. The first step is to figure out generally what is being said and who is saying it. The information in section 2.1.4 of this chapter gave you processes for tracking the information you find; this section will provide strategies for finding information.

2.3.1 | How to Research When You Know Very Little About Your Topic

If you do not know much about your topic, you have to start by educating yourself on the big picture. Treatises and hornbooks are a good way to get a general understanding of a topic. Your reference librarian can point you to a relevant hornbook or treatise if you are unable to get oriented yourself. Once you have a general understanding of your topic, you can start to narrow it down and refine your research.

Treatises and hornbooks often reference primary sources, so a logical second step would be to read those primary sources; in other words, go to the original source. If you access the primary sources through one of the Big Three, you should find it fairly easy to locate

Research Steps
1. Consult the broadest authority necessary to give you working knowledge to move forward.
2. Use footnotes and citations to locate other relevant sources.
3. Check to see who has cited the source and author.
4. Use annotations to find relevant primary and secondary sources.

other primary and secondary sources. For statutes, the annotations lead you into ALRs, articles, other secondary sources, and cases. For cases, the databases provide easy access to other cases, articles, ALRs, and other secondary sources that cite or explain the original case.

As you read through a source, make a note of any other sources cited therein that might be relevant to your topic. Those are sources you will want to pull and read. For each source you consult, determine what other sources have cited it or the author generally. Reading sources that cite a source or author you intend to use on your project will likely lead you to valuable information for your project.

Consider this example from the treatise by Wayne LaFave, *Search and Seizure: A Treatise on the Fourth Amendment* § 9.1 (October 2018 Update):

In 1960 a leading criminal law scholar noted with dismay that the issue of "whether the police have the right to stop and question a suspect, without his consent, in the absence of grounds for an arrest" had been "largely ignored by commentators and dealt with ambiguously by most courts."[1] The situation changed dramatically shortly thereafter, however. In the early 1960's, the police practice commonly and euphemistically referred to as "stop and frisk"[2] became a most popular topic in the law reviews,[3] and was dealt with by a number of courts in a more forthright manner.[4] This development reached its zenith when the Supreme Court for the first time directly confronted[5] this issue in *Terry v. Ohio*[6] and two companion cases.[7]

The footnotes provide:

1. Remington, *The Law Relating to "On the Street" Detention, Questioning and Frisking of Suspected Persons and Police Arrest Privileges in General*, 51 J. Crim. L.C. & P.S. 386, 390 (1960).

2. The terms "stop" and "frisk" are used herein as convenient ways of referring to distinct police practices, and their use is not intended to suggest that the words themselves aid in resolving the difficult constitutional issues concerning these practices. See text at note 32 infra.

3. *See* Abrams, *Constitutional Limitations on Detention for Investigation*, 52 Iowa L. Rev. 1093 (1967); Bator & Vorenberg, *Arrest, Detention, Interrogation and the Right to Counsel: Basic Problems and Possible Legislative Solutions*, 66 Colum. L. Rev. 62 (1966); Kuh, *In-Field Interrogation: Stop, Question, Detention and Frisk*, 3 Crim. L. Bull. 597 (1967); Kuh, *Reflections on New York's "Stop-and-Frisk" Law and Its Claimed Unconstitutionality*, 56 J. Crim. L.C. & P.S. 32 (1965); LaFave, *Improving Police Performance Through the Exclusionary Rule—Part I: Current Police and Local Court Practices*, 30 Mo. L. Rev. 391, 427–55 (1965); LaFave, *Detention for Investigation by the Police: An Analysis of Current Practices*, 1962 Wash. U. L.Q. 331; Leagre, *The Fourth Amendment and the Law of Arrest*, 54 J. Crim. L.C. & P.S. 393, 406–16 (1963); Oberman & Finkel, *Constitutional Arguments Against "Stop and Frisk"*, 3 Crim. L. Bull. 441 (1967); Pilcher, *The Law and Practice of Field Interrogation*, 58 J. Crim. L.C. & P.S. 465 (1967); Reich, *Police Questioning of Law Abiding Citizens*, 75 Yale L.J. 1161 (1966); Reiss & Black, *Interrogation and the Criminal Process*, 374 Annals 47 (1967); Romayne, *The Right to Investigate and New York's "Stop and Frisk" Law*, 33 Fordham L. Rev. 211 (1964); Schoenfeld, *The "Stop and Frisk" Law Is Unconstitutional*, 17 Syracuse L. Rev. 627 (1966); Schwartz, *Stop and Frisk (A Case Study in Judicial Control of the Police)*, 58 J. Crim. L.C. & P.S. 433 (1967); Siegel, *The New York "Frisk" and "Knock-Not" Statutes: Are They Constitutional?*, 30 Brooklyn L. Rev. 274 (1964); Souris, *Stop and Frisk or Arrest and Search— The Use and Misuse of Euphemisms*, 57 J. Crim. L.C. & P.S. 251 (1966); Stern, *Stop and Frisk: An Historical Answer to a Modern Problem*, 58 J. Crim. L.C. & P.S. 532 (1967); Tiffany, *Field Interrogation: Administrative, Judicial and Legislative Approaches*, 43 Denver L.J. 389 (1966); Younger, *Stop and Frisk: "Say It Like It Is"*, 58 J. Crim. L.C. & P.S. 293 (1967); Wolbrette, *Detention for Questioning in Louisiana*, 39 Tul. L. Rev. 69 (1964). The subject also received attention in several books; see W. LaFave, Arrest 344–47 (1965); W. Schaefer, The Suspect and Society 23–26, 40–43 (1967); L. Tiffany, D. McIntyre & D. Rotenberg, Detection of Crime 5–94 (1967).

4. *E.g., People v. Mickelson*, 59 Cal. 2d 448, 30 Cal. Rptr. 18, 380 P.2d 658 (1963); *Commonwealth v. Lehan*, 347 Mass. 197, 196 N.E.2d 840 (1964); *State v. Dilley*, 49 N.J. 460, 231 A.2d 353 (1967); *People v. Rivera*, 14 N.Y.2d 441, 252 N.Y.S.2d 458, 201 N.E.2d 32 (1964); *State v. Terry*, 5 Ohio App. 2d 122, 214 N.E.2d 114 (1966); *Commonwealth v. Hicks*, 209 Pa. Super. 1, 223 A.2d 873 (1966).

5. The Court avoided the issue on two prior occasions. *See Rios v. United States*, 364 U.S. 253, 80 S. Ct. 1431, 4 L. Ed. 2d 1688 (1960); *Henry v. United States*, 361 U.S. 98, 80 S. Ct. 168, 4 L. Ed. 2d 134 (1959).

6. *Terry v. Ohio*, 392 U.S. 1, 88 S. Ct. 1868, 20 L. Ed. 2d 889 (1968). Thirty years after the case was decided, Terry was given a thorough assessment by over 30 authorities in a remarkable symposium running over 800 pages. *See Symposium*, 72 St. John's L. Rev. 721 (1998). Although all the articles are worth reading, special mention must be made of Barrett, *Deciding the Stop and Frisk Cases: A Look Inside the Supreme Court's Conference*, 72 St. John's L. Rev. 749 (1998), which, based upon the papers of several Justices, provides a fascinating look at how the Terry decision came to be written as it was and the contributions of various Justices to the final product. For other interesting looks back at Terry, see Bandes, *Terry v. Ohio in Hindsight: The Perils of Predicting the Past*, 16 Const. Comm. 491 (1999); Butler, *"A Long Step Down the Totalitarian Path": Justice Douglas's Great Dissent in Terry v. Ohio*, 79 Miss. L.J. 9 (2009); Katz, *Terry v. Ohio at Thirty-Five: A Revisionist View*, 74 Miss. L.J. 423 (2004); Miller, *The Warren Court's Regulatory Revolution in Criminal Procedure*, 43 Conn. L. Rev. 1, 48–65 (2010); Weaver, *Investigation and Discretion: The* Terry *Revolution at Forty (Almost)*, 109 Penn St. L. Rev. 1205 (2005). *See* Steiker, *Terry Unbounded*, 82 Miss. L.J. 329 (2013); Swartz, *Terry v. Ohio at 50: What It Created, What It Has Meant, Is It Under Attack and Is the Court Opening the Door to Police Misconduct?*, 38 N. Ill. U. L. Rev. 45 (2017); *Note*, 47 Harv. C.R.-C.L. L. Rev. 573 (2012); and the seven articles constituting *Symposium,* Terry *at Fifty*, 15 Ohio St. J. Crim. L. 1–131 (2017).

7. They were *Sibron v. New York* and Peters v. New York, reported together at 392 U.S. 40, 88 S. Ct. 1889, 20 L. Ed. 2d 917 (1968).

The cases in this example are all primary sources and the articles and books are secondary sources. Assuming this section of the treatise is relevant to your scholarly project, to be thorough, you should pull each source to determine how it relates to your scholarly project. For the cases, you want to consult the citing authorities to determine how they have been treated in more recent history and to search for other law review articles that may be on point for the scholarly project. For the secondary sources, you should identify any portions that are particularly relevant to your project and read the sources cited in any footnotes in those sections. You should also identify other sources that have cited the secondary source to determine how it has been treated more recently.

2.3.2 | How to Research When You Know Something About Your Topic

If you know a little bit about your topic, then you probably will not need to start by reading a broad, general source like a treatise. Instead, you can begin more precisely. For example, if you want to expose a statute as flawed or problematic, begin by reading the statute and annotation. From there, find all cases and secondary sources that analyze the problematic aspect of the statute. Then, review the sources cited in those secondary sources and cases, and identify relevant sources that have cited the secondary sources and cases.

If you look up Florida Statute § 776.012 on Westlaw, you will see the following categories in the annotation:

1. Construction and application	18. Defenses
1.5. Retroactive application	19. Burden of proof
2. Arrests	20. Admissibility of evidence
3. Deadly force	21. Sufficiency of evidence
4. Imminent threat	22. Comments of counsel
5. Provocation	23. Declaratory judgment
6. Unlawful activity	24. Summary judgment
7. Retreat	25. Jury questions
8. Warnings	25. Fact questions
9. Armed kidnapping	26-30. Jury instructions
10. Nondeadly force	27. Self defense, jury instructions
11. Forcible felony exception	28. Cure, jury instructions
12. Employment	29. Certiorari, jury instructions
13. Ineffective counsel	30. Reversible error, jury instructions
14. Qualified immunity	31. Sentence
15. Evidentiary hearings	31.5. Civil actions
16. Res judicata	32. Review
17. Pleadings	33. Prohibition

If you identify the categories applicable to your scholarly project, you can easily zoom in on relevant cases.

The following law review articles all cite the statute, so you will want to read them:

1. *Applying nineteenth century ideas to a twenty-first century problem: The law of self-defense and gang-related homicide,* Dr. Anthony Simones, 20 S. Ill. U. L.J. 589 (Spring 1996).

2. *A call for change: A contextual-configurative analysis of Florida's "Stand Your Ground" laws*, Elizabeth Megale, 68 U. Miami L. Rev. 1051 (Summer 2014).
3. *Florida's "Stand Your Ground" law: The actual effects and the need for clarification*, Zachary L. Weaver, 63 U. Miami L. Rev. 395 (Oct. 2008).
4. *A fresh cut in an old wound—A critical analysis of the Trayvon Martin killing: The public outcry, the prosecutors' discretion, and the Stand Your Ground Law*, Tamara F. Lawson, 23 U. Fla. J.L. & Pub. Pol'y 271 (December 2012).
5. *"He's a black male ... something is wrong with him!" The role of race in the stand your ground debate*, D. Marvin Jones, 68 U. Miami L. Rev. 1025 (Summer 2014).
6. *Race to incarcerate: Punitive impulse and the bid to repeal stand your ground*, Aya Gruber, 68 U. Miami L. Rev. 961 (Summer 2014).
7. *Real men advance, real women retreat: Stand your ground, battered women's syndrome, and violence as male privilege*, Mary Ann Franks, 68 U. Miami L. Rev. 1099 (Summer 2014).
8. *"Stand Your Ground" laws: International human rights law implications*, Ahmad Abuznaid, Caroline Bettinger-Lopez, Charlotte Cassel, and Meena Jagannath, 68 U. Miami L. Rev. 1129 (Summer 2014).

If you are conducting a national survey of Stand Your Ground laws, you will also want to consult the A.L.R.:

1. 60 American Law Reports, Federal 204, *When Does Police Officer's Use of Force During Arrest Become So Excessive as to Constitute Violation of Constitutional Rights, Imposing Liability Under Federal Civil Rights Act of 1871 (42 U.S.C.A. § 1983).*
2. 76 American Law Reports 6th 1, *Construction and Application of "Make My Day" and "Stand Your Ground" Statutes.*
3. 73 American Law Reports 4th 993, *Standard for Determination of Reasonableness of Criminal Defendant's Belief, for Purposes of Self-Defense Claim, that Physical Force Is Necessary—Modern Cases.*
4. 43 American Law Reports 3d 221, *Homicide: Modern Status of Rules as to Burden and Quantum of Proof to Show Self-Defense.*
5. 91 American Law Reports 2d 1095, *Right of Prosecution to Writ of Certiorari in Criminal Case.*
6. 18 American Law Reports 1279, *Homicide: Duty to Retreat When Not on One's Own Premises.*
7. 25 American Law Reports 1007, *Homicide as Affected by Humanitarian Motives.*
8. 68 American Law Reports 1108, *What Amounts to Violation of Statute Forbidding Comment by Prosecuting Attorney on Failure of Accused to Testify.*
9. 114 American Law Reports 634, *Danger or Apparent Danger of Death or Great Bodily Harm as Condition of Self-Defense in Prosecution for Assault as Distinguished from Prosecution for Homicide.*
10. 169 American Law Reports 315, *Comment Note.—Duty in Instructing Jury in Criminal Prosecution to Explain and Define Offense Charged.*

2.3.3 | Natural Language and Boolean Searching

Most law students and academics are at least familiar with the concepts of natural language and Boolean searching. Natural language searching tends to be easier in the earlier stages of a project because it does not require the same level of precision that Boolean searching does. Often, in the beginning, you will not have developed the vocabulary necessary to craft effective Boolean searches. It can be frustrating to run Boolean searches that return no results simply because you do not have enough information to create precise search terms.

As you progress through a project, Boolean searching becomes more practical because you familiarize yourself with the topic and how others are talking about it. Boolean searching is more precise than natural language searching, so when done effectively, you do not have to weed through many irrelevant search results. It can make the research process more satisfying. Many databases offer guided advanced searches or charts with their Boolean terms and connectors. The following chart identifies some of the most common Boolean search terms.

THE MOST COMMON BOOLEAN SEARCH TERMS

&	AND	Sample search terms:
/s	In same sentence	1. "self defense" OR "stand your ground" (will pull resources that use the phrases: self defense, self-defense, or stand your ground)
Or	OR	
+s	Preceding within sentence	
/p	In same paragraph	2. "stand your ground" /s Florida (will pull resources that use the word Florida in the same sentence as the phrase stand your ground)
" "	Exact phrase	
+p	Preceding within paragraph	
%	But not	3. driv! /s auto! OR car* OR vehicle* OR truck* (will pull resources that use the word drive, driver, driven, drives, or driving when they appear in the same sentence as either auto, autos, automobiles, automobile, car, cars, vehicle, vehicles, truck, or trucks).
/n	Within n terms of	
!	Root expander	
+n	Preceding within n terms of	
*	Universal character	
#	Prefix to turn of plurals and equivalents	

2.3.4 | Non-Legal Sources

The strategies explained in sections 2.2.1, 2.2.2, and 2.2.3 of this chapter will not necessarily lead you to all the relevant non-legal sources you might need to consult. Sometimes, a law review article may include a citation to a non-legal source, and that is a source you will likely want to study. More than likely, however, you will need to include strategies for exploring relevant non-legal sources when drafting your research plan. Consider what agencies or special interest groups might be collecting information relevant to your topic. A basic Google search might help you identify agencies and groups connected to your topic. For example, if your topic is about the legalization of marijuana, you might want to know what cannabis rights groups are doing and saying about the matter. Similarly, if you are studying prison reform, you might want to know what the Department of Justice data reveals about prison populations. Once you identify one or two reliable non-legal sources, they will likely connect you to a number of other relevant non-legal sources. Additionally, your reference librarian can help you identify and obtain copies of non-legal sources relevant to your project.

2.4 | WHEN AM I DONE?

Never. Of course, you will come to natural stopping points, but the reality is that you will likely revisit your research even when you are in the advanced stages of editing your final project. A better question to ask is: "How do I know when I am ready to move on to the writing?" The answer to that question is a little easier. First, you want to figure out if you have answered all the questions you have for now. In other words, have you gotten to the point where you cannot think of any more questions to ask, refine, or eliminate? If so, you are probably ready to begin digging deeper into the research in preparation for writing.

In this first phase of research, you are largely focused on refining your topic, figuring out what has been said, and who has said it. That requires a somewhat superficial reading of the resources you plan to use because you need to glean just enough understanding to figure out how to organize it on your tracking chart. Make sure you have been tracking your impressions so that you do not forget the general relevance of the source.

In the next stage, you will move into prioritizing the resources, verifying reliability, and reading more carefully. Chapters 3 and 4 offer strategies for how to manage this process. As you dig into the sources, you will inevitably develop more questions that will require more research. The research will become increasingly fine-tuned and focused to answer those precise questions uncovered by your analysis of the topic. Research conducted in later phases of the project tends to be more manageable and less overwhelming.

NEVER FORGET, YOU **CAN** DO THIS!

SQUELCH THE IMPOSTOR

The impostor voice may have you questioning:

- How can I possibly read everything out there?
- What unique idea could I possibly have?

Here is what you can do:

- Refine your questions
- Talk to your mentor
- Update your topic selection essay
- Begin organizing and categorizing resources
- Start taking notes and questioning the ideas in your resources

---

Research can be the most exhilarating and the most frustrating aspect of a scholarly project. The very nature of a scholarly project is frustrating because you are wrestling with tensions and inconsistencies in the law—problems with no easy solutions. While it is incredibly exciting to find the information you are looking for, it can be equally frustrating when information eludes you. You will inevitably experience disappointment if the research conflicts with your original thesis. If this occurs, remember that you must learn from the research. It is never correct to reach a conclusion that the research does not support. Your options under these circumstances may be to continue researching to determine whether there is another way to view the issue or whether there is different research that would support your original conclusion. You *must* also consider the likelihood that you need to adjust your final conclusion. Asking additional questions, documenting your impressions, writing out your thoughts, continuing the research, and talking with those in your scholarly support community will help you resolve this issue.

The key to effective research is keeping an open mind and following your agenda. It is perfectly natural to update the agenda, but you must do so in a deliberate and thoughtful way to avoid getting off track. As you progress through the other stages, you will thank yourself for following a deliberate and thorough research plan.

ASSIGNMENT

Create a research plan and working bibliography. A sample of this assignment is located in Appendixes II and III. The research plan should include:

1. A list of questions to be answered
2. A list of potential sources
3. A timeline for researching
4. A chart for tracking:
   a. Databases
   b. Search terms
   c. Brief description of source and how you intend to use it

The working bibliography should list, in alphabetical order, all your sources in correct citation format with a brief description of the nature and content of the source. Zotero would make this part of the assignment *very easy* to complete.

CHAPTER **3**

How Do I Know This Is Worth Talking More About?

Preemption Brainstorm

Do I have a well-formulated thesis? If not, how can I use the research process to refine my thesis?

What information should I track to help me refine my thesis and determine who has said what about my topic?

What does the source say and how does it fit in with my thesis?

How is my thesis different from the source's thesis?

As we saw in Chapter 1, your thesis must be original, unique, and novel. The way to determine whether your topic fits these criteria is to conduct a preemption check. So, once you have selected a topic, the *next critical step* is to conduct a preemption check. Preemption checking helps writers determine what has already been said about a topic, who has said it, and whether the issue has effectively been resolved.

Preemption checking will involve most of the strategies explained in Chapter 2, but preemption checking utilizes those processes for a precise purpose. These strategies are used broadly to gather breadth of information early in the research process. Chapter 4 provides guidance for how to use the same research strategies to gather depth of information later in the research process. Focusing on breadth first will help you confirm that your topic is original, unique, and novel.

3.1 | IDENTIFYING NOVELTY AND UNIQUENESS

As noted in Chapter 1, your novel idea does not need to be completely unrelated to other articles that have already been written. You may find that a lot of scholars have written about your topic generally but that you wish to offer a novel or unique perspective on that topic. Just because another scholar has written generally on the topic does not necessarily mean you have been preempted.

Sometimes it is easy to figure out whether you have been preempted. For example, if you choose to analyze a circuit split on a particular legal issue and the United States Supreme Court resolves the circuit split before you finish your article, you have been preempted. In other words, once the Supreme Court has resolved the circuit split, you do not have a unique or novel solution to an existing problem because the problem no longer exists. In this case, you might be able to adjust the approach in the article to address a unique or novel issue that accounts for the Supreme Court decision, or you may wish to discard your piece altogether and pursue a different topic.

Other times, it can be difficult to figure out whether you have been preempted. It can be challenging to determine whether an article on your same topic is too similar to what you want to say. This is where a good mentor comes in handy. Speaking with your mentor about whether an article or legal decision is preemptive will help you figure out whether you should continue to pursue your topic. Often, your mentor can help you refine your perspective so that you don't have to abandon your topic altogether. Other times, you may decide to change your topic because the area you originally wanted to pursue is simply too saturated. Ultimately, you want your article stand out. That generally means you want to choose a topic that has not been written about too much by too many different authors. All this being said, your ideas are unlikely to be identical to another scholar's, so chances are you will be able to take the unique approach you have already decided to pursue.

In Chapters 1 and 2, the concept of entering into a scholarly conversation was introduced. The benefit to entering a conversation is that you know the topic is one that is ripe for exploration because other scholars are exploring it. The risk, of course, is that you may not have anything new or novel to say yourself. Additionally, if you are a novice in the subject area, questioning a long-time expert may not be the wisest strategy since you likely do not have the expertise to understand the nuances and intricacies of the issues. You also run the risk of becoming so focused on rebutting or responding to another scholar's argument that you unnecessarily limit your audience to only those who have read the other author. Scholarship that merely rebuts another scholar is not likely to be as comprehensive as it should be, and your argument may not even stand on its own. When you enter into conversation with another scholar, it is important to ensure that your arguments stand alone while you acknowledge other scholars in the field, explain how your thesis fits into the broader conversation, and respectfully reveal the flaws in other scholars' positions while demonstrating the superiority of your own position.

3.2 | PREEMPTION PROCESS

The process of preemption checking can seem tedious and overwhelming at times. The key to managing the workload is to make a plan and stick to it. Preemption checking should be the first step in the research plan you developed in Chapter 2 because the steps for conducting a preemption check require you to engage in the research process. You will want to be deliberate about the databases you search initially so that you can efficiently determine whether you have been preempted.

> Preemption checking is an integral part of the research process. Treating it as a separate component will make it seem tedious and overwhelming. Allow the process to propel your project naturally through the research stage.

3.2.1 | Alerts and Notifications

If you are working with a topic that you know may get preempted, you should set up alerts on your preferred Big Three database so that you receive notifications when the law changes in that area. For example, if you are examining a circuit split and a case is pending at the Supreme Court, you can set up an alert to tell you when there has been action on the case. Similarly, if you are tracking proposed legislation on an issue, you can set up an alert to be informed about when votes or hearings are held on the law. To set up an alert, follow these steps:

1. *Westlaw:* Click on the Notifications tab, click on Create Alert, select the type of alert you would like to create, and follow the instructions for creating the alert.

2. *Lexis:* Perform a search and click the bell next to Results For at the top of the page, and select your preferred options for monitoring and delivery.

3. *Bloomberg:* Perform a search and click the Create Alert bell above the search results, and select your preferred options for monitoring and delivery.

Most of the time, though, you will not be researching a topic that is obviously at risk for preemption. Therefore, it will be challenging to set up an alert system. The best you can hope for is to conduct a thorough investigation into what has already been written. Until the time you submit your article for publication, you will need to continually update your sources to make sure that you have not missed any new publications.

3.2.2 | Databases

Unless you are tracking a specific statute or line of cases, the best databases for conducting a preemption check are the Index to Legal Periodicals, HEINOnline, and SSRN. More information about these databases is available in Chapter 2. All three of these databases provide abundant information about articles covering diverse topics. It is important to at least skim every article that you think may address your topic so that you can accurately determine whether you have been preempted by another scholar. Also, you should run a variety of searches using different search terms in each database. That way, you can ensure that you have located every potentially preemptive article that exists. In your searches, you may come across another author's research agenda. If you choose a topic that another scholar has listed on a research agenda, you should absolutely make contact to inform the author that you have tapped into the research agenda. That way, you can determine whether the author has an article in progress and whether it is likely to be published before you complete your article.

Most people treat preemption checking as part of the regular research process. There is no reason to double your efforts by thinking about preemption checking as a completely separate process from your research. Obviously, as you identify articles on the same topic, you will want to track those resources so that you can come back and study them more carefully when you move into the next stage of researching your project. The process of preemption checking will help you identify all of those sources that you will likely use to write your final article, so make sure to take notes of your impressions so that the information is not lost in the future. It is important to do a comprehensive and thorough preemption check early so that you do not waste valuable time working on your paper only to find out months later that you have been preempted.

NEVER FORGET, YOU **CAN** DO THIS!

SQUELCH THE IMPOSTOR

The impostor voice may have you questioning:

- What is my unique perspective?
- Has everything I want to say already been said?

Here is what you can do:

- Talk to your mentor
- Take notes and question your sources
- Ask more questions of yourself
- Be curious
- Avoid thinking about your grade or long-term impact of your scholarship

---

During preemption checking, you may start to feel like you will never develop your own unique voice on any topic. You will inevitably experience impostor syndrome. It is important to implement strategies for overcoming feelings of inadequacy. Talking to your support community, mentors, and peers about the process; discussing your research with others; and taking notes about your ongoing questions related to the topic are all ways you can manage impostor syndrome and feelings of inadequacy. As you discuss the topic with others, you will realize that you know much more than you think you do, and as you track questions prompted by your research, you will inevitably find a hole that you can fill with your unique thoughts on the topic.

Drafting a scholarly paper takes patience and persistence. By following the steps outlined in this book, you will surely achieve your goal of drafting a scholarly analysis on a unique topic of importance.

ASSIGNMENT

Draft a 500- to 1,000-word essay identifying the leading scholars in the field and summarizing their positions on your topic. An example is provided in Appendix IV.

CHAPTER 4

Do I Really Have to Read Everything That's Out There?

Verification Brainstorm

Why is it important to prioritize resources? What makes a source reliable?
What makes a source unreliable?
Why are university presses more reliable than self-publications?
What kinds of authors are most reliable?
How can you gauge an author's intellectual integrity?
How do you identify bias in others' writing?
How do you identify bias in your own writing?
Is it important to read work you disagree with?

Now that you are making some good headway with the research itself, you might find that you are starting to feel overwhelmed by the sheer volume of resources out there. In this chapter, you'll learn strategies for managing the research so that you can use it effectively.

Scholarly writing is a process that should satisfy your intellectual curiosity. While it involves significant work, it should not leave you feeling like a broken beast of burden. The key is to prioritize resources and then purposefully read them. In short, you do not need to thoroughly read everything that has ever been written on your general topic. What is more, you SHOULD NOT try to read everything. Reading everything tenuously related to your topic will exhaust you, it will distract you from your central question, and it will burn you out. Instead, manage your time effectively by implementing the following strategies and techniques.

4.1 | PRIORITIZE RESOURCES

Special interest groups are organizations that seek particular policy outcomes, typically through political lobbying, and may receive advantages in the political process. Special interest groups are inherently biased in favor of their cause, and they bear no responsibility for disclosing this bias or the details of any adverse interests. Some examples include the NRA, Brady Campaign to Prevent Gun Violence, ACLU, and Americans for Prosperity.

What other special interest groups can you name?

In other legal writing courses, you were probably taught to prioritize resources beginning with the highest and most recent primary mandatory authority, followed by primary persuasive sources, and, finally, secondary sources. This method of prioritization does not work well for scholarly writing, however, because you are typically not writing for a particular jurisdiction. Recall that focusing on a particular jurisdiction is typically ill-advised for scholarship because it unnecessarily limits your audience and generally provides for a less comprehensive analysis of an issue. If you desire to be published, limiting your scholarship to a single jurisdiction will likely limit your opportunities for publication, too.

The concepts of persuasive and mandatory primary authority are largely inapplicable to scholarly writing. Even if you are focusing on a particular jurisdiction, scholarly writing is supposed to go beyond merely explaining what the law is; it is supposed to analyze the impact, significance, shortcomings, or other aspects of the law. Secondary sources provide bountiful examination of these very aspects. Thus, reliable secondary sources are generally high priority resources for someone engaged in scholarly writing.

Prioritize resources by considering the reliability of the source itself, and the substance of the source, instead of prioritizing by ranking resources as mandatory, persuasive, primary, or secondary. Consider the following sources as they might relate to a question regarding whether Florida's Stand Your Ground statutory scheme legalizes murder[1]: (1) Florida Stand Your Ground statutes; (2) Florida Supreme Court decisions on Stand Your Ground cases; (3) Florida appellate court decisions on Stand Your Ground cases; (4) newspaper articles regarding deaths in

---

1. This same topic will be revisited in Chapter 5 on analytical frameworks.

Stand Your Ground cases; (5) law review articles on Florida's Stand Your Ground laws; and (6) blog posts on Florida's Stand Your Ground laws.

If you are a practicing attorney arguing your case before a court, the most important sources are the statutes and cases, with priority being given to supreme court cases over appellate court cases. If you are a scholar exploring the sociological and cultural impact of Stand Your Ground laws, blogs and newspaper articles might be your best source of information. If you are a scholar documenting the evolution of the law and the treatment by the courts, you will likely rely on both primary and secondary sources, and the priority you give those resources will be dictated by the substance of your argument. For example, if you are interested in identifying what prompted the change from Duty to Retreat to Stand Your Ground in 2006, you might prioritize your resources this way:

- High: the former statute
- High: the statute passed in 2006
- High: legislative documents such as bills, memos, and hearings
- High: sources about the American Legislative Exchange Commission
- Mid: law review articles analyzing Duty to Retreat and Stand Your Ground published around the time the law was passed
- Mid: NRA interest in Stand Your Ground legislation
- Mid: criminology studies or papers on Stand Your Ground and gun violence
- Low: newspapers, social media, and periodicals

On the other hand, if your primary interest is to document the NRA's influence on legislatures and the impact on gun control, you might prioritize your resources this way:

- High: sources about the American Legislative Exchange Commission
- High: legislative documents such as bills, memos, and hearings
- High: criminology studies on gun violence/murders/self-defense
- Mid: NRA interest in Stand Your Ground legislation
- Mid: the former statute
- Mid: the statute passed in 2006
- Mid: law review articles analyzing Duty to Retreat and Stand Your Ground published around the time the law was passed
- Mid: newspapers, social media, and periodicals

Although you will likely initially organize your thoughts around sources, eventually you will synthesize the information from these sources and organize your final paper around concepts, not sources.

4.1.1 | Source Reliability

A source is reliable when it utilizes verifiable accurate facts, data, or information. It is not always easy to recognize whether a source is reliable, however. Sometimes, a source may seem like it is based on verifiable facts, data, or information when it is in fact not reliable. In fact, some unreliable "news" sources practically masquerade as reliable sources by adopting names similar to well-known and historically reliable publishers. Consider the *New York Post* as an example—its name sounds similar to *The New York Times* and the *Washington Post*, both newspapers that have published award-winning journalism for well over a century. The *New York Post*, on the other hand, is a sensationalist tabloid that tends to make emotionally charged hyperbolic claims, replete with grammatical and punctuation errors, and it either does not disclose underlying fact sources or misrepresents the substance of the underlying fact source. Other unreliable sources go so far as to spoof reliable websites by imitating the logo and website layout of a reliable source but using a slightly different web address. Pay careful attention to the sources you select and verify the information is indeed accurate *and* from a reputable website.

Here are some strategies for ensuring that a source is indeed reliable.

4.1.1.1 | Identify the Publisher

Certain publications are inherently reliable because of the nature of the review process prior to publication. Publications that have been reviewed or edited by someone other than the author are inherently reliable because the information has been reviewed and verified before publication. Resources that are not reviewed by an external party or that are published by special interest groups are not inherently reliable. That is not to say that the source is unequivocally unreliable, however; it simply means that you must take additional steps to verify the information before relying on the source. You should never cite a less reliable source without corroborating the information with an inherently reliable source. Always go to the original source and interpret the information for yourself.

The following chart provides a non-exhaustive list of publications categorized by reliability:

PUBLICATIONS CATEGORIZED BY RELIABILITY

INHERENTLY RELIABLE PUBLICATIONS	LESS RELIABLE PUBLICATIONS
University Press Publications	Self-Published Books or Other Writings
Peer-Reviewed/Edited Publications	Special Interest Group Publications
Government Publications	Wikipedia
State Bar Publications	Internet Publications
Law Reviews	Blogs/Tweets/Facebook

4.1.1.2 | Identify the Author

Books and other publications written by an expert in the field are inherently reliable. Experts have cultivated robust knowledge through research and study—their work is typically reliable. Similarly, authors who have been cited by other scholars are recognized for their expertise in a certain field. Their writing is also inherently reliable. Authors who have not been cited or who are publishing works on behalf of special interest groups or who otherwise demonstrate bias are not inherently reliable. Their writing would need to be verified by an inherently reliable source.

Some ways to assess whether an author has cultivated expertise include:

- How long the author has been studying the subject matter
- How many studies or research projects the author has developed
- How many other authorities recognize the expertise of the author

Can you think of other ways to determine expertise?

4.1.1.3 | Identify the Purpose

Work that is written for the purpose of educating or informing is typically based on research and study, so these sources are inherently reliable. Some examples are learned treatises, textbooks, hornbooks, or law reviews. Work that is written primarily for entertainment or profit-making purposes, however, is generally unreliable. These sources often rely on inflammatory hyperbole designed to provoke an emotional response in the audience. These sources also tend to be poorly written, as evidenced by grammar and punctuation errors. Similarly, propaganda materials published by special interest groups or other biased authors are generally unreliable.

In addition to examining the publisher, author, and purpose, here are some additional questions you can ask to gauge a source's reliability.

- **Are there footnotes or endnotes?** A source that uses footnotes or endnotes provides the reader with information about all the sources the author relied on in writing the piece. A source is reliable if the footnotes demonstrate the author has utilized reliable sources and has cited multiple other authors. You will also want to ensure that the author has accurately represented the content of the sources cited by going to the original source. In other words, do the cited works indeed say what the author represents the cited works say? You should be skeptical of a source if the footnotes cite only to other works by that same author or if the cited sources are inherently unreliable.

Sometimes you will need to look to other sources to determine whether a particular method is reliable. For example, in 1998, Andrew Wakefield published a paper claiming that he had conducted a study proving that vaccines cause autism. His study has since been disproven by other experts in the field who examined his study and exposed the questionable methodologies. Wakefield has been discredited, and his paper is an unreliable source.

- **Has the source been cited by other sources?** The more a source is cited by other authors, the higher its indicia of reliability. If a source has been heavily criticized, utilizes questionable methods, or has been exposed as unreliable, it may mean the source is not reliable. You will need to dig deeper to determine whether the criticism is rooted in reliable facts, data, and information. If the criticism seems well founded, you should not rely on the source as an authority for your position. On the other hand, if you remain unconvinced by the criticism or the criticism simply reveals another perspective without delegitimizing the rationale developed in the source itself, it may remain a reliable source. Always go to the original sources and reach your own conclusions. Also, consider whether it is a relatively new source—if so, that may account for the fact that it has not yet been cited. By the same token, if the source is particularly controversial, it may simply be that other scholars are not yet ready to engage in that conversation. If it meets other indicia of reliability, then it is likely reliable.

- **How recently was the source published?** It is important to rely on sources that convey current information. Depending on your topic, a source published 20 years ago may now be outdated. For example, an article examining incarceration rates in the 1990s will not provide accurate data about incarceration rates in 2018. If you are doing a comparative study, however, you may well need to rely on a 1990s study to provide a baseline comparison with modern trends. Additionally, it is important to note that some old sources remain authoritative. For example, Prosser on Torts or Chemerinsky on Constitutional Law are "old" sources, but they are reliable. Old sources are periodically updated, so you need to ensure you are relying on a recent edition. You will want to carefully consider your purpose in writing when trying to determine whether a source is too outdated to be reliable.
- **Does the author demonstrate intellectual integrity?** An author demonstrates intellectual integrity in a variety of ways: (1) writing clearly and concisely; (2) revealing well-reasoned conclusions based on data and information; (3) disclosing biases; (4) addressing counterarguments or alternative systems of thought; and (5) precisely stating assumptions.

4.1.2 | Substance of the Source

Once you have identified reliable publications, it is time to determine which of these sources are important for your particular purposes. Just because a source is inherently reliable does not mean that you need to read it in its entirety. It may be that the source does not squarely address your topic or that only a portion of the source is relevant to your topic.

Step 1: Skim all the sources to determine whether the author has raised a vital question relevant to your question. If so, that source probably merits a more thorough review. It is important to take notes during this stage. If you are using pen and paper, writing notes, highlighting, and tabbing the source is a good way to begin note-taking. You will also want to write down your impressions in a notebook. In advance, think about using a system for color-coding or tagging information so you can be consistent and easily find important information during the writing phase. If you are taking notes electronically, you can use many of the same systems for highlighting and commenting. On Zotero, you can even create tags so you can search for specific information during the writing phase. Whenever you are documenting your impressions in a separate document, be sure to include a reference to the source and page number that sparked the thought. That way, you can easily recall the citation during the writing phase.

This chart can help you track the sources as you conduct the initial skim, and it emphasizes the most important information you should be documenting at this stage. This information can be noted as you are conducting your preemption check, too, and you could easily integrate it into the research tracking chart you created in Chapter 2.

TRACKING SOURCES

TITLE/AUTHOR	INDICIA OF RELIABILITY	SYNOPSIS	USE?
Taking the time to list the sources in correct *Bluebook* form will make it easier to track resources and it will save you countless hours when it comes time to finalize footnotes in the final stages.	Guided by the strategies in the previous section, state the reasons why this source is reliable.	Include a brief description of the source and explain how it might be helpful. For example, if chapter 3 of a treatise is helpful to the central question you pose, then state so in this space.	Yes/No

Step 2: Review the chart and set aside any sources marked "No" in the fourth column. They are not resources that should command your attention at this stage. You probably do not want to discard or otherwise lose these sources, however, because they may become relevant as you continue to develop your thesis.

Step 3: Prioritize the sources marked "Yes" in the last column. Your particular topic will dictate how you prioritize these resources. If you know very little about your topic, you may want to prioritize a broad resource, such as a treatise, so that you cultivate a strong foundation of knowledge on the general topic. If you already have a clear understanding of the topic generally, then you probably want to prioritize sources that more particularly address the nuances of your topic. As you prioritize the sources, take a moment to set out a general order in which you will read the resources.

4.2 | READ WITH PURPOSE

After you have prioritized sources, you will want to determine the treatment you will provide each source. The most important sources that examine nuanced issues related to your topic will need thorough reading. Indeed, those sources may need to be read multiple times in their entirety. Other sources may only be tangentially relevant to your central research question, so a more cursory review may be appropriate. You'll also want to focus on the portions of the sources that are relevant to your topic. For example, a treatise in its entirety is likely not relevant to your research question. More likely, a chapter or even a subsection of a chapter is all that is relevant. You do not necessarily need to read the entire treatise in detail. Instead, focus on the most relevant portions.

> **Checklist for Managing Research**
> 1. Identify reliable sources.
> 2. Prioritize sources relevant to your topic.
> 3. Thoroughly read and re-read the most relevant sources.
> 4. Cursorily review less relevant *sources.*

You may find it helpful to indicate which sources require thorough review and those that do not. As you work through the materials, it may provide relief from mental fatigue to intersperse lighter cursory reviews with the materials demanding a heavier cognitive effort.

For the sources needing a lighter cursory review, you will want to highlight important passages, make notes in the margin or on a separate paper about the significance of the information, and jot down your own ideas about the information being communicated. Make sure to document the source and page number when taking notes in a separate document. These notes will help you easily access important information when you are ready to write.

4.3 | WORKSHEET FOR DEVELOPING RESEARCH SUMMARY

For the sources requiring a more thorough review, it is important to take a methodological approach to ensure you do not miss important information. You will likely read a given source multiple times, and you will need to make notes about your impressions as you read as well as document any questions that arise. Consider working with resources in print. Reading on a computer screen or other device promotes skimming, which is not the best way to ensure accurate research or interpretation of other sources, whereas reading an actual book or printout forces the eyes to concentrate on a single page at a time. It is also easy to make accurate notes on a printed page, and later in the research process, it will be easier to compare sources side by side if they are in print.

The following worksheet provides guidance for how you should process and thoughtfully consider sources you intend to thoroughly review.

WORKSHEET FOR DEVELOPING RESEARCH SUMMARY

1. The main purpose of this article/essay/book is (state as accurately as possible the author's purpose for writing this article):
2. The key question that the author addresses is (figure out the key question in the mind of the author when it was written):
3. The most important information in this article is (figure out the facts, experiences, and data the author is using to support the conclusion):
4. The main inferences/conclusions in this article are (identify the key conclusions presented in the article):
5. The key concepts we need to understand in this article are (figure out the most important ideas you need to understand in order to understand the author's line of reasoning and identify what the author means by those concepts):
6. The main assumptions underlying the author's thinking are (figure out what the author is taking for granted or that might be questioned):
7. If we take this line of reasoning seriously, the implications are (what consequences are likely to follow if people take the author's line of reasoning seriously?):
8. If we fail to take this line of reasoning seriously, the implications are (what consequences are likely to follow if people ignore the author's reasoning?):
9. The main points of view presented in this article are (what is the author looking at, and how is the author seeing it?):

NEVER FORGET, YOU **CAN** DO THIS!

SQUELCH THE IMPOSTOR

The impostor voice may have you questioning:

- Have I refined my research enough?
- Do I have the stamina to do all this work?
- But I really should read everything, shouldn't I?

Here is what you can do:

- Take the research in bite-size pieces
- Talk to your mentor
- Follow your schedule
- Take breaks
- Get rest
- Eat healthy food
- Exercise
- Avoid thinking about your grade or long-term impact of your scholarship

---

Pursuing the strategies outlined in this chapter will convert the mountain of research into a manageable molehill. It is important to skim everything you find to ensure you have not been preempted, but the only resources that you **must** study and revisit are those that you intend to use in your article.

This short checklist will keep you on track:

- Identify reliable sources
- Prioritize sources relevant to your topic
- Thoroughly read and re-read the most relevant sources
- Cursorily review less relevant sources

Whether you rely on the source for support or counterargument, any source you ultimately cite must be studied and carefully analyzed to ensure it advances your thesis. Also keep in mind that you may not necessarily cite a source that you have carefully studied. Sometimes, scholars feel that they must cite to any source they have invested time in analyzing because, if they do not, they will have "wasted" their time. Sometimes, though, the greatest value of your time investment is the realization that you should not, or need not, cite to a particular source.

ASSIGNMENT

Prepare a research summary between 2,500 and 3,000 words explaining what other sources have said about the topic you chose and how these other sources fit with the thesis you formulated. A sample research summary is available in Appendix V. Organize the summary topically, not by resource, and coherently synthesize the information from all sources.

CHAPTER **5**

How Do I Use All This Information?

Analytical Framework Brainstorm

What is my purpose?

What is the issue?

What information must I rely on?

What interpretation or inference must I make?

What key concepts must I rely on?

What assumptions have I made?

Even with the most finely tuned thesis, a scholar could write any number of analyses and reach a variety of conclusions. An analytical framework provides structure and context for the development and presentation of your scholarly analysis. Analytical frameworks provide different lenses through which to consider similar legal questions.

In the context of law, analytical frameworks facilitate a systematic approach to solving legal problems. Believe it or not, you are familiar with, and have even utilized and scrutinized, analytical frameworks. You might not be familiar with the phrase "analytical frameworks," but as a law student or legal professional, you scrutinize analytical frameworks any time you study a case, and you utilize analytical frameworks when you rely on a rule of law to support legal argument. In the context of a real or hypothetical case, the analytical framework commonly follows the structure of the rule, but other policy-based or sociological frameworks sometimes drive the analysis.

To be sure, it is difficult to find a standardized definition of what "analytical framework" means, but at the core, the analytical framework is simply a systematic method of inquiry or problem-solving. In the academic context, some scholars interchange the phrases theoretical framework, conceptual framework, and analytical framework. It is beyond the scope of this book to study the intricate and nuanced differences between these concepts. For our purposes, you could potentially use a theoretical or conceptual framework as the analytical framework for your article, so do not let yourself get too bogged down trying to figure out whether you have identified an analytical framework or a conceptual one.

Instead, you should start focusing on whether you can identify systematic methods of inquiry in the works you are reading. Then, you should try to determine which systematic approach (or combination of systematic approaches) you might utilize for your own article. As explained in more detail in Chapter 6, once you begin the writing phase, you will utilize an organizational paradigm to provide *physical* structure to your article. The analytical framework is necessary to provide *conceptual* structure to your article. In other words, it is the glue that holds the ideas together while the organizational paradigm dictates the method and mode of exposition in the final written piece.

It may help to think of the organizational paradigm as a cake pan with the analytical framework as a recipe. Depending on the recipe, your cake can have a different flavor, texture, or quality, but the shape and appearance of the cakes will be similar regardless of the recipe. The same is true of scholarship—what you say will vary and be influenced by the analytical framework, but the way you say it will be predictably molded by the organizational paradigm.

Thus, while you may have inquired into your thesis in a given order as you fleshed out ideas and created an analytical framework, those steps will not necessarily explicitly appear in your final product; and if they appear at all, they will likely be in a different order as necessitated by your organizational paradigm.

5.1 | SYSTEMATIC METHODS OF INQUIRY

Advanced and well-reasoned analysis includes the following components: purpose, issue, information, interpretation and inference, concepts, assumptions, implications, consequences, and point of view.

When it comes to wedding cakes, a common question is: Do you want it to look good or taste good? With scholarship, you can have both if you develop a strong analytical framework and utilize a predictable organizational paradigm for the exposition of your ideas.

Photo credit: *Low Country Wedding Cake at Pin Point Heritage Museum, Savannah, Georgia* by Rich Burkhart.

Whatever analytical framework you choose or develop, it must account for these components.

As you progress through your project, it is important to consider all of these components in the context of your own writing as well as with regard to the sources you are using. Although the first example used in this chapter explicitly identifies its analytical framework, a lot of scholarly writing does not. The student comment example in this chapter identifies an area of law that lacks a framework and proposes a workable framework, but it does not explicitly identify the analytical framework supporting the conclusion that the existing law lacks a framework. If your source does not describe the analytical framework itself, you should attempt to identify the analytical framework by identifying the critical components.

5.1.1 | Checklist for Your Project

- *Purpose*—Purpose is inextricably intertwined with audience. As explained in Chapter 1, audience is sometimes easy to ascertain. It may be your professor, a review board, or colleagues. Sometimes, you may be addressing a friendly audience who you know is receptive to your position, or, at the other end of the spectrum, you may be addressing a hostile audience who is unwilling to be persuaded. Generally, scholars are motivated by more than just earning a grade. Perhaps you are curious and want to know more about an area of law. Maybe you want to effect change in the law or reveal an injustice. It could be that you want to document trends in the law over time. As you work through refining your topic and collecting research, you should continually ask yourself:

- What am I trying to accomplish?
- What is my central aim?
- Why am I writing?

- *Issue*—The issue is the ultimate question you decide to answer. It is inherently narrower than the initial topic you wrote about in Chapter 1. Numerous issues can arise from a single topic. Consider, for example, the topic of Florida's Stand Your Ground laws. A scholar may write a comparative article analyzing how Florida's statutory scheme compares to those of other states, or the scholar may write an article exposing a constitutional harm and offering a solution, or the scholar may write an article about the cultural implications of the statutory scheme, to name just a few. As you develop your article, you may find that it is easy to lose focus or fall off track. That is why it is important to define your issue clearly and early in the process. Tracking additional questions is also a good way to stay focused on the issue while simultaneously creating a future research agenda. As you work through refining your topic and collecting research, you should continually ask yourself:

- What question am I raising?
- What question am I addressing?
- Am I considering the complexities in the question?

- *Information*—All scholarly analysis is dependent on information, and that information comes from researching. If you write an article without doing any research and without reference to any information other than your own personal experience, the end product is not scholarship, it is mere opinion. Scholars rely on information to justify their conclusions. Information may take the form of data, results from studies conducted by the scholar or other reliable entities, statutes and cases, or research conducted by other scholars.

As you work through refining your topic and collecting research, you should continually ask yourself:

- What original source information am I using to support my conclusions?
- What experience have I had to support my claims?
- What additional information do I need to settle this question?

- *Inferences*—Inferences are the connective tissue binding your understanding of the significance of the information you have been researching. Your job as a scholar is not to merely report what the information is; rather, your job is to explain the significance of the information in light of the issue as you have defined it. By explicitly identifying the inferences you make, you help your audience understand the purpose and significance of your scholarship. As you work through refining your topic and collecting research, you should continually ask yourself:

- How did I reach this conclusion?
- Is there another way to interpret the information?
- Have I entered into a conversation with other scholars?

- *Concepts*—Most issues relate to law and society beyond the scope of any given article. Part of creating a connection with your audience involves demonstrating the relevance of the issue to other areas of law, even if a full exploration of the other area is beyond the scope of your project. Understanding related concepts helps you and your audience grasp the significance of your scholarship. You may also be able to utilize analytical frameworks from other related areas to develop your thesis. As you work through refining your topic and collecting research, you should continually ask yourself:

- What areas of law are implicated by my thesis?
- What other areas of scholarly study are implicated by my thesis?
- How can I explain my thesis?

- *Assumptions*—Making assumptions is a natural brain activity in humans. We process so much information that making assumptions is a basic survival skill. Assumptions, however, can lead to bias or misinterpretation of data and information. Scholars must continually question their assumptions to ensure accurate and correct interpretation of the information collected through research. Disclosing these assumptions also aids the audience in understanding how to read your scholarship. As you work through refining your topic and collecting research, you should continually ask yourself:

- What am I taking for granted?
- Why have I reached my conclusion?
- What assumptions have led me to my conclusion?

- *Implications*—Legal scholarship matters in large part because it alerts its audience to important issues in the law. Many articles act as warnings and offer solutions to problems that already exist. Other articles may predict future problems and offer strategies for avoiding those problems. Directly stating the implications of your article will help your audience understand why it should care about the issue at all. As you work through refining your topic and collecting research, you should continually ask yourself:

  - What are the consequences of my conclusions?
  - How will my theory operate in practice?
  - How will my conclusions impact the law, culture, and society?

- *Point of view*—Addressing competing points of view is one of the easiest ways to establish credibility with your audience. By disclosing other theories and methods of analyzing an issue, you build rapport with your audience and help the audience understand all the ways to think about an issue. Identifying other points of view also helps you to evaluate potential weaknesses in your own position and forces you to explain why your point of view is superior to another that already exists. As you work through refining your topic and collecting research, you should continually ask yourself:

  - How will I include alternate points of view?
  - How does my point of view square with other points of view?
  - How is my viewpoint justified vis-à-vis other viewpoints?

5.1.2 | Checklist for Sources

Remember, an analytical framework provides a system for figuring out the problem, but it necessarily relies on certain assumptions, data, concepts, and theories that influence the ultimate conclusions. As researchers, we often take for granted information that we already know, and we also assume that what we already know is correct. It is important to permit yourself to question what you think you already know, and it is important to question the conclusions reached by other authors whose work you intend to use in your own scholarship. Remember, always look up the original sources cited by other authors. Additionally, if you can identify the analytical framework the author uses, it will be easier for you to identify all the assumptions, perspectives, and concepts that are influencing the ultimate conclusion. You do not need to process this checklist for every resource you consult, but you should use this checklist for any resource you intend to utilize to support your own analysis. Once you have written your own paper, you will want to use this checklist to verify your analytical framework. In Appendix IX, you will find two articles that have been annotated using this checklist.

- What is the topic of the reading?
- What is the setting (place and time)?
- What is the thesis? Recall a thesis differs from a topic in that it includes the writer's position on the topic.
- What evidence supports the author's argument?
- How is the work organized?
- What questions is the author interested in?
- What does the author take for granted?
- What does the author assume?
- What information and evidence does the author utilize?
- Does the author disclose any bias?
- Does the author's work conflict with others? Does the author account for this conflict?
- How will the author's theories operate in practice?
- Has the author impacted the law, culture, or society? If not, how would the author's proposals impact the law, culture, and society?
- What aspect of the work resonates with you?
- How has this writing shaped your understanding of the issue?

5.2 | UNIVERSAL INTELLECTUAL STANDARDS[1]

In addition to providing a systematic approach to legal analysis, using an analytical framework ensures the analysis comports with Universal

---

1. The information in this section is adapted from Richard Paul & Linda Elder, *Critical Thinking: Concepts & Tools* (2014).

Intellectual Standards. In both your own writing as well as the sources you intend to use to support your analysis, you must ensure the reasoning is sound, systematic, and intelligent. In essence, the analytical framework is the systematic approach that provides a check to ensure your analysis is sound and intelligent.

Clarity	• Clarity is a gateway standard. If something is unclear, its accuracy cannot be verified. Questions to help you determine clarity: Could you elaborate further on that point? Could you express it another way? Could you illustrate it? Could you give an example?
Accuracy	• Even if a statement is clear, it may simply be untrue. Is the statement supported by other authorities? Has the statement been called into question by other authorities?
Precision	• Accurate and clear statements may still lack sufficient detail or precision to support the analysis. Does the statement provide enough detail to understand the implications of the proposition? What additional information might you want to know?
Relevance	• Sometimes statements may be clear, accurate, and precise, but are simply irrelevant to the analysis. How is the statement connected to the overall question? How does the statement bear on the issue?
Depth	• Scholarly legal analysis should address the complexities inherent in your thesis. Are you dealing with the most significant factors? Have you tackled the most difficult questions? Have you asked every "why" there is to ask?
Breadth	• Scholarly legal analysis should also consider other relevant viewpoints. Is there another way to look at the question? What would this look like from a conservative viewpoint? What about a liberal one?
Logic	• Frequently, once a writer delves into the research, the research may support a conclusion different than the one initially anticipated. Instead of trying to force a conclusion you desire, allow the research to guide you toward a logical conclusion. Does the analysis lead to a logical conclusion? Does the analysis make sense in light of the research? Do your conclusions make sense? Are you internally consistent?
Fairness	• Fairness requires you to treat other viewpoints and sources in good faith. We naturally think from our own perspective which means we usually privilege our own position. Fairness implies that you treat all relevant viewpoints equally without reference to your own feelings or interests. Because we tend to be biased in favor of our own viewpoint, it is important to keep the standard of fairness at the forefront of our thinking. Have you distorted information to maintain your desired perspective or outcome? Have you unfairly attacked the author rather than the method? Have you carefully unpacked the flawed argument?

Focusing on Universal Intellectual Standards will help you ensure your analysis is sound and complete. With any research project, there is always a risk that your initial hypothesis is disproven. What should you do if you discover that your research does not support your thesis? Without question, you must rework your thesis. Scholars must be willing to learn and change their minds about things that they think they know when the research calls for a change. Speaking from personal experience, I had to completely reverse my thesis when writing my first three articles because I proved myself wrong during the research and initial drafting phases. My analytical frameworks provided a systematic method of inquiry to ensure that my conclusions were ultimately sound and intelligent.

Changing your thesis may require you to revisit an earlier stage in the process. Perhaps you need to rethink how you have defined the issue. Maybe you need to conduct more research. What is certain is that you will need to invest more time in your project. Failure to adapt your thesis to the research will inevitably lead to your credibility being questioned. A thesis that is unsupported by research does not comport with the Universal Intellectual Standards and does not constitute sound analysis. If you develop a strong analytical framework, you, too, will naturally ensure the standards are met because the framework itself demands a systematic method of inquiry.

5.3 | SPECIFIC FRAMEWORKS

Most of the resources you will use incorporate some sort of analytical framework, although many articles do not explicitly identify the framework. Few authors invent a framework from whole cloth, although some scholars do spend their entire careers seeking to develop complete theories of jurisprudence for the purpose of solving complex and multi-faceted legal problems. You will likely not want to undertake the task of developing a new analytical framework for a variety of reasons, not the least of which is, as a new scholar, you are still learning how to identify and work with frameworks. If you are reading this book, you likely do not yet have the experience to invent a framework on your own.

Analytical frameworks can derive from a number of sources, but most authors rely on some philosophy of law or normative jurisprudence.

In recent years, it has even become more widely accepted in the legal academy to rely on interdisciplinary frameworks. Frameworks that derive from philosophy of law tend to provide for a more descriptive approach to figuring out the law, while normative and interdisciplinary frameworks provide for a more prescriptive approach. A descriptive approach typically describes the issue and its implications, while a prescriptive approach not only describes the problem but also offers a solution to the problem.

The following are just a few examples of sources from which you might derive your analytical framework.

5.3.1 | Philosophy of Law

Philosophy of law is the philosophical analysis and study of the law and legal institutions. If you have taken a jurisprudence course, you probably have some familiarity with some of the concepts. If you are not familiar with philosophy of law or jurisprudence, your mentor should be able to guide you in finding sources relevant to your topic.

Philosophy of law can be broken down into three broad categories: analytic jurisprudence, normative jurisprudence, and critical theories of law. Analytic jurisprudence seeks to understand the essence of the law and to identify what differentiates the law from other systems of norms. Normative jurisprudence takes a more specific focus to examine the normative, evaluative, and prescriptive issues of law, such as purposes of punishment and obligations to obey the law. Finally, critical theories of law expose legal systems, institutions, and laws to ensure transparency and general understanding. Typically, critical legal scholars identify systemic injustice caused by the law and propose solutions to the injustices. Although most philosophies of law are too broad to provide a working analytical framework, most analytical frameworks derive from some philosophy of law. The tables below provide details about some of the most common philosophies of American law, but keep in mind these lists are not exhaustive.

ANALYTIC JURISPRUDENCE

Natural law	Legal positivism	Legal realism	Legal interpretivism
finds ultimate authority in nature and demands that the laws of man submit to those of nature. Natural law theorists believe a man-made law is not a true law when it is contrary to natural law.	finds ultimate legal authority in the social rules or practices that identify certain norms as laws. H. L. A. Hart is the premier voice contending that the law is simply a system of social rules to guide the conduct of members of society and secondary rules that regulate how the primary rules may be changed.	finds ultimate legal authority in the actual practices of courts, law offices, and police stations, rather than in the rules and doctrines set forth in statutes or learned treatises.	finds ultimate legal authority in society taking into consideration moral truths about the justification for societal practices.

NORMATIVE JURISPRUDENCE

Utilitarianism posits that laws should be created so as to produce the best consequences. Defining what the best consequence might be is a critical part of any analysis that uses utilitarianism as a framework.	Deontology posits that laws should protect individual autonomy, liberty, and rights.	Libertarianism would impose a market ideology on legal systems, positing that minimal government is essential to a free society and that the primary function of law should be enforcement of contracts. The market will naturally produce social order.

CRITICAL LEGAL STUDIES

Critical Race Theory examines the relationship between race, law, and power and typically advocates for change to legal institutions to promote justice, equity, and equality.	**Critical Feminist Theory** examines the relationship between gender, law, and power, and typically advocates for change to legal institutions to promote justice, equity, and equality.	**Critical Class Theory** examines the relationship between class, wealth, and poverty vis-à-vis law and power, typically advocating for change to legal institutions to promote justice, equity, and equality.

In addition to these philosophies of law, many legal scholars engage in interdisciplinary work where they rely on analytical frameworks from other fields such as philosophy, sociology, or criminology, to name a few. Most critical studies, for example, rely on some other area of law, such as philosophy, economics, history, sociology, or criminology.

Scholars disagree about the legitimacy of interdisciplinary work. Legal purists are of the mind that philosophy of law provides enough of a framework for the pure study of law and reliance upon other fields of study is wrong. Interdisciplinarians see the law as inextricably integrated with every other sociological and cultural system that exists. To them, failure to study related concepts provides an incomplete and erroneous understanding not only of the law itself, but also of its implications. If you consider relying on a framework developed for another field, you will need to seriously consider your audience's receptivity to the interdisciplinary approach as well as your ability to justify using the approach at all.

5.4 | IDENTIFYING AND USING AN ANALYTICAL FRAMEWORK

In this section, we will study an excerpt from a law review article to practice identifying an analytical framework. Inherent in this guided study is the identification of a systematic methodology and Universal Intellectual Standards.

The following excerpt is a snapshot of the introduction to an article that is particularly explicit regarding the analytical framework it will utilize. The entire article has been reproduced in Appendix IX and is annotated with the notes consistent with the practices set forth in this book.

Notice how the title communicates the author's purpose: to change Florida's Stand Your Ground Laws.

A Call for Change:
A Contextual-Configurative Analysis of Florida's "Stand Your Ground" Laws

ELIZABETH MEGALE

Section II will explain the framework and Section III will apply it.

I. INTRODUCTION

Public response to the shooting death of Trayvon Martin evidenced a drastic schism in community values. To some, the problem of "Stand Your Ground" represents purely a race issue that not only perpetuates endemic racial tensions amongst members of society,[1] but also generally protects whites more often than blacks.[2] On the other hand, some view the statutory scheme as a non-racist[3] protection of individual liberties that makes the community safer.[4] These two perspectives lie at the opposite ends of the spectrum, and both perspectives tend to oversimplify a complex issue.

In tracking the media coverage, protests, and commentary related to Florida's most recent "Stand Your Ground" cases, it is readily apparent that the various interest groups and individuals weighing in are sharply

The author identifies competing points of view and criticizes their oversimplification of a complex issue.

---

1. Michael H. Cottman, *Commentary: Zimmerman Acquittal Says it's Open Season on Black Males*, BLACK AM. WEB (July 14, 2013), http://blackamericaweb.com/2013/07/14/zimmerman-acquittal-black-teens/.
2. *Id.*
3. Matt Wilstein, *Ted Cruz Tells Trayvon's Mother Why Stand Your Ground Laws Can't Possibly Be 'Racist*,' MEDIAITE (Oct. 29, 2013), http://www.mediaite.com/tv/ted-cruz-tells-trayvons-mother-why-stand-your-ground-laws-cant-possibly-be-racist.
4. Abby Goodnough, *Florida Expands Right to Use Deadly Force in Self-Defense*, N.Y. TIMES (Apr. 27, 2005), http://www.nytimes.com/2005/04/27/national/27shoot.html.

1051

1052   UNIVERSITY OF MIAMI LAW REVIEW   [Vol. 68:1051]

> Do you think the author treats the opposing viewpoints fairly? From the introduction, you may not have enough information to know.

> The author explains that this framework was not created for use in this context, but explains why it is a valid framework for analysis of the questions contemplated by this article.

divided.[5] This disagreement occurs for two principle reasons. First, the participants embrace fundamentally different value structures, so their acceptance of the legitimacy of Florida's "Stand Your Ground" law will naturally create dissonance. Second, most viewpoints being advanced are far too myopic to account for the multi-faceted issues presented by Florida's version of "Stand Your Ground."

This Article attempts to account for each of the competing viewpoints related to the statutory scheme. This author's position is that in legalizing certain types of homicide by decriminalizing killings and other acts of violence involving self-defense,[6] Florida has exchanged respect for human dignity with cold self-import.[7] To examine the process by which this transformation occurred, this Article relies on a jurisprudential model, created by Yale professors Harold Lasswell and Myres McDougal, for the preservation of human dignity.[8] It is important to note that this theory of legal inquiry was intended to be applicable to both micro and macro analyses,[9] though most scholars have employed it as a tool for studying international law and politics.[10] The peculiar feature of this model, however, is that it also specifically contemplates individuals, making it uniquely suited to the inquiry of any legal system.[11]

As a central premise, it establishes that effective[12] law requires the existence of both authority and control.[13] Authority and control manifest when laws are created consistently with commonly held community values.[14] By the same token, if a law is inconsistent with commonly held values, it may lose its authority, control, or both.[15] In the case of Florida's "Stand Your Ground" statutory scheme, this Article suggests that the turmoil following the shooting death of Trayvon Martin and the continuing media attention of other shooting deaths since that time illustrate the inconsistency between the law and relevant human values.

---

5. Elizabeth Megale, *Disaster Unaverted: Reconciling the Desire for Safe and Secure State with the Grim Realities of Stand Your Ground*, 37 AM. J. TRIAL ADVOC. 255, 282 (2013).

6. *Id.* at 257.

7. *Id.*; Elizabeth Megale, *Deadly Combinations, How Self-Defense Laws Pairing Immunity with a Presumption of Fear Allow Criminals to 'Get Away with Murder,'* 34 AM. J. TRIAL ADVOC. 105 (2010).

8. HAROLD D. LASSWELL & MYERS S. MCDOUGAL, JURISPRUDENCE FOR A FREE SOCIETY (1992).

9. *Id.* at 335; *see also* WINSTON P. NAGAN, CONTEXTUAL-CONFIGURATION JURISPRUDENCE: THE LAW, SCIENCE, AND POLICIES OF HUMAN DIGNITY 3 (2013).

10. NAGAN, *supra* note 9, at vi.

11. *Id.* at i.

12. The Lasswell/McDougal model predates modern legal legitimacy discourse, though it employs similar vocabulary. Modern theories about legitimacy of the law are beyond the scope of this Article.

13. LASSWELL & MCDOUGAL, *supra* note 8, at 400.

14. *Id.*

15. *Id.* at 401.

A CALL FOR CHANGE 1053

The legal theory mapped out by Lasswell and McDougal employs a discrete vocabulary attributing particularized meanings to words, which are sometimes inconsistent with common parlance.[16] Throughout this Article, these terms will be defined in the words of the authors and used as intended within the jurisprudential context.[17] The analytical framework creates a launching point with identification of an outcome relevant to a particular value situation.[18] From there, pre- and post-outcomes can be determined.[19] Once outcomes are identified, the community participants must be identified.[20] The value situation is assessed by analyzing the participants, their values, and the strategies used to leverage their values to gain command over others and achieve a specific outcome and effect.[21] Section II provides the background for this normative framework.

Section III applies this jurisprudential framework in the context of Florida's "Stand Your Ground" statutes. It begins the legal analysis by identifying the decision to enact Florida's "Stand Your Ground" as the central outcome giving rise to the present value situation. The pre- and post-outcomes will be analyzed together with the participants, their values, and strategies for leveraging to achieve the desired outcome. The effects will then be identified and interpreted to reach the conclusion that Florida's "Stand Your Ground" law is inconsistent with commonly held community values. Finally, Section IV concludes by examining the implications of the analysis and suggesting reforms for aligning the law with community values.

> The author sets forth a clear and precise roadmap for how the article will explain and utilize the analytical framework to resolve whether Florida's Stand Your Ground laws should be changed.

II. NORMATIVE FRAMEWORK

Jurisprudence for a Free Society[22] is the two-volume magnum opus of Myres McDougal and Harold Lasswell. Labeled contextual-configurative jurisprudence,[23] it is a normative response to the tension cre-

---

16. *Id.* at 391–97 ("It is beyond dispute that new modes of discourse are difficult to grasp and assess. In part, this comes about because the processes of thought and of communication typically receive scant attention during formative years. Although vocabularies are taught, they are seldom examined as phenomena whose fundamental principles ought to be part of the intellectual equipment of every educated member of society. As a result, it is much more difficult than need be for educated persons to master relatively new and systematic modes of discourse.").
17. EMILE DURKHEIM, SUICIDE: A STUDY IN SOCIOLOGY 41 (1951) (providing particularized definitions is not unusual because "words of everyday language, like the concepts they express are always susceptible of more than one meaning, and the scholar employing them in their accepted use without further definition would risk serious misunderstanding").
18. LASSWELL & McDOUGAL, *supra* note 8, at 379.
19. *Id.*
20. *Id.* at 381.
21. *Id.*
22. *Id.*
23. *Id.* at vi.

Notice how, from the beginning, the analytical framework begins to shape how the overarching question is framed, the analysis of the competing viewpoints, and the systematic method of inquiry the writer will follow when analyzing the issues surrounding Florida's Stand Your Ground laws. Moreover, every single point in the checklists in sections 5.1.1 and 5.1.2 of this chapter are either addressed or foreshadowed in this relatively short introduction section. We see that the author states a purpose and identifies the issues, that she foreshadows the information she will rely upon in supporting her conclusions, and that she introduces many of the concepts, assumptions, and implications in the paper. She is forthright regarding her viewpoint and potential biases.

The writing is also clear and concise. Each sentence includes a reference to another source, so at a glance it seems accurate and precise. As a diligent scholar, you would of course want to check the sources to ensure the author has treated them fairly and presented the information accurately. From the introduction, it also appears that the author is using a framework that requires substantial depth and breadth of analysis. The author explains how the framework is relevant, and the roadmap foreshadows a logical analysis to follow.

Here is an example of scholarly work written by a student, but this one does not identify the overarching analytical framework quite so explicitly. Her thesis is that North Carolina campaign finance law lacks cohesion and that judicial analysis has lacked a workable analytical framework. Her article proposes an analytical framework for resolving campaign finance issues.

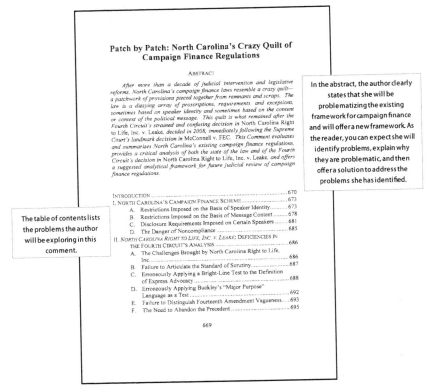

Patch by Patch: North Carolina's Crazy Quilt of Campaign Finance Regulations

ABSTRACT

After more than a decade of judicial intervention and legislative reforms, North Carolina's campaign finance laws resemble a crazy quilt— a patchwork of provisions pieced together from remnants and scraps. The law is a dizzying array of proscriptions, requirements, and exceptions, sometimes based on speaker identity and sometimes based on the content or context of the political message. This quilt is what remained after the Fourth Circuit's strained and confusing decision in North Carolina Right to Life, Inc. v. Leake, decided in 2008, immediately following the Supreme Court's landmark decision in McConnell v. FEC. This Comment evaluates and summarizes North Carolina's existing campaign finance regulations, provides a critical analysis of both the state of the law and of the Fourth Circuit's decision in North Carolina Right to Life, Inc. v. Leake, and offers a suggested analytical framework for future judicial review of campaign finance regulations.

In the abstract, the author clearly states that she will be problematizing the existing framework for campaign finance and will offer a new framework. As the reader, you can expect she will identify problems, explain why they are problematic, and then offer a solution to address the problems she has identified.

The table of contents lists the problems the author will be exploring in this comment.

669

INTRODUCTION

Modern political campaigns are dominated by political ads and the money required to produce and air them. Candidates and Political Action Committees break new fundraising records every election cycle.[1] By July 31, 2016, Hillary Clinton and Donald Trump, along with their Super PACs and party committees, raised over $1 billion for the 2016 presidential contest.[2] Here in North Carolina in the same period, candidates for state and local races raised more than $38 million.[3] Independent political groups spent another $33.1 million, with more than $16 million spent on the gubernatorial race alone.[4]

Campaign finance regulations seek to ensure that candidates raising such large sums of money are not doing so in exchange for political favors, and if they are, that the public has sufficient information available to hold them accountable. These regulations pose a tricky balancing act for the federal and state governments. Political speech is vital to our democracy and has been the bedrock of our nation's history.[5] Citizens expect the

The introduction begins by broadly identifying the two competing interests that have led to the problem of campaign finance.

---

1. Paul Blumenthal, *Get Ready for the Most Expensive Senate Races of All Time*, HUFFINGTON POST (Sept. 30, 2016, 4:11 AM), https://perma.cc/A85U-4ZWQ.

2. Anu Narayanswamy, Darla Cameron & Matea Gold, *Campaign 2016: Money Raised as of July 31*, WASH. POST (July 31, 2016), https://perma.cc/VB3Y-TF7Q.

3. Ctr. for Responsive Politics, *North Carolina, State Summary, 2016 Cycle*, OPENSECRETS.ORG, https://perma.cc/A6G7-K2EW.

4. Alex Kotch, *North Carolina's 2016 State Elections Smashed Outside Spending Records*, FACING SOUTH (Feb. 22, 2017), https://perma.cc/T8VK-63ZE.

5. Whitney v. California, 274 U.S. 357, 375 (1927) (Brandeis, J., concurring). The Founders

> believed that freedom to think as you will and to speak as you think are means indispensable to the discovery and spread of political truth .... They knew ... that it is hazardous to discourage thought, hope and imagination; that fear breeds repression; that repression breeds hate; that hate menaces stable government; that

greatest freedom when they engage in political speech. But, for the last century, free-flowing political discourse has had to yield to protections against the threat of corruption. As candidates continue to appeal to anonymous donors who pour millions of dollars into state and national campaigns, the public is apt to suspect that political favors will be exchanged for those donations. When the public perceives corruption in the political process, distrust of government often follows, and that can be as damaging to our system of government as the constraint of speech.

As a result, federal and state governments have sought to carefully thread the needle—permitting the broadest free speech possible while also ensuring that campaign contributions do not result in corruption or seriously undermine the public's confidence in our electoral system. That struggle has resulted in a set of regulations and exceptions so confusing that an average citizen could easily run afoul of the law without ever intending to do so.[6] As the Fourth Circuit noted:

> It is no unfounded fear that one day the regulation of elections may resemble the Internal Revenue Code, and that impossible complexity may take root in the very area where freedom from intrusive governmental oversight should matter most."[7]

If we have not yet reached that day, it is fast approaching.

For more than a decade, North Carolina has made piecemeal revisions to its campaign finance laws, amending, repealing, or replacing sections of the law in response to court orders.[8] The result is a code that has lost its original purpose. It is a quilt stitched together without a pattern. The average citizen is left unsure what the law is, with his speech chilled by the threat of criminal sanction if he fails to adequately understand how to comply with the law. In its current form, North Carolina's campaign

---

the path of safety lies in the opportunity to discuss freely supposed grievances and proposed remedies; and that the fitting remedy for evil counsels is good ones.

Id.

6. *See* Citizens United v. FEC, 558 U.S. 310, 335–36 (2010) (holding that the Federal Election Commission's two-part, eleven-factor balancing test amounted to a prior restraint on speech because an average speaker who desired to avoid criminal liability would need to ask the government whether his speech was regulated).

7. N.C. Right to Life, Inc. v. Leake (*NCRL III*), 525 F.3d 274, 296 (4th Cir. 2008).

8. *See* Act of May 4, 1999, no. 31, 1999 N.C. Sess. Laws 34 (revising the definition of "political committee" in response to the holding in N.C. Right to Life, Inc. v. Bartlett, 168 F.3d 705, 712–13 (4th Cir. 1999)); Act of Aug. 19, 2007, no. 391, § 3, 2007 N.C. Sess. Laws 1150, 1152 (repealing the $3,000 rebuttable presumption that had previously been used to classify issue advocacy after the test was held unconstitutional in N.C. Right to Life, Inc. v. Leake, 344 F.3d 418, 430 (4th Cir. 2003)); Act of Aug. 2, 2008, no. 150, 2008 N.C. Sess. Laws 605 (titled in part as "An Act . . . to Respond to the Decision of the 4th Circuit U.S. Court of Appeals in North Carolina Right to Life v. Leake").

Here the author hearkens to deeply-held values dear to the American people. She is providing a broad context and clearly stating the significance and importance of what she is saying.

The author is essentially saying that the reason the law has become such a mess is because there has not been a systematic approach. Piecemeal legislation is the antithesis of an analytical framework—it is ineffective to try to solve legal problems without a systematic method of inquiry. In other words, an analytical framework is essential.

672   CAMPBELL LAW REVIEW   [Vol. 40:2

finance regulations fail to accomplish the government's goals of encouraging political participation while limiting the possibility and perception of corruption.

This Comment will begin by providing an overview of North Carolina's campaign finance regime, explaining which individuals and organizations are subject to regulation and which types of speech are subject to regulation. It will also explain how the North Carolina Board of Elections[9] uses disclosure reporting requirements along with civil and criminal penalties to fulfill its duty to regulate campaign finance.

Part II offers a critique of the Fourth Circuit Court of Appeals' decision in *North Carolina Right to Life, Inc. v. Leake*,[10] which struck two provisions of North Carolina's campaign finance laws as facially unconstitutional. Rather than analyzing the law's ability to achieve a governmental interest without burdening constitutionally protected speech, the court subjected the law to bright-line tests that it incorrectly adopted and applied.

Part III proposes a framework for future review of challenges to campaign finance regulations. This framework suggests that the court proceed by (1) identifying the type of burden imposed by the regulation, (2) selecting the appropriate level of constitutional scrutiny, (3) determining whether the method of regulation chosen is capable of achieving that stated purpose, and (4) determining whether the law incidentally burdens protected speech that the government need not regulate in order to accomplish its purpose. Finally, the court should assess the law for vagueness under both the First and Fourteenth Amendments.

This Comment concludes by asserting that what remains of North Carolina's campaign finance regime is incapable of achieving the

---

9. On December 16, 2016, the Bi-Partisan Ethics, Elections and Court Reform Act was enacted and signed by outgoing Governor Pat McCrory. S. 4, 2016 Gen. Assemb., 4th Extra Sess. (N.C. 2016). The Act combined the North Carolina Board of Elections and the North Carolina Ethics Commission into a new board designated The North Carolina Bipartisan State Board of Elections and Ethics Enforcement. The incoming Governor, Roy Cooper, challenged the new act and a preliminary injunction was issued blocking all portions of the law from taking effect. Cooper v. Berger, No. 16 CVS 15636, 2017 WL 1433242 (N.C. Super. Ct. Jan. 6, 2017). The Act was repealed and replaced by the Bipartisan Board of Elections and Ethics Enforcement Act five months later. S. 68, 2017 Gen. Assemb., Reg. Sess. (N.C. 2017). The portions of the Act which provided for the composition of the new board were found unconstitutional by the North Carolina Supreme Court. Cooper v. Berger, 809 S.E.2d 98 (N.C. 2018). The legislature again sought to combine the board and commission immediately following the court's holding. H.B. 90, 2018 Gen. Assemb., Reg. Sess. (N.C. 2018). For the sake of clarity, throughout this Article the board is referred to as the Board of Elections.

10. *NCRL III*, 525 F.3d 274.

The framework proposed by the author identifies a multi-step process to ensure integrity and soundness of decision-making when campaign finance issues arise.

The author explicitly states what she will be criticizing and how she will criticize it. Her thesis is clearly stated: the court erred when it failed to "analyz[e] the law's ability to achieve a governmental interest without burdening constitutionally protected speech" and instead "subjected the law to bright-line tests that it incorrectly adopted and applied."

The author concludes by emphasizing the significance of the problem subject of this comment.

governmental interest that is purportedly the justification for its existence. Instead, the law unconstitutionally chills free speech. The resulting patchwork of regulation is so complex that an average citizen cannot understand it and, without the assistance of an attorney, could face criminal penalties for innocently violating the law through the simple act of collectively associating and advocating for a candidate.

I.   NORTH CAROLINA'S CAMPAIGN FINANCE SCHEME

North Carolina's statutory scheme for regulating campaign finance restricts political speech in three primary ways. It imposes restrictions on the basis of the speaker's identity; it imposes restrictions on the basis of the content of certain messages; and it imposes disclosure requirements on certain speakers and messages. The statute uses civil and criminal penalties to enforce the law. The following sections will summarize those restrictions, requirements, and penalties.

A.   *Restrictions Imposed on the Basis of Speaker Identity*

North Carolina's statutes identify seven types of speakers subject to regulation: (1) individuals,[11] (2) candidates,[12] (3) for-profit corporations,[13] (4) non-profit corporations,[14] (5) segregated funds created by corporations or labor unions,[15] (6) political parties and their affiliated party committees,[16] and (7) any other organization which has "the major purpose to support or oppose" the nomination, election, or defeat of a candidate (political action committees, colloquially known as PACs).[17]   The regulations impose different burdens on the different types of speakers,

11. *See generally* N.C. GEN. STAT. §§ 163A-1410 to -1505 (2017) ("Regulating Contributions and Expenditures in Political Campaigns"). Registered lobbyists are subject to more stringent regulations. *Id.* § 163A-1427. Discussion of the constitutionality of these restrictions is beyond the scope of this Comment; however, for a more thorough discussion on the constitutionality of these restrictions, see *N.C. Right to Life, Inc. v. Bartlett*, 3 F. Supp. 2d 675 (E.D.N.C. 1998).
12. §§ 163A-1411(9), -1475(2).
13. *Id.* §§ 163A-1411(24), -1436.
14. *Id.* § 163A-1436(h).
15. *Id.* § 163A-1436(g); *see also id.* § 163A-1436(d).
16. *Id.* §§ 163A-1411(76), -1416 to -1417.
17. *Id.* § 163A-1411(74)(d).   The statute defines a political committee as "a combination of two or more individuals ... that makes ... contributions or expenditures and has ... the major purpose to support or oppose the nomination or election of one or more clearly identified candidates." *Id.* § 163A-1411(74).

In these excerpts, the analytical frameworks have facilitated the analysis and its presentation to the audience in an intelligent and thoughtful way. In your own paper, using an analytical framework will help you do the same.

If you are still wondering, "what in the world is an analytical framework?" that is normal! This abstract concept is hard to understand until you start digging into the research and you realize that all reliable scholarship has some sort of framework. The framework is simply a systematic and methodological inquiry. If you are worried that you will not be able to develop a framework for your project, that is normal, too! Fear not—if you follow the steps in this book, your analytical framework will naturally unfold. Remember, it is not necessary to label or name your framework; what is important is that your framework ensures that the Universal Intellectual Standards are met and the components of a systematic method of inquiry are present.

You will undoubtedly uncover myriad articles with strong analytical frameworks in the course of your research, but if you are interested in seeing other particularly good examples of analytical frameworks, consider reading these articles:

1. Lucille A. Jewel, *Bourdieu and American Legal Education: How Law Schools Reproduce Social Stratification and Class Hierarchy*, 56 Buff. L. Rev. 1155 (2008).
2. Teri A. McMurtry-Chubb, *#SayHerName #BlackWomensLivesMatter: State Violence in Policing the Black Female Body*, 67 Mercer L. Rev. 651 (2016).
3. Elizabeth Megale, *The Invisible Man: How the Sex Offender Registry Results in Social Death*, 2 J.L. & Soc. Deviance 92 (2011).
4. Song Richardson and Phillip Atiba Goff, *Self-Defense and the Suspicion Heuristic*, 294 Iowa L. Rev. 293 (2013).

NEVER FORGET, YOU **CAN** DO THIS!

SQUELCH THE IMPOSTOR

The impostor voice may have you questioning:

- How in the world will I ever figure out my analytical framework?
- Who am I to question any other scholar?

Here is what you can do:

- Practice using the checklist with all your most important sources
- Talk to your mentor
- Develop a methodological system for working through your sources
- Write down what you like about other scholars' approaches
- Start working through your own ideas using the checklist
- Avoid thinking about your grade or long-term impact of your scholarship

Remember that you do not need to invent your own analytical framework for your scholarly analysis. On the contrary, you establish credibility by identifying a relevant framework and utilizing it to analyze the question you have identified. Identifying and choosing an analytical framework can seem daunting at first, especially if you have not delved deeply into the research yet. The best way to become familiar with analytical frameworks is to read scholarly analysis. You will start to recognize the papers that effectively utilize analytical frameworks, and how the effective use of the framework helps the author advance the thesis.

Appendix IX contains the entirety of the two articles excerpted above. You can review the annotated articles in their entirety to gain practice at identifying and studying analytical frameworks. You can also study the articles you have pulled for your own research project and engage in the same type of analysis demonstrated in this chapter. Chances are you will ultimately choose a framework that has already been utilized in your area of study.

ASSIGNMENT

Identify an analytical framework you wish to use for your scholarly paper and respond to the following:

1. Describe the method of inquiry demanded by the framework.
2. Explain why the framework is relevant to this project.
3. Outline how the framework will guide your written analysis.
4. Identify others who have used or criticized this framework.
5. List any potential assumptions, inferences, or biases inherent in the framework.
6. Identify any theory of law or jurisprudence from which the framework derives.

An example is provided in Appendix VI.

CHAPTER **6**

Putting Pen to Paper

Writing Phase Brainstorm

Why is what I'm saying important?

Who will want to read my article—who is my audience?

How do I know what I'm saying is accurate?

Have I documented my sources appropriately?

What are my own biases?

How have I protected the integrity of my work from my bias?

Throughout the research process, you have been engaged in many pre-writing activities, such as writing a topic selection essay, a preemption report, and a research plan and summary. These pre-writing assignments have guided you in refining your thesis and planning exactly what you want to say.

Now, it is time to put pen to paper and write. Like other phases of this project, the writing process is often not linear and occurs in multiple recursive phases. It could be that you have already written a good deal of substantive background information in drafting your topic selection essay, preemption report, and research summary. You may find that you have solid ideas about what you want to add to the scholarly conversation, or you may find that you are battling the impostor voice as you try to develop your own thoughts about the information you have found. Either way, it is important to continue on systematically.

So far, your assignments may have been largely organized around sources. This is the phase where you must finally synthesize the ideas from all your sources and begin organizing around concepts, not sources. This is also the phase where you must decide on a physical organizational structure and title for your article. After completing the assignment in Chapter 5, you should have developed a solid analytical framework for the concepts your article will develop, and the annotated outline you draft in this chapter will facilitate the exposition of your thesis through the context of the analytical framework.

As you put pen to paper, it is important to remember your audience, your purpose, and your central issue. Creating an outline can help you synthesize your analysis within the bounds of a workable analytical framework. All the assignments you have completed throughout this book have forced you to do much of the pre-writing that is necessary for a project of this nature, and working from those as your starting point will help you manage your time and ensure you remain focused. It is also important to set reasonable expectations for yourself. The first scholarly article you write will likely take you a long time to complete. As you complete more projects, you will gain fluidity as you become more familiar and comfortable with the process.

Try to consistently dedicate time to completing your project and take the liberty of working on discrete sections of your project instead of attempting to write the entire paper from beginning to end. Chunking the tasks will make the process easier to manage. Expect to spend much more time on revising and editing than on initially writing. It is important to get some words down on the page even if they do not accurately communicate your entire thought at first. During the revision and editing phases, you can refine your ideas, rearrange your sentences and paragraphs, and supplement the initial draft. Finally, actively seek the satisfaction that comes from learning and from accomplishing a significant aspiration—set interim goals so that you can monitor and track your progress, take breaks as necessary, and revisit earlier phases of the process when you start to hit a roadblock. Also, revisit the Introduction of this book from time to time to remind yourself of how to use each chapter during the various stages of the project.

6.1 | PRELIMINARIES

Before you actually begin writing, it is helpful to take inventory of where you are in the process and where you need to go. Having a clear idea of what you know and how that relates to what you need to draft will help you finalize your document with as little frustration as possible.

6.1.1 | Understanding Where You Are in the Process

Any legal analysis project requires the writer to engage in the creative process. The creative process is a five-step recursive progression that aids the writer in developing ideas, finding answers, and proving those answers with verified research. It involves:

Step 1: Insight
Step 2: Saturation
Step 3: Incubation
Step 4: Revelation!
Step 5: Verification

You have been engaged in various phases of the creative process since you started reading this book and working on your project. You may even have already noticed its recursive nature. For example, when you initially chose your topic, you identified a first insight. Throughout the research process you have been saturating. As you have used the research to refine your topic, you have been moving between developing new insights and saturating. You have also incubated while considering the research, and you have undoubtedly had at least one revelation. Putting pen to paper is the final verification step.

As you write, you may discover that you need to revisit a prior step—perhaps you need more research on a certain point, or perhaps you need to incubate a bit more on an idea you thought you had worked out. The writing process teases out potential weaknesses in your analysis and it forces you to wrestle with the most challenging concepts of your thesis. As you write, take time to pause when you need to revisit an earlier step. There is no reason to think you must write every word of the final product from beginning to end in one fell swoop.

6.1.2 | Understanding What You Are Drafting

There are many types of scholarly documents that you could write, such as a case note, comment, article, or dissertation, to name a few. The principles in this book can help you write any type of scholarly analysis, but you should have a clear idea of what type of document you are writing before you start putting pen to paper so that you do not waste time tangled up in drafts that go nowhere.

6.1.2.1 | Case Note[1]

A case note is a scholarly analysis of a single case. This type of scholarly analysis is typically written by a law student for a law review. Compared to other types of scholarly documents, the case note is relatively short. It introduces the case and sets forth the facts before delving into analysis of the rationale and reasoning. The writer should focus on the significance of the case and the implications of the court's opinion.

6.1.2.2 | Comment

A comment is similar to a case note in that it is written by a law student for law review, but it is much broader in that it covers a particular issue in a discrete area of law and typically analyzes more than one case, statute, or other source of law. The writer should focus on the significance of the issue identified in the particular area of law and offer some sort of resolution. Comments often adopt a problem/solution organizational paradigm. Organizational paradigms will be discussed in more detail in section 6.2 of this chapter.

6.1.2.3 | Article

An article is substantively similar to a comment, but it is usually written by a law professor or scholar who has already graduated from law school. An article identifies a unique question of legal significance in a particular area of law and examines all the sources of law related to that question. Like comments, articles often adopt a problem/solution organizational paradigm, although any of the paradigms detailed in section 6.2.1 could work for an article.

---

1. Some law schools use different terminology for student-written scholarship. For example, at some law schools, what is described as a note here is considered a comment and what is described as a comment here is called a note.

6.1.2.4 | Dissertation

A dissertation is a lengthy comprehensive scholarly analysis typically written during the course of post-graduate studies, such as in pursuit of an LL.M., Ph.D., or S.J.D. Like an article, it identifies a unique question of legal significance in a particular area of law and examines all the sources of law related to that question. While it may adopt a problem/solution organizational paradigm, it is also well suited to some of the other options described in section 6.2 of this chapter.

Once you have determined what type of document you are drafting, make sure you understand any applicable conventions such as page limits, font, margins, spacing, and citation. For most U.S. legal publications, publishers will expect citations to be in footnotes using Bluebook citation conventions. International publications may require other conventions, such as OSCOLA. Appendixes X and XI of this book provide a list of references for understanding citation conventions, grammar and punctuation, and the editing process.

6.2 | ORGANIZATIONAL PARADIGMS

ARCHITECTURAL ELEVATION

Image credit: Eric Brehm, *Court Atkins Group*, Bluffton, SC.

As you begin, it can be helpful to identify an organizational paradigm that would facilitate your analysis. In Chapter 5, I compared the relationship between the organizational paradigm and analytical framework to the relationship between a cake pan and a recipe. You could also think of it another way, with the organizational paradigm functioning like an architectural elevation foreshadowing what the completed project will actually look like, while the analytical framework functions as the blueprint providing the systematic method for ensuring integrity of the ideas conveyed in the completed project. It is important to keep in mind that the organizational paradigm is the overarching physical design of your article, while the analytical framework provides a systematic method of inquiry to ensure conceptual cohesion.

The most common paradigms are case notes, comparisons, problem/solutions, cause and effect, and historical analysis. The information provided here is an overview of the most common paradigms. For deeper treatment of these paradigms, see *Legal Writing in the Disciplines* by Teri McMurtry-Chubb.

6.2.1 | Case Note Paradigm

The case note paradigm has five major components: introduction, background, statement of the case, analysis, and conclusion. The rhetorical purpose of the introduction is to provide your reader with information about your ultimate claim and roadmap the rest of the article. In case notes, the introduction often provides a brief factual background for the case being studied, an explanation of why the case is significant and why the author chose the case, and a brief statement of the issues raised in the case. The background section provides the legal context for how the case arose in light of the facts relevant to the particular case. The statement of the case provides a thorough brief of what occurred in the case. The analysis section provides the author's perspective on the rationale and legal significance of the case. The conclusion wraps up the analysis with a statement about the significance and impact of the case.

The broad outline for a case note paradigm would look something like this:

> I. Introduction
> II. Background
> III. Statement of the Case
> IV. Analysis
> V. Conclusion

6.2.2 | Comparative Paradigm

The comparative paradigm is typically used to compare law from different jurisdictions, such as domestic and international law or federal and state law. The components include an introduction, analysis, counteranalysis, and conclusion. The rhetorical purpose of the introduction is to identify the issue and roadmap the rest of the article. A good introduction often sets forth a compelling story or hypothetical to emphasize the importance of the issue to the reader. The analysis and counteranalysis sections set up the comparison of how the issue is handled by competing jurisdictions. The conclusion typically suggests that one jurisdiction's approach is better than the other, or it may suggest a third approach altogether.

The broad outline for a comparative paradigm would look like either of these:

I. Introduction II. Analysis I III. Counteranalysis I IV. Analysis II V. Counteranalysis II VI. Conclusion	I. Introduction II. Analysis I and II III. Counteranalysis I and II IV. Conclusion

6.2.3 | Problem/Solution Paradigm

The problem/solution paradigm is a common structure in scholarly legal articles. It identifies a discrete problem in a particular area of law, analyzes the problem, and proposes a solution to the problem. The rhetorical purpose of the introduction is to identify the issue and roadmap the rest of the article. A good introduction often sets forth a compelling story or hypothetical to emphasize the importance of the issue to the reader. The history and background section defines the problem itself while the analysis section studies the causes, scope, and impact of the problem. The proposed solution offers a strategy for solving the problem and should address the issues raised in the analysis section. Any proposed solution should be tested to ensure that it is indeed a workable solution. Weaknesses or drawbacks to the solution should also be disclosed to the reader. The conclusion emphasizes to the reader why this solution is the best approach for this particular problem.

The broad outline for a problem/solution paradigm would look like this:

> I. Introduction
> II. History/Background of Problem
> III. Analysis of the Cause, Scope, and Impact of the Problem
> IV. Proposed Solution
> V. Conclusion

6.2.4 | Historical Paradigm

Historical studies tend to be interesting, but for a nascent scholar, it may be challenging to move beyond a recitation of historical facts to a critical analysis of whether law has or has not changed, followed by questioning why and evaluating the significance. The difference depends on whether you take a humanities approach or a social science one.[2] In the words of Markus Dubber: "The point of historical analysis of law is to trace the genealogy of law, or legality, over the longue durée in a particular legal-political project in order to bring into clearer relief its normative features, which then drive the critical analysis of legal norms and practices within that (temporally and spatially limited) project."[3] Historical studies can also provide insight into the "textual and structural . . . premises of mainstream views."[4] The components of a historical paradigm are introduction, exposition of relevant history, critique, and conclusion. The rhetorical purpose of the introduction is to describe the purpose of the historical study and roadmap the rest of the article. A good introduction may define a certain principle or maxim whose evolution will be explained later in the article, or it may tell a compelling story of some past tragedy caused by a significant legal or political project. The introduction should hook the reader by demonstrating the importance of the article. The exposition documents the changes, or lack thereof, in law over the relevant time period. The critique reveals the significance of the historical evolution and may identify enduring myths that became

---

2. Teri McMurtry-Chubb, *Legal Writing in the Disciplines* 54-55 (2012).

3. Markus D. Dubber, *Legal History as Legal Scholarship: Doctrinalism, Interdisciplinarity, and Critical Analysis of Law* (July 13, 2017). *Oxford Handbook of Historical Legal Research* (2016). Available at SSRN: https://ssrn.com/abstract=3002587.

4. Martin S. Flaherty, *History Right: Historical Scholarship, Original Understanding, and Treaties as Supreme Law of the Land* Response, 99 Colum. L. Rev. 2095, 2096 (1999). Incidentally, this Response is a good example of entering into a conversation with another scholar.

entrenched during a significant historical moment. It may also offer lessons or a cautionary tale. The conclusion recaps the article and may offer strategies for avoiding a repeat of history or for deconstructing damaging yet enduring myths. A historical study may compare two different legal systems, as well.

The broad outline for a historical paradigm would look like either of these:

I. Introduction II. Exposition of Relevant History III. Critique IV. Conclusion

I. Introduction II. Exposition of Relevant History in System A III. Exposition of Relevant History in System B IV. Critique V. Conclusion

6.2.5 | Choosing the Best Paradigm for the Analytical Framework

Any organizational paradigm could facilitate your analytical framework; in other words, your analytical framework is not necessarily going to demand you choose any particular paradigm over another. Your organizational paradigm is dictated by what you ultimately want to say while your analytical framework is how you justify and validate what you are saying.

For example, if you have chosen a critical race analytical framework, here are some ideas for how you could use each paradigm:

- **Case note paradigm:** You could analyze a particular case to reveal a problematic race-related issue and critique the court's analysis using critical race theory to support your analysis.

I. Introduce racial significance of *Brown* II. Explain the background of the case (use *Plessy* and other intermediate cases) III. Brief the facts of the case (tell the story of *Brown* and the companion cases) IV. Analyze the rationale of *Brown* V. State conclusion emphasizing the significance of *Brown* for desegregation and the hope for equality

- **Comparative paradigm:** You could use critical race theory to compare the racial impacts of laws, like Stand Your Ground and Duty to Retreat laws, across the United States.

I. Introduce racial significance of Stand Your Ground and Duty to Retreat laws
II. Analyze racial impact 1 under Stand Your Ground
III. Analyze racial impact 1 under Duty to Retreat
IV. Analyze racial impact 2 under Stand Your Ground
V. Analyze racial impact 2 under Duty to Retreat
VI. Conclude by emphasizing significance of each

I. Introduce racial significance of Stand Your Ground and Duty to Retreat laws
II. Analyze all racial impacts of Stand Your Ground laws
III. Analyze all racial impacts of Duty to Retreat laws
IV. Conclude by emphasizing significance of analysis

- **Problem/solution paradigm:** You could use critical race theory to expose problematic racial consequences of a law and offer a solution to address those issues.

I. Introduce racial problems created by Stand Your Ground laws
II. Describe or explain how problem developed or manifests
III. Analyze the cause, scope, and impact
IV. Propose a solution to solve the problem
V. Conclude by emphasizing the need to implement the solution

- **History:** You could use critical race theory to document how systemic racism has been historically entrenched in a given political system and critique the apparatuses that have perpetuated discrimination and bias.

I. Introduce historical significance of *Plessy, Brown,* and *Milliken*
II. Exposition of relevant history of the cases
III. Critique deeply entrenched myths and legacies
IV. Conclude by emphasizing significance of analysis

I. Introduce racial significance of treatment of heroin and crack-cocaine
II. Exposition of relevant history of war on drugs
III. Exposition of relevant history of opioid epidemic
IV. Critique systems that have entrenched disparate treatment along race lines
V. Conclude by emphasizing significance of analysis

6.3 | THE ANNOTATED OUTLINE

An annotated outline is simply a very detailed outline that includes references to the sources that support the ideas you advance. Once you have determined which organizational paradigm to use, you can begin fleshing out the outline that will guide the remainder of the writing process.

Each major Roman numeral may have multiple subsections depending on how many discrete points you will make. It should include all of the relevant research information from your research summary as well as your own analysis. This is the stage where you finally get to add in your unique perspective and thoughts on the research you have collected. In creating the annotated outline, it is not necessary to start from scratch; instead, begin by using the research summary you have already created to fill in the outline. If your research summary was organized around sources, this is the moment to shift the organization around concepts. Make sure you have synthesized the information from various sources and noted the significance of the information. If you have been using a color-coded system or tags, you already have a fairly good idea of the general topics and sub-topics of your article. As you organize around concepts, you may change the order multiple times until you achieve the best flow for exposition of your thesis.

Until now, the assignments have focused on collecting external information, but in the outline, you should begin adding your own thoughts about the significance of the information. The major differences between the outline and the research summary are: (1) the outline includes your own thoughts; and (2) it is organized around concepts, not sources. This outline will serve as the guide for the rest of your writing. The transition from research summary to annotated outline looks something like this:

RESEARCH SUMMARY	ANNOTATED OUTLINE

● Source 1:
  ○ Relevant point about Topic A1 (include page number)
  ○ Relevant point about Topic C7 (include page number)
  ○ Relevant point about Topic A4 (include page number)
● Source 2:
  ○ Relevant point about Topic C2-C7 (include page number)
● Source 3
  ○ Relevant point about Topic B (include page number)
  ○ Relevant point about Topic A1-A10 (include page number)
	● Topic A
	  ○ Relevant point supported by Source 1 (include page number)
	  ○ Relevant point supported by Source 3 (include page number)
	  ○ My thoughts about these relevant points
	● Topic B
	  ○ Relevant point supported by Source 3 (include page number)
	  ○ Relevant point supported by Source 3 (include page number)
	  ○ My thoughts about these relevant points
	● Topic C
	  ○ Relevant point supported by Source 1 (include page number)
	  ○ Relevant point supported by Source 2 (include page number)
	  ○ My thoughts about these relevant points

As you finalize your outline, you should begin working on ideas for your title and introduction. A title should convey the substance and significance of your article. From the title, a reader should know why your article is worth reading. Although some scholars try to write clever or catchy titles, a clever title is not necessary and can even backfire. It is better to begin with a descriptive title and then work on editing it into something more refined. Use precise words to convey the substance and significance.

The introduction should begin with a compelling hook. Often, the introduction takes the form of a story or a hypothetical. Your reader should know from the first paragraph why the issue you are exploring matters. If you create a hypothetical, make sure it is realistic. Similarly, if you use a real story, make sure it is accurate. You do not want to lose credibility right from the start.

Your ideas for title and introduction do not need to be finalized in the outlining phase. In fact, you could even write your introduction last, after you have written out most of the paper. I personally find that spending time trying to write a compelling introduction before my analysis is complete is an exercise in frustration. Frequently, I do not know how to hook my reader until I have written most of the analysis. Other writers, however, find the introduction to be the easiest and most fun part to write. Maybe your scholarly project was inspired by a particular story that you are ready to tell before you have written any of the analysis. If so, writing out the introduction may be a good way to get words on paper for a first draft. Some writers also use the roadmap in the introduction as an anchor to ensure they are not getting off track in the writing. If you have a detailed annotated outline, though, it will serve the same purpose as an initial draft of the introductory roadmap. Additionally, the background and analytical sections of your article are the most important parts of your paper, and you will not necessarily know the best way to roadmap those for the reader until they have been written. Working from an outline gives you more flexibility in determining how to organize the flow, synthesize information, and situate your own ideas into the analysis.

Be careful if you decide to write your introduction first because your impressions about the significance of the story will, and should, evolve as you develop the written analysis. I cannot stress enough how much your ideas will change throughout the entirety of the scholarly process. Even if you think you have figured out your analysis in the researching and pre-writing stages, the process of writing the article will inevitably cause you to question those conclusions. That is the point. You will inevitably need to revisit your research or conduct additional research. You will need to re-evaluate your notes and initial conclusions. Writing the introduction before you have fully fleshed out the analysis can cause you to become entrenched in a certain mindset, making it difficult to be led by the research. My best advice is to include your ideas about how you want to approach the title and introduction in the outline, but write these sections out only after your substantive analysis is mostly complete.

6.4 | DISCIPLINED WRITING

Discipline is an important and critical skill for every phase of a scholarly project, but it is especially important during the writing phase. Writing can sometimes be exhausting because it requires intense focus and stillness. It can also be exhilarating when you work through a challenging concept and are able to clearly and concisely articulate a complicated issue to your client. Discipline is essential to helping writers face the emotionally and physically taxing aspects of writing. Discipline forces you to continue writing when your body and mind want to quit. Discipline also forces you to take breaks to care for your body and mind when they need it. Discipline ensures you are mindful of incorporating all those components that establish your credibility and make your scholarship sound: reliable sources, Universal Intellectual Standards, and a workable analytical framework.

6.4.1 | Create a Schedule

Once you have created the outline, it will be helpful to set a schedule for writing. You may decide to keep the same schedule that you have been using throughout the research stage, or you may find that you need to update it. Many people like to set aside time every day for writing. Daily writing helps you keep momentum and feel like you are hitting milestones toward the completion of the final project. If you have a detailed outline, you can easily work on small, manageable chunks of the article.

On the other hand, some scholars may find that daily writing is less productive because they cannot fully flesh out any part of the document in a 30- or 45-minute window. Instead, some writers prefer to set aside large blocks of time, three to five hours or more, to work on the writing project. Whatever schedule you choose, stick to it. Setting goals for completing certain sections of the paper will incentivize you to work consistently and diligently.

6.4.2 | Create a Plan of Attack

Rarely does a law review article get written straight through from beginning to end. Typically, authors write discrete sections, sometimes out of order, and then put them together as a whole at the end of the writing phase. That is why creating a thorough and detailed outline is so important. If you have a detailed outline, you can easily track which sections have been written, how they fit together, and how you will ultimately marry all the pieces in a final document.

When you are creating the plan, focus first on what you already know. Often, fleshing out the history or background section not only advances the overall written project, but it helps you continue to flesh out your own ideas for the later analysis. Writing the introduction or conclusion first may lead to frustration down the road because your hypothesis will change as you continue to develop your written analysis.

6.5 | PLAGIARISM

Integrity is your most prized asset as a scholar—never compromise it by presenting another's idea as your own. Plagiarism, whether intentional or reckless, is theft. You must cite a source for every single idea that is not your own original idea; when in doubt, cite. The consequences of plagiarism include loss of your reputation, a failing grade if you are writing for a school project, disciplinary proceedings, or even legal proceedings.

Plagiarism occurs when you use someone else's ideas or words and present them as your own. If you are quoting directly from another source, use quotation marks and include a citation to the original source. Remember to properly signal any changes or adaptations you have made to a quote. The following table shows the most common adaptations made to quotes:

THE MOST COMMON ADAPTATIONS MADE TO QUOTES

. . .	Ellipsis demonstrate text that has been deleted from the original quote
[ ] [a]t (original: At) Jail[] (original: Jails) [parent] (original: mother)	Brackets demonstrate a change from the original text. For example, a single lowercase letter in brackets signals a change from a capital letter in the original quote. Brackets sometimes appear at the end of a word to change it from singular to plural, or an entire word may be bracketed when new text is embedded into the quote.
, .	Commas and periods belong inside quotation marks.
: ;	Colons and semicolons belong outside quotation marks
? !	Question marks and exclamation points belong inside quotes only if they are part of the original quote.

To avoid plagiarism, nearly every sentence in most sections of your paper will need a footnote with a citation. If you are not sure whether you should cite, go ahead and include a citation to the source that sparked the idea. To ensure accuracy, it is imperative that you read the sources cited within the sources you are relying upon. For example, if you intend to rely on a claim made in Article A, you must read the corresponding footnote in Article A and pull any source Article A cites. If Article A pulled the idea from another source, you definitely need to read that other source, and you will likely need to cite both Article A and the source Article A cites for the proposition. Following the research strategies outlined in Chapters 2, 3, and 4 of this book will help you ensure you are citing all the relevant sources in support of your thesis.

Finally, before submitting your paper, you likely want to have it checked for plagiarism. A number of online programs, such as SafeAssign or Turnitin, allow you to upload your paper and have it electronically checked for matches to other sources on the Internet. If you are writing a paper for a school assignment, your professor may require you to submit it through a plagiarism checker prior to submission. Your professor is likely to run a plagiarism check on your paper, as well. Because of the nature of a scholarly project, you will likely have a high rate of matches to other sources. So long as the text that matches other sources is properly cited within your document, however, you will successfully avoid plagiarism.

6.6 | FOOTNOTES

In legal scholarly writing, citations most commonly appear in footnotes. Nearly every sentence in a legal academic paper will require a footnote. Footnotes may be a simple citation to the original source, or they may include the citation along with a lengthier explanation. Consider the following excerpt from Elizabeth Esther Berenguer, *The Color of Fear: A Cognitive-Rhetorical Analysis of How Florida's Subjective Fear Standard in Stand Your Ground Cases Ratifies Racism*, 76 Md. L. Rev. 726 (2017):

courts have wrestled with applying the subjective intent standard.[13] Recently, the Florida Supreme Court utilized a reasonable man standard in interpreting Stand Your Ground[14]; in response, the legislature proposed a number of bills evidencing its original intent to create a subjective fear standard to protect *innocent* people from prosecution.[15] Although these most recent bills have not yet successfully passed the legislature, the rhetoric that supports these proposed bills mirrors the original debates and conversations that led to the 2005 enactment of Stand Your Ground.[16]

14. *Bretherick.* 170 So. 3d at 770.

Notice how footnote 14 is a simple citation footnote. This is a short cite, so we can assume Bretherick has previously been cited. This footnote provides no additional explanation, so we can expect any analysis to appear in the text of the article.

15. The Florida Supreme Court's ruling in *Bretherick* led to a number of bills proposing to enact different standards. *See, e.g.*, S. 344, 118th Leg., Reg. Sess. (Fla. 2015) (proposing to shift the burden of proof to the prosecution to disprove a defendant's immunity claim beyond a reasonable doubt); S. 1100, 118th Leg., Reg. Sess. (Fla. 2015) (proposing to require an overt act from the attacker before reasonable force may be used); S. 228, 118th Leg., Reg. Sess. (Fla. 2015) (as filed) (proposing to prohibit courts from imposing minimum mandatory sentences on defendants that committed certain acts using a firearm if they find that the defendants subjectively believes the use of force was justified); S. 228, 118th Leg., Reg. Sess. (Fla. 2015) (as substituted by S. Comm. on Criminal Justice) (proposing to eliminate aggravated assault from the list of crimes mandating courts to impose a minimum sentence). Most recently, on March 15, 2017, the Florida Senate voted to approve CS/SB 128, which requires a court to grant a defendant pretrial immunity unless the State proves beyond a reasonable doubt that the defendant is not immune. As of the date of this publication, the Florida House is considering the measure.

In addition to observing two different styles of footnotes, in this sample you can also see how every idea cites to an authoritative source. After each period, and sometimes even in the middle of a sentence, a footnote is placed to identify the supporting source. As you read through law review articles related to your project, notice how footnotes are used and allow those articles to guide you in good footnote practices. Be careful

Notice how footnote 15 provides much more text than footnote 14. In the text, the author references "a number of bills." The substance of each bill is not the primary focus of the article, however, so clogging the text would not have been the best approach. The author included the relevant information in a footnote so the reader can read it if the reader wants to know more detail. The reader can also choose to continue reading the text to focus on the main purpose of the article.

in early drafts not to use *id.*, *supra*, and *infra*. These forms of short citing will not provide you with enough information about your citation if you end up moving text around in later drafts. It can be very frustrating to lose an antecedent cite and then have to revisit all your sources to figure out where the idea originated.

6.7 | MECHANICS

As you begin writing, it is important not to get bogged down in the details of choosing the perfect word or ensuring citations are in proper format in the early stages. Expect to work through multiple drafts in the writing, revising, editing, proofreading, and polishing stages. In the later stages you can work on refining word choice and finalizing citations. In the initial drafting, when you are still formulating ideas, it is important to simply get words on the paper. You might find that you spend two hours staring at a blank screen before the fount of inspiration begins to flow—that is okay! It is part of this process.

Once you begin writing, use a shorthand cite form to track your sources (you do not want to have to retrace your sources in later stages).

Helpful Hints

Save each draft with a new name so you can find information that is "accidentally" lost.

Never delete ANYTHING. Cut words you would delete and paste them into a separate document. That way, you can easily access them if they become relevant in the future.

This shorthand form should give you enough information to locate the source and page number that supports the assertion. A good practice might be to include the author or title of the source along with the page number.

Upon fleshing out and writing down all your ideas, you can begin the processes of editing, proofreading, and polishing. You should plan to have multiple drafts—perhaps as many as 50 or more. Save new drafts with a new name or version number so you do not lose earlier versions. You may need an earlier version if you accidentally delete a section or lose a later version. Back up your work on the cloud or other back-up drive. You do not want to lose your work.

Appendix XI offers a revising/editing/proofreading checklist that may be helpful to you as you go through this process. During the revising and editing stages, you may find that you adjust the organization quite a bit. Whole sections may get moved around, so it is important that your footnotes contain sufficient information for you to be able to find your source later on. For example, if you use "*id.*" in a footnote and then move that section, the anterior cite that "*id.*" referenced will be lost and you will have no idea what source "*id.*" refers to. It is a better practice to use the author name or an abbreviated title and page number for shorthand citations in earlier drafts. You will also want to draft your table of contents and abstract toward the end of all your writing.

Not all articles require a table of contents and an abstract. If your article is particularly long, or if your publisher requires either or both, definitely include them. Also, if you plan to post your article on SSRN, having an abstract and a table of contents will make it easily accessible to other scholars. The table of contents can be built through the automatic generator in most word processors. You will want to use descriptive subheadings for your table of contents so a reader can easily identify the progression of your thesis analysis. The abstract can be adapted from your most recent iteration of your topic selection essay. Abstracts usually consist of a single paragraph that succinctly describes your thesis and the significance of your article. Study abstracts from some of your sources to see common ways of drafting abstracts. Choose a style that speaks to you and matches your analytical framework and organizational paradigm.

Once you move into the proofreading stage, you will likely not be making major changes to the overall order and flow of ideas. This stage is an ideal time to get citations in order and to double check grammar, usage, and punctuation. Appendix XI has some helpful tips for editing and Appendix X includes a refresher on citation format.

NEVER FORGET, YOU **CAN** DO THIS!

SQUELCH THE IMPOSTOR

The impostor voice may have you questioning:

- How will I ever finish?
- How will I ever cover everything I want to say?

Here is what you can do:

- Frequently consult your outline
- Revisit your research and conduct new research to verify your conclusions

- Stick to a systematic method of inquiry to preserve the Universal Intellectual Standards
- Remind yourself that you do not have to answer every question out there
- Create an agenda for future scholarly research
- Follow a schedule
- Set interim goals and celebrate accomplishing each one
- Talk with your mentor frequently
- Get interim and periodic feedback on your written work
- Give yourself breaks from thinking about the project

While the writing stage may initially seem daunting, you can manage the intensity with good preparation. Make sure you have worked through the earlier chapters of this book to whittle down your idea to a manageable topic. Complete the preemption check and research summary. Decide what your analytical framework/systematic mode of inquiry will be and choose an organizational paradigm. Know what type of document you intend to draft. Finally, convert your research summary into a detailed annotated outline. This detailed outline will moor you as you flesh out your ideas, and it will ultimately become your final paper as you fill in the details. As you write, focus on one part of your outline at a time and focus only on that section. Your outline should be detailed enough so that each point of your outline will become a paragraph (or maybe two or three paragraphs) in your final paper. By remaining focused, you can easily document your progress and see your paper taking shape. Writing from your outline will help minimize the feeling of being overwhelmed and frustrated.

ASSIGNMENT

Draft an annotated outline that merges and expands the working bibliography and research summary to provide a structure for drafting the final paper. An example is provided in Appendix VII. It should include, at a minimum, the components of whatever organizational paradigm you have chosen. Each section should include detailed explanation and as many subsections as necessary to completely address the thesis. Correct citations supporting each assertion must be included in the outline.

Draft an abstract by refining your topic selection essay to account for the analytical framework and organizational paradigm you have chosen.

Sample Topic Selection Essay

As you read through the Sample below, notice how nearly every sentence serves a specific function. The purpose of this assignment is not to create superfluous work for you. Rather, the purpose is to help you identify a path upon which to embark. There is no need to write ad nauseum, but it is important to write enough to understand the direction in which your next steps must head. Using the questions in Chapter 1 as a guide will help you maintain focus and will force you to begin thinking more critically about the topic you want to explore. Also keep in mind that your first draft of the topic selection essay will need to be updated periodically as you finish your preemption check, begin your research, and dig deeply into your research. It will eventually become your abstract.

ESSAY

After Trayvon Martin was shot and killed, I, a law professor and former defense——1 attorney, had the opportunity to speak on a panel alongside Dennis Baxley (sponsor of the bill), Judge O.H. Eaton, and State Attorney Aramis Donnell (at the time a criminal defense attorney). As we answered questions about the lawfulness of the shooting, all three legal professionals resoundingly agreed that the language of Florida's Stand Your Ground statutory scheme permitted the shooting. The language of the statute is so broad that, once a person's fear is triggered, it permits that person to stand his or her ground even once the purported danger has subsided. In response, Dennis Baxley stated that such a result had not been his or the legislature's intention. He went on to say that he was not a lawyer and did not understand what the words of the statute meant. The audience was aghast.

---

1 This paragraph explains why you have chosen this topic. It emphasizes your personal interest and demonstrates why a broader audience might be interested in this topic. It also begins to explain the parameters of the issue.

I began to question the authority of the law even more upon hearing that the legislature did not understand the law well enough to understand its implications prior to voting on it. The purpose of this paper is to determine whether a law is legitimate

2 ——— when the legislature does not understand it and when it has consequences contrary to public desire. In my preliminary research, I have discovered a theory of jurisprudence

3 ——— called Contextual-Configurative Jurisprudence. It was developed by two Yale professors, Laswell and McDougal, for the purpose of studying international law. They identify a number of features that should exist when a law is legitimate. I plan to apply this theory to Florida's Stand Your Ground statutory scheme to prove that it is not authoritative.

4 ——— I expect that explaining the jurisprudential theory in an understandable way applicable to a domestic law may be challenging. If I cannot find a way to apply it, I may need to abandon the article entirely. Ultimately, my goal is to provide support for

5 ——— individuals attempting to challenge the law either by introducing new legislation or by making constitutional challenges in court. While many scholars have criticized the

6 ——— consequences of the law, few have questioned its authority. Most scholars advocate for an application contrary to the plain language, but those solutions would require compromise to the integrity of our delicate system of checks and balances. If the law can be stricken as unconstitutional, the positive societal impact is much broader and consistent on an individual level.

---

2 This sentence identifies the purpose and broad topic of the paper. At this stage, the thesis is not fully fleshed out, and it really should not be. It becomes more refined as you progress through the process.

3 Applying a theory of jurisprudence in a new context is how I intend to offer a new perspective on Stand Your Ground analysis.

4 Here I identify some of the challenges that can be expected in this project.

5 Identifying an ultimate goal is a good way to stay centered when the topic is not yet refined to a specific thesis.

6 This sentence offers a preliminary look at what other scholars have said about Stand Your Ground. At this stage, I still must complete significant research to determine who has said what about Stand Your Ground.

APPENDIX II

Sample Research Plan

This Sample Research Plan is one created fairly early in the research process before preemption checking has taken place. At this stage, you should have a lot of questions, and you may not be able to predict the search terms you will use to answer every question. As you progress through the research, you will track your results and write down the searches you perform so you can effectively track your progress. As you begin to read through the research, you will eliminate some questions, add some questions, and track the answers to your questions. You can simultaneously draft your research summary as you move through your research plan by tracking the answers to your questions in a separate document that becomes your research summary.

PLAN

Timeframe	Task/Question	Purpose/Questions	Search Terms & Results
Weeks 1–4	Study Harold D. Lasswell & Myers S. McDougal, *Jurisprudence for a Free Society* (1992) (book that will provide analytical framework)	Identify components of analytical framework	I purchased this resource after reading Nagan so that I could study the primary source analyzed in that textbook.

Timeframe	Task/Question	Purpose/Questions	Search Terms & Results
Weeks 1–4	Study Winston P. Nagan, *Contextual-Configuration Jurisprudence: The Law, Science, and Policies of Human Dignity* (2013) (book that analyzes Lasswell & McDougal work)	Provides analysis of Lasswell & McDougal work.	I came across this book when I was conducting research for another purpose. It sparked the idea that I could use this framework in the Stand Your Ground context.
Weeks 1–4	Search HEINOnline and consult with research librarians to determine whether this framework has been used in other contexts.	Will this framework be useful in analyzing Stand Your Ground? Will it advance my thesis that Stand Your Ground is not law?	Author search for Lasswell & McDougal; Author search for Nagan; keyword search "contextual configurative jurisprudence" and "jurisprudence for a free society"
Weeks 5–8	Study Florida legislative history—Database: Online Sunshine—FL legislative website. Pull statutes. Pull proposed bills. Find committee hearing transcripts/draft bills/memos and any other legislative material available	How did SYG become law? Why did it become law? What other laws did the legislature consider?	

1 —
2 —
3 —

1 Sometimes as you are researching for another project, you may find a source that sparks an idea for another project. In my case, I came across the Nagan text and wanted to look at Stand Your Ground through this lens. After reading Nagan, it was imperative that I pull the original source, *Jurisprudence for a Free Society* and read it for myself.

2 During the preemption checking phase, I need to know whether the framework has been criticized, and if so, how and why. I also need to know if it has ever been used in this context.

3 Because this is my third article on Stand Your Ground, I already have a lot of this background information. I definitely know the statute numbers, so pulling this information and the other legislative history will be fairly easy.

Timeframe	Task/Question	Purpose/Questions	Search Terms & Results
Weeks 7–10	Determine what sectors of society are satisfied with SYG and which are not. Sources: news, newspapers, blogs, magazines, editorials	How do we know if SYG is working? How do we know if society approves?	TBD ———————— 4
Weeks 7–10	Identify key players around SYG – Online Sunshine legislative materials; HEINOnline other scholars (look to their original sources)	What motivates them? What is the source of their influence? Why does public outcry not matter? Who is hurt by Stand Your Ground? Who benefits from Stand Your Ground? Should society care about the sanctity of life? If not, why not? If so, why?	TBD ———————— 5

---

4 Because I am interested in Stand Your Ground issues, I already have a number of newspaper, magazine, and blog articles that report Floridians are opposed to Stand Your Ground. I will use those as a starting point for locating other sources that will help me prove society's position.

5 As I dig deeper into the research on society's position, I should naturally identify some of the key players. I also know, from the legislative history, who some of the key players were in drafting, proposing, and passing the law. I also know who has been vocally opposed to the law.

Timeframe	Task/Question	Purpose/Questions	Search Terms & Results
Weeks 7–10	Study other scholarly work—Source HEINOnline and consult with research librarians	Has anyone else taken this approach to studying SYG? Can this framework be applied this way? What are the pros and cons of SYG? Is it significant that FL is far from the mainstream? Is it true that FL is far from the mainstream?	TBD
Weeks 8–12	Study the impact of SYG. Find DOJ or FL statistics on deaths, racial disparities, etc. Consult with research librarians for best databases.	Is SYG really as bad as it seems? Does it keep society safer? Are certain groups more at risk than others?	TBD

6   After identifying the participants, I can use HEINOnline and other similar resources to find out background information about their motivations, their philosophies, their goals, and other similar information. When I first create my research plan, I do not have enough information to draft search terms, but I will update my research plan with questions and terms as I move through the research process.

APPENDIX **III**

Sample Working Bibliography

The following working bibliography is fairly complete. In the initial stages, you may only have a handful of sources on your list. As you near completion of your project, however, your list should be quite robust. If you track sources along the way, it will be easier to finalize your footnotes and citations in the final editing stages. If you are using a program like Zotero, it will automatically track your sources and create the bibliography for you.

BIBLIOGRAPHY

Sources by Type

I. Academic Articles and Books
II. News Articles
III. Cases ───1
IV Statutes
IV. Miscellaneous

I. Academic Articles and Books

Michael C. Dorf, *Identity Politics and the Second Amendment*, 73 Fordham L. Rev. 549────2 (2004).

Robert E. Dreschel, *Media Ethics and Media Law : The Transformation of Moral Obligation into Legal Principle,* 6 Notre Dame J.L. Ethics & Pub. Pol'y 5 (1992).

Harold D. Lasswell & Myers S. McDougal, *Jurisprudence for a Free Society* (New Haven Press, 1992).

Scott Medlock, *NRA = No Rational Argument? How the National Rifle Association Exploits Public Irrationality*, 11 Tex. J. C.L. & C.R. 39 (2005).

---

1 Organizing by category helps the author easily find sources once the bibliography has a significant number of sources.

2 Notice that the sources are alphabetized for ease of reference within each category.

Elizabeth Megale, *Deadly Combinations: How Self-Defense Laws Pairing Immunity with a Presumption of Fear Allow Criminals to Get Away with Murder*, 34 Am. J. Trial Advoc. 105 (2010).

Elizabeth Megale, *Disaster Unaverted: Reconciling the Desire for a Safe and Secure State with the Grim Realities of Stand Your Ground*, 37 Am. J. Trial Advoc. 1 (2014).

Elizabeth Megale, *The Invisible Man: How the Sex Offender Registry Results in Social Death*, 2 J.L. Soc. Deviance 92 (2011).

Winston P. Nagan, *Contextual-Configurative Jurisprudence: The Law, Science and Policies of Human Dignity* 01 (Vandeplas Publishing, LLC 2013).

Francisco Valdes, *Unpacking Hetero-Patriarchy: Tracing the Conflation of Sex, Gender and Sexual Orientation to Its Origins*, 8 Yale J.L. & Human. 161 (1996).

3———II. News Articles

Joel Achenbach, Scott Higham & Sari Horwitz, *How NRA's True Believers Converted a Marksmanship Group into a Mighty Gun Lobby*, The Washington Post, Jan. 12, 2013, http://www.washingtonpost.com/politics/how-nras-true-believers-converted-a-marksmanship-group-into-a-mighty-gun-lobby/2013/01/12/51c62288-59b9-11e2-88d0-c4cf65c3ad15_story.html.

Steve Almasy, *Dad's Texting to Daughter Sparks Argument, Fatal Shooting in Movie Theater*, CNN, Jan. 13, 2014, http://www.cnn.com/2014/01/13/justice/florida-movie-theater-shooting/.

Curt Anderson, *Despite Outcry, Stand-Ground Law Repeals Unlikely*, Wisconsin Gazette, July 27, 2013, http://www.wisconsingazette.com/national-gaze/despite-outcry-stand-ground-law-repeals-unlikely.html.

Wilson Andrews, Kat Downs, Dan Keating & Karen Yourish, *How the NRA Exerts Influence over Congress*, The Washington Post, Jan. 15, 2013, http://www.washingtonpost.com/wp-srv/special/politics/nra-congress/.

Walker Bragman, *The Culture of Guns and Misinformation*, Huffington Post, Mar. 27, 2013, http://www.huffingtonpost.com/walker-bragman/guns-misinformation_b_2553021.html.

Ethan Bronner, *Adultery, an Ancient Crime Still on Many Books*, The New York Times, Nov. 14, 2012, http://www.nytimes.com/2012/11/15/us/adultery-an-ancient-crime-still-on-many-books.html?_r=0.

Elizabeth Chuck, *Mothers of Victims Plead for Changes to Stand-Your-Ground Laws*, U.S. News, Oct. 29, 2013, http://usnews.nbcnews.com/_news/2013/10/29/21231481-mothers-of-victims-plead-for-changes-to-stand-your-ground-laws?lite.

Seth Cline, *Firepower: Gun Control Opponents Outspend Opposition 25-to-1*, U.S. News & World Report, July 24, 2012, http://www.usnews.com/news/articles/2012/07/24/firepower-gun-control-opponents-outspend-opposition-25-to-1.

---

3 Although news articles are not always the most authoritative source, the article ultimately produced with this bibliography specifically studied the tension between legislation and public sentiment. One of the best ways to document public sentiment is to consult contemporary cultural sources, like the news.

Michael H. Cottman, *Commentary: Zimmerman Acquittal Says It's Open Season on Black Males*, Black America Web, July 14, 2013, http://blackamericaweb.com/2013/07/14/zimmerman-acquittal-black-teens/.

John Daly, *The Mainstream Media Have Made the Conservative Media Prophets*, Bernard Goldberg, Nov. 30, 2013, http://www.bernardgoldberg.com/mainstream-media-made-conservative-media-prophets/.

Michael George, *Justifiable Homicides Double Since "Stand Your Ground,"* ABC Action News, Mar. 27, 2012, http://www.abcactionnews.com/dpp/news/local_news/investigations/i-team-justifiable-homicides-double-since-stand-your-ground.

Jerry Lansen, *In Trayvon Martin Case, Media Need to Examine Their Own Role*, Huffington Post, Apr. 2, 2012, http://www.huffingtonpost.com/jerry-lanson/critique-of-trayvon-martin-coverage_b_1393453.html.

Alee MacGillis, *This Is How the NRA Ends: A Bigger, Richer, Meaner Gun-Control Movement Has Arrived*, New Republic, May 28, 2013, http://www.newrepublic.com/node/113292/.

Tim Murphy, *Justifiable Homicides Up 200 Percent in Florida Post Stand Your Ground*, Mother Jones, Sept. 16, 2013, http://www.motherjones.com/mojo/2013/09/stand-your-ground-justifiable-homicide-increase statistics.

Tim Murphy, *Map: Is Adultery Illegal?*, Mother Jones, Nov. 29, 2011, http://www.motherjones.com/mojo/2011/11/is-adultery-illegal-map.

Jack Maddox, *Florida Teen Dead After Row That Began with Loud-Music Complaint, Suspect Jailed*, CNN, Nov. 27, 2012, http://www.cnn.com/2012/11/26/us/florida-music-shooting/.

Kurt Nimmo, *Stand Your Ground Upheld in Florida Despite Efforts of Obama's DOJ*, The Daily Drudge Report, Nov. 8, 2013, http://thedailydrudgereport.com/2013/11/08/mainstream-mixup/stand-your-ground-upheld-in-florida-despite-efforts-of-obamas-doj/.

Frank Rich, *Stop Beating a Dead Fox*, New York, Jan. 26, 2014, http://nymag.com/news/frank-rich/fox-news-2014-2/.

Rebekka Schramm, *Georgia Democrats Try to Repeal "Stand Your Ground" Law*, CBS Atlanta, Mar. 27, 2012, http://www.cbsatlanta.com/story/17262525/georgia-democrats-try-to-repeal-stand-your-ground-law.

Daniella Silva, *Florida Panel Rejects Bill to Repeal "Stand Your Ground,"* U.S. News on NBC News.com, Nov. 7, 2013, http://usnews.nbcnews.com/_news/2013/11/07/21353112-florida-panel-rejects-bill-to-repeal-stand-your-ground?lite.

Philip Smith, *Justice Dept. Wants More Drug Clemency Applicants*, Stop the Drug War, Jan. 30, 2014, http://stopthedrugwar.org/chronicle/2014/jan/30/justice_dept_wants_more_drug_cle.

Joe Strupp, *Former NRA President: We Helped Draft Florida's "Stand Your Ground" Law*, Media Matters for America, Mar. 27, 2012, http://mediamatters.org/blog/2012/03/27/former-nra-president-we-helped-draft-floridas-s/185254.

Brian Walsh, *Liberal Media Shrug at Bloomberg's Big Ad Buy*, U.S. News & World Report, Mar. 28, 2013, http://www.usnews.com/opinion/blogs/brian-walsh/2013/03/28/the-hypocrisy-of-liberal-medias-silence-on-bloombergs-gun-blitz.

115

David Westin, *Divided We Stand (But How Divided Are We Really?)*, Huffington Post, Jan. 10, 2013, http://www.huffingtonpost.com/david-westin/election-media-politics_b_2109093.html.

Larry Womack, *The Real Problem with Media Today? The Audience*, Huffington Post, Mar. 18, 2012, http://www.huffingtonpost.com/larry-womack/the-real-problem-with-the_1_b_1207888.html.

4———III. Cases

State v. Lash, 16 N.J.L. 380, 381 (1838).
S.B. v. S.J.B., 258 N.J. Super. 151, 155-156 (Ch. Div. 1992).

IV. Statutes

California's Proposition 215, SB 420, HSC § 11357-11362.9.
Colo. Rev. Stat. § 25-1.5-106, 1 CCR 212-1, -2.
Fla. Stat. Ann. §§ 776.012-013, 776.032.
Washington Initiative 502, Wash. Rev. Code Chapter 69.51a.

V. Miscellaneous

Brady Campaign to Prevent Gun Violence, *Our History*, Brady Campaign to Prevent Gun Violence, http://www.bradycampaign.org/?q=our-history.

Dream Defenders, *The Crisis*, Dream Defenders, http://dreamdefenders.org/thecrisis/.

Magna Carta, 1215.

Mayors Against Illegal Guns, *Coalition History*, Mayors Against Illegal Guns, http://www.mayorsagainstillegalguns.org/html/about/history.shtml.

Moms Demand Action, *About Moms Demand Action for Gun Sense in America*, Moms Demand Action, http://momsdemandaction.org/about/.

National Association for the Advancement of Colored People, *NAACP: 100 Years of History*, http://www.naacp.org/pages/naacp-history.

National Rifle Association, *About Us: A Brief History of the NRA*, http://home.nra.org/history/document/about.

ProCon.org, *History of Marijuana as Medicine—2900 BC to Present*, Aug. 13, 2013, http://medicalmarijuana.procon.org/view.timeline.php?timelineID=000026#1900-1949.

Testimony of Jonathan E. Lowy on *Stand Your Ground: Civil Rights and Public Safety Implications of the Expanded Use of Deadly Force,* before the United States Senate, Oct. 29, 2013.

---

4 Compare the working bibliography to the final article in Appendix IX. How many of the sources in the working bibliography made it into the final article? How many more sources are in the article?

Sample Leading Scholar's Essay

This sample essay provides an overview of the discourse on Florida's Stand Your Ground law from the relevant time period for the Megale article that appears in Appendix IX: 2005-2013. Note that it is not in a traditional essay format. This assignment is intended to guide you in creating a working document that meets your needs. The purpose is to confirm your preemption check and ensure that your thesis is refined and unique. For me, a list tends to be more helpful than a multi-paragraph essay, but other scholars find it helpful to flesh out the existing scholarship in more detail at this stage. The format is not important. What is important is that you identify what other scholars have said and create a document that will help you determine whether you have been preempted. This document will also integrate with your research plan and research summary assignments insofar as you may need to rely on these sources in proving your thesis.

ESSAY

For the relevant time period, HEINOnline turns up 58 articles on Stand Your Ground. The following is a list of the articles covering issues most related to the central thesis of the contextual-configurative piece.

1. Tamara Rice Lave, *Shoot to Kill: A Critical Look at Stand Your Ground Laws*, 67 U. Miami————1 L. Rev. 827 (2012-2013). In this essay, the author analyzes the role the NRA played in passing Stand Your Ground legislation.
2. Anthony Hall, *A Stand for Justice—Examining Why Stand Your Ground Laws Negatively Impact African Americans*, 7 S. Region Black Students Ass'n L.J. 95 (2013). This author takes a critical race approach to analyzing Stand Your Ground.

---

1 For a preemption check, you may only need a short description of the article to remind yourself of the article's content. At this stage, you should have read the source in sufficient detail that you know how the source relates to your thesis. When you draft the research summary, you should expand these notes to include more detail about the author's specific position and arguments in support. The research summary will also include questions and critiques you have about the author's thesis.

3. Louis N. Schulze, Jr., *Of Trayvon Martin, George Zimmerman, and Legal Expressivism: Why Massachusetts Should Stand Its Ground on Stand Your Ground*, 47 New Eng. L. Rev. on Remand 34 (2012). Essay analyzing society's collective reinterpretation of the boundaries of use of force.

4. Elizabeth Megale, *Disaster Unaverted: Reconciling the Desire for a Safe and Secure State with the Grim Realities of Stand Your Ground*, 37 Am. J. Trial Advoc. 255 (2013). My article argues that Florida's Stand Your Ground law has shifted societal norms and effectively legalized homicide.

5. Luevonda P. Ross, *Transmogrification of Self-Defense by National Rifle Association–Inspired Statutes: From the Doctrine of Retreat to the Right to Stand Your Ground*, 35 S.U. L. Rev. 1 (2007-2008). The article analyzes the push by the NRA for Stand Your Ground laws through a critical race lens.

6. Tamara F. Lawson, *A Fresh Cut in an Old Wound—A Critical Analysis of the Trayvon Martin Killing: The Public Outcry, the Prosecutor's Discretion, and the Stand Your Ground Law*, 23 U. Fla. J.L. & Pub. Pol'y 271 (2012). This article analyzes the killing of Trayvon Martin through a critical race lens.

2——— 7. Pearl Goldman, *Criminal Law: 2007-2010 Survey of Florida Law*, 35 Nova L. Rev. 95 (2010 2011).

8. Adam Harris Kurland, *Not the Last Word, but Likely the Last Prosecution: Understanding the U.S. Department of Justice's Evaluation of Whether to Authorize a Successive Federal Prosecution in the Trayvon Martin Killing*, 61 UCLA L. Rev. Discourse 206 (2013). This article analyzes whether George Zimmerman could have been subject to federal prosecution after his acquittal in state court.

9. Elizabeth B. Megale, *Deadly Combinations: How Self-Defense Laws Pairing Immunity with a Presumption of Fear Allow Criminals to Get Away with Murder*, 34 Am. J. Trial Advoc. 105 (2010). Article problematizes Stand Your Ground and predicts murder and unaccountability will ensue.

10. Joshu Harris, *The Real Reasons the Trayvon Martin Case Should Be a Criminal Justice Poster Child*, 61 Drake L. Rev. Discourse 46 (2013). Argues that Stand Your Ground is radical and has a disparate racial impact.

11. Jonathan Feingold & Karen Lorang, *Defusing Implicit Bias*, 59 UCLA L. Rev. Discourse 210 (2011). Analyzes Florida's Stand Your Ground through a critical race lens.

12. Renee Lettow Lerner, *The Worldwide Popular Revolt Against Proportionality in Self-Defense Law*, 2 J.L. Econ. & Pol'y 331 (2006). This article critically analyzes elite notions of proportionality.

13. Cynthia Lee, *Making Race Salient: Trayvon Martin and Implicit Bias in a Not Yet Post-Racial Society*, 91 N.C. L. Rev. 1555 (2012-2013). This article analyzes implicit bias in the context of Stand Your Ground.

---

2 At this stage, you want to include every potentially relevant source on your list. Later, as you read through the sources more carefully, you may find that you do not need to include each one in your research summary or final paper. At this stage, however, you do not yet know exactly how each source will ultimately relate, so you will want to track them all on this list.

14. L. Song Richardson & Phillip Atiba Goff, *Self Defense and the Suspicion Heuristic*, 98 Iowa L. Rev. 293 (2012-2013). This article analyzes Stand Your Ground through a critical race lens.

15. Allison Boldt, *Rhetoric vs. Reality: ALEC's Disguise as a Nonprofit Despite Its Extensive Lobbying*, 34 Hamline J. Pub. L. & Pol'y 35 (2012). Critically analyzes ALEC as a participant in the legislative process.

While many scholars critique Stand Your Ground, no scholar has taken a comprehensive look at all the participants and their relationships to the legislative process and each other. No author has written an article using the contextual-configurative framework. It does not appear this thesis has been preempted, and there is some related scholarship analyzing some participants that could inform the contextual-configurative piece.

Sample Research Summary

The research summary that appears below is a sample of a first draft summary completed fairly early in the research process. The research summary should be a living document that you revise continually until you are ready to draft your annotated outline. Some drafts of the research summary may include resources that ultimately do not make it into your paper. In early drafts, your research summary may not be detailed enough, and you will need to add in more detail as you re-read your sources and gain a better understanding of the materials. In the annotations below, I have made notes about where the research summary could incorporate more detail in a future draft.

Some authors prefer to create a more bare-bones research summary and save the detail for the writing process. You will develop your own style, but I encourage you as a novice to spend the time fleshing out the research in the research summary through multiple drafts so that the actual drafting of the paper is not so tedious. If you can figure out exactly what the research means and what the relationships are between the competing voices already engaged in the discourse, then the writing will not be as challenging. Once you become more comfortable with the scholarly writing process, you may find that you can effectively draft a full paper from a sparse research summary because you are more familiar with the materials and do not need to write down all your thoughts about the sources during a preliminary stage. As a novice, though, one advantage to writing a detailed research summary is that you can essentially cut and paste your analysis into your final paper and revise and edit to match the format and style. If you spend time doing the hard work up front, you will save yourself time and headache later in the process.

SUMMARY

The most important part of the research for this particular project is developing the analytical framework. In writing my last article, my very strong feeling was that Florida's Stand Your Ground laws were not legitimate because they are inconsistent with community values and desires. I came across *Jurisprudence for a Free Society* (Harold D. Lasswell & Myers S. McDougal, *Jurisprudence for a* Free *Society* (New Haven Press, 1992)), which provides a framework for analyzing whether a government is lawful and——— 1 should be recognized. It was developed to be used in the context of international law, specifically for the purpose of determining when a change in government is legitimate. For this project I would like to utilize this framework to determine whether Florida's Stand Your Ground law is a valid law.

The framework requires identifying participants and analyzing whether the law has both authority and control. For this to exist, law must be consistent with community-held values (page 1052). This framework provides a guide for determining community-held values and evaluating whether they exist. To better understand the framework, I have consulted Winston P. Nagan, *Contextual-Configurative Jurisprudence : The Law, Science and Policies of Human Dignity* 01 (Vandeplas Publishing, LLC, 2013). Nagan was a student of Lasswell and McDougal. His text on *Jurisprudence for a Free Society* makes the framework accessible and a bit easier to understand. I plan to use this resource to verify my understanding of the original text.

I have also gone back and consulted my two previous articles on Stand Your Ground: Elizabeth Megale, *Deadly Combinations, How Self-Defense Laws Pairing Immunity with a Presumption of Fear Allow Criminals to Get Away with Murder*, 34 Am. J. Trial Advoc. 105 (2010), and Elizabeth Megale, *Disaster Unaverted: Reconciling the*——— 2 *Desire for a Safe and Secure State with the Grim Realities of Stand Your Ground*, 37 Am. J. Trial Advoc. 1 (2014). The first article argued that Stand Your Ground did not actually make society safer, contrary to the legislature's assertion. The second argued that Stand Your Ground effectively legalized homicide. These articles provide in-depth analysis of the meaning of the statutes, but in this article I want to go beyond just the words of the statute. I want to look at whether the law is consistent with community-held values.

In thinking about community, articles analyzing the impact of Stand Your Gound on the community, especially communities of color, are critical. Tamara Rice Lave, *Shoot to Kill: A Critical Look at Stand Your Ground Laws*, 67 U. Miami L. Rev. 827 (2012-2013), and Anthony Hall, *A Stand for Justice—Examining Why Stand Your Ground Laws Negatively Impact African Americans*, 7 S. Region Black Students Ass'n L.J. 95 (2013), are both arti-cles that look at the impact on communities of color. Both of these authors argue that——— 3 African Americans are disparately impacted by Stand Your Ground. These conclusions

---

1 The next phase of the research summary would need to include much more detail about the framework, its components, and its operation.

2 When you are building on your own work, you may not need to include as much detail in your research summary because you are obviously already familiar with what you have written in the past.

3 The research summary should track ongoing questions such as whether the conclusions reached by other scholars are

supported by the data. In a future draft, this section would be fleshed out to provide more detail about exactly how the authors reached their conclusions. If the authors are relying on anecdotal evidence instead of hard data collected by law enforcement, their arguments are probably not reliable, and these sources may not make it into the final paper. If they do make it in, it will probably be for the purpose of rebutting their conclusions.

may not be supported by data, however. The *Tampa Bay Times* has been collecting data on homicides wherein the shooter has claimed protection under Stand Your Ground. *Florida's Stand Your Ground Law Cases*, Tampa Bay Times, http ://www.tampabay.com/stand-your-ground-law. Based on the raw data, disparate racial impact is not readily apparent. I explore this unexpected result in *Disaster Unaverted*.

Based on preliminary research, it appears that two major participants are the NRA and ALEC. Several articles explore these groups and the role the gun lobby has played 4———in the sweeping Stand Your Ground legislation passed across the nation. In *NRA = No Rational Argument? How the National Rifle Association Exploits Public Irrationality*, 11 Tex. J. C.L. & C.R. 39 (2005), Scott Medlock explores the myth of fear and its power to manipulate public sentiment. In *Self Defense and the Suspicion Heuristic*, 98 Iowa L. Rev. 293 (2012-2013), L. Song Richardson and Phillip Atiba Goff explain how fear reinforces the suspicion heuristic to justify violence even when fear is not rational. In her article, Tamara Rice Lave also analyzes the role the NRA played in passing Stand Your Ground legislation. Similarly, in *Transmogrification of Self-Defense by National Rifle Association–Inspired Statutes: From the Doctrine of Retreat to the Right to Stand Your Ground*, 35 S.U. L. Rev. 1 (2007-2008), the author problematizes the push by the NRA for Stand Your Ground laws. It is impossible to discuss the NRA's legislative role without considering ALEC. In *Rhetoric vs. Reality: ALEC's Disguise as a Nonprofit Despite Its Extensive Lobbying*, 34 Hamline J. Pub. L. & Pol'y 35 (2012), the author analyzes ALEC as a participant in the legislative process and criticizes its disguise as a nonprofit.

My next steps are to dig deeper into these sources to flesh out the motivations of 5———the participants I have already identified. I also need to identify other participants and their motivations.

---

4 This part of the research summary alludes to an intertwining of gun rights issues and racially disparate impacts of Stand Your Ground laws. A future draft of the research summary would flesh out this interconnectivity more explicitly. It would also include sources more directly tied to the NRA and ALEC to establish their goals and purposes in advancing Stand Your Ground legislation across the nation.

5 An early stage research summary should include at least some general notes about next steps. You may have more specific questions to log here or in your research plan, too.

APPENDIX **VI**

Sample Analytical Framework Exercise

This sample exercise provides answers to the questions found at the end of Chapter 5. If you are intimately familiar with the analytical framework you wish to use, answering these questions may not be challenging. On the other hand, you may find yourself struggling to find a label for the method or approach you wish to take. The purpose of this document is to guide you in thinking critically about how you intend to approach the analysis of your thesis. It does not matter so much whether you can identify the correct label. It is much more important that you be able to identify the methodology and process you will use for analyzing your thesis.

Additionally, you may find that you cannot answer every question all at once. You may find that you need to begin working on your outline a bit before you can fully conceptualize how the analytical framework will guide the written analysis. Like other stages of this process, you should revisit this assignment to work through those challenges as you progress.

EXERCISE

1. Describe the Method of Inquiry Demanded by the Framework

Contextual-configurative analysis demands a methodological inquiry into community-held values. Community-held values are the cornerstone of the analysis because they are what legitimize law. According to Lasswell and McDougal, a law is legitimate when it has authority and control over the community, and authority and control simultaneously exist only when the law is consistent with community-held values. To utilize this framework, community members must be identified and their values must be defined.

2. Explain Why the Framework Is Relevant to This Project

In this paper, my goal is to prove that Stand Your Ground laws are not legitimate because they are inconsistent with community values. The entire purpose of this framework is to measure whether laws are consistent with community values, so it is an appropriate tool for advancing this particular project.

3. Outline How the Framework Will Guide Your Written Analysis

1 ———— a. Effective law requires the existence of both authority and control.

   i. Authority and control manifest when laws are created consistently with commonly held community values.

   ii. If a law is inconsistent with commonly held values, it may lose its authority, control, or both.

b. Process:

   i. Identify outcome relevant to a particular value situation, then identify pre- and post-outcomes.

   ii. Identify community participants.

   iii. Assess value situation by analyzing participants, their values, and the strategies used to leverage their values to gain command over others and achieve a specific outcome and effect.

4. Identify Others Who Have Used or Criticized This Framework

Winston P. Nagan, *Contextual-Configurative Jurisprudence: The Law, Science and Policies of Human Dignity* (Vandeplas Publishing, LLC, 2013) is a textbook that explains contextual-configurative jurisprudence. All reviews I have found are positive, but I cannot find that it has ever been used to evaluate domestic law. Because it is an international framework, I could draw criticism for using it in a context for which it was not intended.

5. List Any Potential Assumptions, Inferences, or Biases Inherent in the Framework

This particular framework intentionally accounts for many biases by acknowledging that not everyone in a given community has an equal voice or shares the same values. That is one of the main appeals of this framework. I think that the framework makes some assumptions about the rationality or predictability of participants. It also requires some inferences about who the participants are and what their values may be.

---

1 This part of the framework could use a lot more fleshing out even though it provides more detail about the framework than the example research summary did. When you review the sample outline in this chapter, notice how much more detail is provided regarding the framework. In your own processes, you can choose to update this assignment separately, or you could simply integrate this part of the process into your annotated outline. The process is intended to be organic to meet your needs as a scholar. Each assignment builds on the previous, and you should revisit earlier assignments as necessary to help you move forward in your project.

6. Identify Any Theory of Law or Jurisprudence from Which the Framework Derives

This framework derives from policy sciences and is an interdisciplinary approach to understanding law in a free society. It is a normative response to legal realism and legal formalism.

APPENDIX **VII**

Sample Annotated Outline

This sample outline uses a traditional format, but this type of formality is not a requirement. You may find at this stage that it is easier for you to begin converting your research summary into an "outline" by drafting short paragraphs of what will ultimately become your final paper. Depending on how intricate the argument is, you might even consider creating a mindmap or some sort of visual flowchart to help you conceptualize the overall organization of your paper. Like the other assignments, this one is intended to help you begin to understand how your own ideas fit into the broader discourse.

As you study this outline, compare it to the final article in Appendix IX. Notice which parts of this outline have been rearranged in the final article and which ones have remained the same. Notice where additional detail appears in the final article. Your outline may go through multiple drafts before you are ready to write, or you may wish to begin drafting after your very first draft. The key is to create an outline that gives you sufficient information so that you can begin to convert each point into its own sentence/paragraph/section.

Having a strong outline also facilitates the writing process by allowing you to focus on discrete sections of the paper. For example, I could focus on drafting the section on the legislature during one period of time without having to even think about drafting anything about the NRA and ALEC. Having the outline gives you fluidity and flexibility in how you budget time to complete your project.

OUTLINE

Title: A Call for Change: A Contextual-Configurative Analysis of Florida's "Stand Your Ground" Laws

I. INTRODUCTION
  a. Identify racial tension issues
    i. Participants embrace fundamentally different value structures, so their acceptance of the legitimacy of Florida's "Stand Your Ground" law will naturally create dissonance.

        1. Cottman, *Zimmerman Acquittal*
        2. Wilstien, *Ted Cruz*
        3. Abby Goodnough, *Florida Expands*
        4. Megale, *Disaster Unaverted*, 40-44
    ii. Most viewpoints being advanced are far too myopic to account for the multi-faceted issues presented by Florida's version of "Stand Your Ground."
        1. Megale, *Deadly Combinations*, 111 ————————————1
  b. In legalizing certain types of homicide by decriminalizing killings and other acts of violence involving self-defense, Florida has exchanged respect for human dignity with cold self-import.
    i. Megale, *Deadly Combinations*, 111
  c. Identify jurisprudential model for the preservation of human dignity.
    i. Theory of legal inquiry was intended to be applicable to both micro and macro analyses.
    ii. Most scholars have employed it as a tool for studying international law and politics.
    iii. Model specifically contemplates individuals.
        1. L&D, 335 ————————————————2
        2. Nagan, 3
  d. Effective law requires the existence of both authority and control.
    i. Authority and control manifest when laws are created consistently with commonly held community values.
    ii. If a law is inconsistent with commonly held values, it may lose its authority, control, or both.
        1. L&D, 401
  e. Florida's "Stand Your Ground" statutory scheme is inconsistent with human values.
  f. Discrete vocabulary — will be defined throughout article.
    i. Durkheim, *Suicide*, 41
  g. Process:
    i. Identify outcome relevant to a particular value situation, then identify pre- and post-outcomes.
    ii. Identify community participants.
    iii. Assess value situation by analyzing participants, their values, and the strategies used to leverage their values to gain command over others and achieve a specific outcome and effect.
        1. L&D, 379-81
  h. Roadmap article.

---

1 Wherever possible, try to note your source and page number so that you do not have difficulty putting your citations in order once the drafting is complete. At this stage, using a shorthand for sources is highly advisable so that you do not lose momentum in the drafting.

2 You will notice that my shorthand sometimes changes for citations throughout the outline. The purpose of this assignment is not to generate precise citations. The purpose is to give yourself notes that you understand so that when you reach the end stages of writing you can easily format citations. There is no need to distract yourself with perfect citations or consistent shorthand at this stage as long as you can understand your notes.

3 ——— II. NORMATIVE FRAMEWORK

    a. Values are manifested through particular outcomes, as follows (L&D, 377):

Value	Outcome
Power	Decision
Enlightenment	Knowledge
Wealth	Transaction
Well-being	Vitality
Skill	Performance
Affection	Cordiality
Respect	Prestige
Rectitude	Rightness

    b. *Jurisprudence for a Free Society* is a normative response to the tension created by the simplicity of other legal theories like legal formalism and legal realism.

       i. "Lasswell's deepest personal commitment was to the creation of a comprehensive theory for inquiry about the individual human being in social process." Nagan, 8

    c. Overview of the legal theory:

       i. Social process and the role of the legal process.

          1. "When two persons influence one another, the process is social, whether the individuals concerned are aware of one another or not. Wherever there is mutual influencing there is community."

          2. Social process involves people pursuing "values through institutions using resources."

          3. Legal processes involve individuals who use institutions and resources to advance values — it would be naïve to consider the law in a vacuum without accounting for the surrounding social process and the reciprocal effects.

            A. L&D, 379-81

    d. The Social Process (Next section pulled from L&D, 337-50)

       i. Human values include power, enlightenment, wealth, well-being, skill, affection, respect, and rectitude.

          1. Power is the making of decisions important to the social context as a whole and enforceable against challengers when necessary by the use of severe sanctions.

---

3 In the sections where I lay out the normative framework, almost every idea will come from another source. This is very common in the early sections of a paper. Nearly every scholarly paper sets up a problem, explains a framework, or otherwise provides background at the beginning of a paper. Your own thoughts typically come in toward the end of the paper.

      2. Enlightenment is the gathering and spreading of information.

      3. Wealth is the production and distribution of goods and services.

      4. Well-being is opportunity for safety, health, and comfort.

      5. Skill is opportunity to acquire and exercise excellence in a particular operation.

      6. Affection is giving and receiving intimacy, friendship, and loyalty.

      7. Respect is recognition and the reciprocal honoring of freedom of choice.

      8. Rectitude refers to responsibility for conduct.

  ii. All eight values appear in communities, but the specifics vary.

  iii. Communities disagree among themselves about how to pursue and prioritize values.

      1. "[I]t is usual to find many degrees of inequality." Pg. 343

  iv. Inequalities arise and create a class system with individuals occupying an elite, mid-elite, or rank and file status.

      1. Values are distributed unevenly throughout communities.

      2. Discrepancies in defining values.

  v. Status does not remain the same across values.

  vi. Initial distribution of values impacts mobility.

      1. Example, an elite in power or wealth generally has more potential to com———4 mand other values than an elite in well-being or respect, at least in Western cultures.

  vii. The potential for a value to be leveraged is related to the perspectives and practices of the individuals in community.

      1. "Perspectives" contemplate the "inner life of those who participate in an interaction," accounting for identity, demands, and expectations. Pg. 347

      2. "Operations" is the behavior of the participants. Pg. 350

      3. "Practices" emerge when behaviors and perspectives emerge in recurrent patterns. Pg. 347

        A. Human beings tend to modify their behavior when they interact with each other, but some "relatively stable patterns emerge." Pg. 347

        B. "Personality"—stable patterns that are separate from the behavior of an individual as affected by the social process. Pg. 349

        C. "Myth"—all the perspectives existing in a given institutional context. Pg. 347

        D. "Technique"—cumulative operations. Pg. 347-48

        E. "Culture"—"distinctive and stable pattern of community values and institutions." Pg. 348

e. Elites dominate sharing and shaping values.

  i. "[E]ach category of value is sought as an end or employed as a means."

  ii. Scope and base values.

---

4 Is it within the scope of this paper to examine why? Probably not. But it is a good topic for a future paper, along with how individuals who do not possess power or wealth could ever have a voice in a capitalistic society. This would be a good idea to jot down for your future research agenda.

       1. Values might be used as a base for augmenting their own scope —consider the adage, "it takes money to make money," as representative of wealth used as a base to expand the scope of wealth. Pg. 340-43

       2. A base value can serve as the impetus for increasing the scope of another value —"money is power" is a notion that represents the use of wealth as a base value to achieve a greater scope of power. Pg. 340-43

       3. To the extent any individual or group commands a particular value, that base may be used to acquire command over other values by shaping and sharing those within the community. Pg. 350

       4. Based upon this system of interaction, it would be possible for a dominant minority to define community values for a weaker majority.

f. Personality related to value determination.

   i. It is "organized in reference to values and employs practices specialized in varying degree to the shaping and sharing of each value." Pg. 350

   ii. "[T]he power-centered personality is of special interest to lawyers and legal scholars. Such a political personality diverges in discernible ways from the wealth-centered, respect-centered, or enlightenment-centered person." Pg. 350

   iii. Personality patterns are observable because personality is embedded in culture while simultaneously representing the individual. Pg. 350

   iv. Personality system is comprised of identification, demands, and expectations. Pg. 350-51

g. Identification is critical to assessing the participants in a given community, as well as their potential command over the shaping and sharing of values.

h. The symbols used by individuals and groups within a community create a system of identification.

   i. "'[I]dentities' are far more numerous than 'bodies,' and relate the biological individuals to one another in many different ways in the pursuit of value goals in various institutional networks." Pg. 351

   ii. Emphasizing individuals and organized groups makes it possible to identify "targets of responsibility." Pg. 351

   iii. Unorganized groups are useful "in examining factors that help to explain conduct." Pg. 351

i. Personality systems involve perspectives, or demands and expectations.

   i. "The demand system is composed of the values sought, and the practices assumed to embody these values." Pg. 352

   ii. Demands can be placed by the self on the self, or they can be placed by the self on others. Pg. 352

   iii. Demands evolve into patterns involving a complex amalgamation of values and particularized demands. Pg. 352

   iv. Intertwined with demands are expectations, which can be either positive or negative and involve the self or others. Pg. 352

   v. The following formula illustrates this point (Pg. 352):

System of expectations = positive expectations concerning demands by self on self

+

negative expectations concerning demands by self on self

+

positive expectations concerning demands by self on others

+

negative expectations concerning demands by self on others

+

positive and negative expectations concerning demands by others on self

+

positive and negative expectations concerning demands by others on others

j. Identification, demands, and expectations, both personal and group, eventually stabilize into myths, which can be subcategorized as doctrine, formula, and miranda. Pg. 353
   i. Doctrine—"abstract propositions that affirm the perspectives of the group." Pg. 353-54
      1. Expressed through symbols of identification coupled with demands and expectations.
      2. Memorialized in canonical documents such as the Declaration of Independence or the Magna Carta.
      3. To give effect to doctrine, formulas are necessary to develop prescriptions and mechanisms ensuring consistent implementation of doctrine.
   ii. Miranda facilitates the understanding of doctrine and provides a mode for interpretation of formulas vis-à-vis doctrine. Pg. 355
   iii. Patterns of myths evolve over time and differ throughout communities. Pg. 355
      1. Dominant myths are those advanced by the elite in any given social structure and may be labeled ideology.
      2. Counter-ideology is the systematization of discontent within communities and requires an "explicit rejection of the established 'ideology.'"
k. Analysis of each of these elements would be impossible without the outward expression of inward processes through communication and collaboration.
   i. "Communication" refers to the signals (including speech and gestures) used to communicate subjective perspectives between various systems. Pg. 357
   ii. Collaboration refers to activities bridging competing perspectives.

l.   MEASURING OUTCOMES.
  i.   Outcomes analysis studies the complex relationships between demands, expectations, and perceptions of identity as well as myths, modes of communication, and value systems.
  ii. "[S]ome outcomes deal directly with the formulation of prescriptions," a component of myth, while others invoke existing prescriptions. Pg. 358
  iii. Prescriptions—normative act sanctioning specific expectations with regard to particular activities. Pg. 359
  iv. Activities promoting any given prescription are common prior to its adoption, as are intelligence missives including collection and analysis of data and planning.
  v.   Through intelligence and promotion activities, community perspectives can be assessed, measured, and influenced.
m. Related to the invocation of prescriptions are the notions of application, termination, and appraisal.
  i.   Invocation of a prescription will include any "initial steps taken to put a prescription into effect." Pg. 359
  ii. Application refers to the point in time when a prescription is finally (not provisionally) characterized as such. Pg. 359
  iii. Terminations refer to the point in time when a prescription ceases. Pg. 359
  iv. Appraisal is the process by which prescriptions are evaluated to assess their functionality vis-à-vis the goals of collective policy and to allocate responsibility for results. Pg. 359
n. These apparatuses create policy systems that assist in identifying patterns of future actions by individuals or groups.
  i.   Interests arise from policies and "refer to events expected to harmonize with value demands." Pg. 360
  ii. Shared interests are referred to as "common" and other incompatible interests are "special." Pg. 360
  iii. System of exclusivity such that "[c]ommon interests are 'inclusive' when the events involved are of considerable importance for all; they are 'exclusive' when the relevant events are of very much greater importance to identifiable sub-groups than to the whole." Pg. 360
o. Working definitions:
  i.   "[A] decision is giving, withholding, rejecting or receiving support in an interaction that affects the entire social context to a significant extent (including the probable use of severe deprivational sanctions against challengers)." Pg. 379
  ii. Knowledge is "a culminating interaction in which information about the past and present, together with estimates of the future, are made available, withheld, rejected or received." Pg. 379
  iii. Transactions are "the giving, withholding, rejecting or receiving of claims to processed (or processable) resources." Pg. 379

  iv. Vitality refers to individual and group health, with an eye toward elongation and preservation of life free from disease, illness, discomfort, or defect. Pg. 379

  v. Performance is evidenced through formal examinations and the appraisal of work product. Pg. 379

  vi. Congeniality is related to loyalty and assessed by examining families and their disruptions, social activities, and clashes between and commitments to one another. Pg. 379

  vii. Prestige requires a method of "taking note of the culminating circumstances in which recognitions are given or received." Pg. 379

  viii. Rightness evolves from sequences of affirmations and inquiries that solidify the moral and ethical conscience. Pg. 379

III. LEGAL PROCESSES

 a. Broad definition of the "law" as "a process of authoritative decision by which the members of a community clarify and implement their common interests." L&D, xxx

 b. Legal system is also an embedded element within the broader social process.

 c. Must be stable enough and dynamic enough to respond to the various demands and expectations of the community.

 d. It both affects, and is affected by, the social process.

 e. All institutions within a society must strike a balance between competing worlds. Pg. 366

  i. Compare inclusive and exclusive interests, or the distribution of base values in a given community. Pg. 366

  ii. Social order is maintained when stability is flexible enough to provide for change as values and interests evolve. Pg. 366

  iii. Dominant majority of the collective may define values, but sometimes, like in apartheid, a powerful minority might have sufficient power to define them.

  iv. Boundaries separating the majority from the minority are always shifting.

   1. Over time individuals and groups who were traditionally excluded from the collective, the "others," find themselves included in the mainstream. *Invisible Man*, 96

   2. Boundaries shift, those who were once included may become outsiders.

   3. Boundaries morph as values and beliefs of the collective evolve.

 f. Law "refers to the 'power institutions' in a community," and power is correlated to decision outcomes. L&D, 379

  i. Processes affecting decisions implicate the balance of authority and control.

  ii. "Control" avers to the "effective impact on the choices being made." L&D, 362

  iii. "Authority" means the "expectations of permissibility, [and] expectations among community members that decision functions are properly performed." L&D, 362

    g. To be law, it must possess both authority and control. L&D, 400
        i. Absence of power means the rule of "law" is an abuse of power.
        ii. The absence of control leads to pretended power, and the absence of authority leads to naked power.
        iii. When authority and control are absent, anarchy and chaos erupt.
        iv. Authority and control derive from members of society when the law is consistent with their values.
    h. Authority and control are manifested through the enactment of various types of codes.
        i. Constitutive codes are the most comprehensive and operate as the formula component of myth to "establish[] a process of authoritative decision and [to] allocate[] permissible participations in the decision process." L&D, 362
        ii. Supervisory codes "refer[] to the more general principles for settlement of controversies between private parties." L&D, 362
        iii. A "'regulative' code refers to the community limits within which private shaping and sharing activities are to be carried on." L&D, 362
        iv. The "'sanctioning and corrective' code includes all the activities designed in appropriate contingencies to maintain conformity to the norms of collective policy." L&D, 362
    i. Sanctioning and corrective code is the only one relevant to this article.
        i. The six permissible objectives of the sanctioning and corrective code are:
            1. Deterrence
                A. "[D]esigned to influence the expectations of potential violators by making the point that compliance is likely to leave one better off than non-compliance." L&D, 363
            2. Prevention
                A. "[D]esigned to influence the expectations of potential violators by making the point that compliance is likely to leave one better off than non-compliance." L&D, 363
                B. Explain how different from deterrence.
            3. Restoration
                A. "[P]utting a stop to acts of violation and as far as possible reinstate the original situation." L&D, 363
            4. Rehabilitation
                A. "[P]utting a stop to acts of violation and as far as possible reinstate the original situation." L&D, 363
                B. "[U]ndo[ing any] deprivations of value occasioned by the impermissible activities." L&D, 363
            5. Reconstruction
                A. Fundamentally alter "prevailing institutions." L&D, 363
            6. Correction
                A. Achieve "personality changes in offenders (an objective paralleling the reconstruction of a group)." L&D, 363

    j. Sovereign's decisions are "an outcome of power," and become authoritative as an outcome of the sovereign's pattern of "established and recognized authoritative practice." Nagan, 92

    k. Social order patterns affect perceptions of stability.

       i. "'[B]uilt-in' regulative practices that identify and negatively sanction acts deviating from shared prescriptions." L&D, 366

    l. Stable prescriptions are simultaneously authoritative and controlling—these are the most supported by society and which, upon violation, are expected to result in punishment. L&D, 366-67 for this section

       i. "Mores" have a tendency to strongly influence societal norms and values.

      ii. "Counter-mores" are prescriptions that individuals expect to be violated even though the community might strongly support the norms.

    iii. Violation of a counter-more is not likely to be punished harshly because "it is perceived that violators cannot be entirely stamped out."

    iv. Mores and counter-mores create social order because they are the only cultural traits involving prescriptions.

     v. Societal norms can evolve such that mores eventually become counter-mores or expediencies.

    vi. This evolutionary process is reciprocal; expediencies may turn into counter-mores and then mores as societal values change.

    vii. Examples:

        1. Cultural shifts in norms related to marijuana use. Prior criminalization——5 to decriminalization to legalization. *History of Marijuana; NYC Mayor Bloomberg: Next Month, No Jail for Marijuana Possession; Marijuana Laws in Louisiana Should Be More Lenient*; Colo. Const. art. XVIII, § 16; Wash. Rev. Code § 69.51A.005(2) (2011).

    viii. Trends of pederasty. Common practice in ancient Greek Society but criminalized today. *Unpacking Hetero-Patriarchy*, 186-87; *Invisible Man*, 146

    ix. Adultery laws in the United States. Crime still on the books, but rarely prosecuted. Treated less harshly in divorce cases. *History of Adultery and Fornication Criminal Laws*; Ala. Code § 13A-13-2(c) (2014); Ariz. Rev. Stat. § 13-1408(A) (2013); Fla. Stat. § 798.01 (2013); Ga. Code § 16-6-19 (2013); Idaho Code § 18-6601 (2014); 720 Ill. Comp. Stat. 5/11-35(b) (2014); Kan. Stat. § 21-5511(b) (2013); Md. Code § 10-501(b) (2014); Mass. Gen. Laws 272 § 14 (2014); Mich. Comp. Laws § 750.30 (2014); Minn. Stat. § 609.36; Miss. Code § 97-21-1 (2013); N.H. Rev. Stat. § 645:3 (2014); N.Y. Adultery Law § 255.17 (McKinney 2014); N.D. Cent. Code § 12.1-20-09(1) (2013); Okla. Stat. § 872 (2013); R.I. Gen. Laws § 11-6-2 (2013); S.C. Code § 16-15-60

---

5 Here is an example of a place where I can use my own examples to illustrate the concepts set up by the framework. While I will offer many more of my own ideas in later sections of this paper, this is one way I can begin to inject my own ideas as related to the sources upon which I ultimately rely.

(2013); Va. Code § 18.2-365 (2013); W. Va. Code § 62-9-20 (2014); Wis. Stat. § 944.16 (2013); 163. Tim Murphy, *Map: Is Adultery Illegal?*, Mother Jones (Nov. 29, 2011, 2:20 PM), http://www.motherjones.com/mojo/2011/11/is-adultery-illegal-map ("State-level adultery provisions are rarely if ever enforced."); 164. Ethan Bronner, *Adultery, an Ancient Crime That Remains on Many Books*, N.Y. Times, Nov. 15, 2012, http://www.nytimes.com/2012/11/15/us/adultery-an-ancient-crime-still-on-manybooks.html?_r=l&; *State v. Lash*, 16 N.J.L. 380, 381 (1838); see also *S.B. v. S.J.B.*, 609 A.2d 124, 126 (N.J. Ch. 1992).

m. Law-culture-law cycle.
  i. Laws are created through the influence of existing values, institutions, and other elements of the social process.
  ii. The law comes into existence by aligning with dominant values to achieve authority and control, and as counter-mores emerge in response to evolving value systems, the law risks losing authority and control over the community.
    1. "An important key to any social order is the severity or the mildness of the value deprivations employed as negative sanctions against any challenger of established norms." L&D, 367

n. Balance of stability and innovation in society/maximization postulate (this section L&D, 368-70).
  i. "[P]olicies are chosen which are expected to yield net value advantages."
  ii. Complex decision-making process.
  iii. "Degrees of unfreedom and freedom [must be distinguished] according to the variety of alternatives open to the responder, and the magnitudes of value indulgence or deprivation involved."
  iv. Outcomes cannot be characterized as "either/or" options, but rather "more or less."
  v. Allows some predictability, particularly with regard to habitual behavior.
  vi. Optimalizes by balancing value indulgences against deprivations to achieve maximum advantages.
  vii. Framing goals to portray optimalization is essential to garnering community support for policies and preserving social order.
  viii. Given the type of institution, policies might be formed by the elite without any input from the mid-elite or rank and file, while in other systems, contribution of the mid-elite and rank and file are essential to the success of the policy and preservation of social order.
  ix. The maximization postulate looks both backward and forward.
  x. Advance goals that will maximize desired values.
  xi. Policies guide goal formation.

o. Social change is a result of legal action because of its interconnectivity with culture traits (mores, counter-mores, and expediencies) (this section L&D, 370-73).

      i. Stability can be maintained by minimizing the nature and degree of changes at any given time.

      ii. Changes can be classified in one of two ways: functional or structural.

         1. Functional changes alter the way the salient elements of the social process interact with each other.

         2. Structural changes "are exhibited in the pattern of value shaping and sharing (changes in priorities, or from wide to narrow distribution, or the reverse), or in basic institutions (in myth or technique)."

         3. Past changes can be studied to predict pathways of future change, and they can also be used as models for achieving desired change.

IV. SCHEMATIC FOR ANALYTICAL FRAMEWORK (cite to L&D for framework) (this section L&D, 379-84)

    a. Value situation surrounding Florida's enactment of a "Stand Your Ground" statutory scheme.

      i. A value situation can be described as a "value shaping and sharing sequence."

    b. "Identification of outcome events is the critical step both in value and institution analysis."

      i. Permits the analysis of the surrounding events, including pre- and post-outcomes.

      ii. Facilitates the identification of base and scope values.

      iii. Characterization of value outcomes facilitates the identification and description of institutional practices in any context.

      iv. Identifying the boundaries of a value situation is critical to correctly identifying the participants and their roles.

         1. Participants — those individuals and groups that shape and share values both formally and informally.

         2. Perspectives — the demands and expectations of the participants.

         3. Base values — values that any given participant possesses that can be used to achieve power and other values.

         4. Strategies — the methods the participants employ to leverage base values.

         5. Outcomes — the resulting concrete events and the general prescriptions.

         6. Effects — "implicate all values, especially those critical to power, decision making, and organizing formalized authority, which will then affect the production and distribution of all values other than power."

    c. Identify strategic patterns of leveraging base values to achieve particular outcomes (cite L&D, 394 this section).

      i. Identify, analyze, and critique the evolution of culture traits and law

      ii. Measuring outcomes "in units of interaction" to assess the value situation, as different units of measure apply to different outcomes.

         1. Example:

           A. Power outcomes (decisions) are measured by votes.

     B. Wealth outcomes (transactions) are measured by prices.

     C. Enlightenment outcomes (knowledge) are measured by "informativeness."

     D. Well-being outcomes (vitality) are measured by "salubrity."

     E. Skill outcomes (performance) are measured by "craftsmanship."

     F. Affection outcomes (cordiality) are measured by "friendliness."

     G. Respect outcomes (prestige) are measured by "distinction."

     H. Rectitude outcomes (rightness) are measured by "morality" or "responsibility."

   d. "[C]all[] attention to connections that might otherwise be overlooked."

6——— V. FLORIDA'S "STAND YOUR GROUND" STATUTES

   a. Outcome: enactment of Florida's "Stand Your Ground" statutes.

     i. Statutes are a result of legislative decision making.

       1. "Decision" is the outcome related to power. L&D, 377

       2. Organize by participants because each pre- and post-effect, base value, and strategy is particular to a given participant.

     ii. Florida's "Stand Your Ground" statutes took effect October 1, 2005. *Deadly Combinations*, 113-14; *Florida's Protection of Persons Bill*, 200.

       1. Prior to the enactment (cite *Deadly Combinations* and prior Florida statute).

         A. Limited defense requiring proof of retreat to the wall, except in "castle" cases.

         B. "Castle"— home and workplace.

         C. Before 2005, Duty to Retreat was the majority rule in most states.

       2. Three key changes with enactment: (*Deadly Combinations*)

         A. Duty to Retreat was eliminated (§ 776.012, Florida Statutes).

           i. Wherever anyone had a right to be, that person is justified in using deadly force to prevent the likelihood of death or great bodily harm.

           ii. Expands the historical notion of castle to anywhere a person has a right to be, even a public place.

         B. Expanded the concept of castle to include vehicles as well as homes, and eliminated workplace (§ 776.013, Florida Statutes).

           i. Presumption of reasonable fear for any castle cases involving the justifiable use of force.

         C. Created immunity for anyone using force.

           i. Prohibits the punishment of an individual claiming self-defense.

           ii. Punishment includes detention, arrest, prosecution, or civil liability.

---

6 This is the section where I begin to interject my own ideas. Some of them come from my previous work, and some ideas are new connections and conclusions I have reached based on studying the issues through the analytical framework.

3. Since enactment, the number of justifiable homicides in Florida has risen dramatically. *Justifiable Homicides up 200%*.
4. Statutes have been liberally interpreted to employ a subjective standard regarding reasonable fear. *Disaster Unaverted*, 45
   A. Instead of determining whether a reasonable man would have feared death or great bodily harm, the question is whether the defendant, in the defendant's circumstances and with the defendant's knowledge, formed a reasonable belief that death or great bodily harm was imminent.
   B. "Getting away with murder" has become easier in Florida.
      i. Maddox, *Florida Teen*
      ii. Almasy, *Dad's Texting*
      iii. Fullard, *License to Kill*
      iv. Lanson, *Media Role*
5. New attention with Trayvon Martin's killing by George Zimmerman. (*Disaster Unaverted*)
   A. Moment the public began to question "Stand Your Ground."
   B. Shooting deaths grab national attention because people wonder——7 whether and to what extent the shooter will be punished.
   C. Claims of reasonable fear grow increasingly preposterous.
   D. Many individuals in Florida feel entitled to shoot and kill for any reason at all.
6. Clash in cultural values — a value situation.
   A. "Stand Your Ground" was promulgated to advance the interests of certain groups. *Deadly Combinations, Beyond Trayvon*
   B. Careless drafting has had far-reaching detrimental impacts in other communities.
   C. Despite strong public outcry for amending the statutes, Florida has not changed the "Stand Your Ground" laws to better represent commonly held values.
   b. Participants
      i. The Florida legislature
         1. Center participant of the value situation presented by Florida's "Stand Your Ground" statutory scheme.
         2. Organization is stable and specializes in the shaping and sharing of human values by making decisions to create prescriptions with an "expectation that severe deprivations will be, or are being, imposed on the challengers of policy and that high indulgences will be, or are being, granted to supporters of policy."

---

7 While many of these conclusions I have reached on my own, I should still find support for the facts I rely on to reach those conclusions. Sometimes, when you are drafting your outline, you cannot readily find the source that sparked the idea. You should still make a note of the thought, but remember that when you finish drafting your article, you will need to cite to original sources in support of your positions.

3. Enacted Florida's "Stand Your Ground" law in 2005.
   A. Prior to 2005, anyone claiming to act in self-defense required to make a prima facie showing of reasonable fear of death or great bodily harm, then prosecutor was tasked with disproving, beyond a reasonable doubt, the claim of self-defense.
   B. Duty to Retreat and the traditional castle doctrine are evolved counter-more.
      i. Discuss the notion of excuse or justification in homicide cases not recognized during medieval times. Society opposes all homicide no matter the reason.
      ii. Modern age, England began to recognize the desire for excusing or justifying certain types of killings.
      iii. Excusable homicide and justifiable homicide evolved from the more of the draconian medieval law to the counter-more of modern law.
      iv. As a counter-more, society continued to embrace the prohibition against homicide, but under certain circumstances the offense was not expected to be punished harshly.
      v. Thus, the principles of Duty to Retreat and the castle doctrine are counter-mores.
4. Florida legislature evolved the counter-mores of Duty to Retreat and castle doctrine in the direction of an expediency.
   A. Not all jurisdictions with "Stand Your Ground" legislation have created an expediency; however, all have at least created a more expansive counter-more than Duty to Retreat.
   B. Florida's "Stand Your Ground" laws legalized homicide.
      i. Converted self-defense into an expediency by eliminating the expectation of any punishment with regard to the justifiable use of force.
5. Legislature influenced by two core values: power and wealth.
   A. Retain office — authority/control.
   B. NRA influence.
      i. Multistate strategy.
      ii. Wealthy lobby group.
      iii. American Legislative Exchange Council.
      iv. Opposition by law enforcement and other groups.
      v. Gun control groups unable to craft a response prior to the legislature's vote.
6. *How NRA's True Believers Converted a Marksmanship Group into a Mighty Gun Lobby; How the NRA and Its Allies Helped Spread a Radical Gun Law Nationwide; Overwhelming legislative support; Why Florida Senate Democrats; Divided We Stand; NRA Fueled; Money Trail; Fla. Gun Law*
   A. Legends of "stranger danger." (*Disaster Unaverted*)
   B. Legends of rampant violence.

      i. Story of James Workman (shot and killed an intruder shortly after Hurricane Ivan). Expose distortion in the legend and reality. Workman did not support the law. *Florida's "Stand Your Ground" Law Was Born of 2004 Case, But Story Has Been Distorted*

7. Two main goals:
   A. Retain its power by ensuring authority and control over constituents.
   B. To maintain authority and control, increase the sense of security and well-being of its constituents.

8. Two values: power and well-being.
   A. Power is the base value because a governmental agency is involved.
   B. Community value—well-being, allows the government to gain command over a scope value to build and ensure its own power.
   C. "Law" is "a process of authoritative decision by which the members of a community clarify and implement their common interests."
   D. Individual legislators want to preserve their positions of power through re-election, and when laws coincide with community interests, citizens are more likely to re-elect legislators.
   E. Through voting, citizens express their consent to governance and vest authority in the legislature.
   F. The legislature exercises control by creating prescriptions, in the form of laws that are then enforced by other legitimate agencies.
   G. The enforcement of laws ensures continued effective control by the government.
      i. Law enforcement agencies will arrest individuals who commit crimes and state attorneys will prosecute those crimes.
      ii. The judicial branch will provide a forum for the prosecution, and upon a showing of guilt, the offender will be punished.
      iii. The concept of mores and counter-mores informs that some crimes will not be prosecuted as readily or punished as harshly as other crimes.
      iv. The decision to prosecute and punish is intimately tied with maintaining control over the constituency.
      v. Government gains control by prosecuting and punishing in a manner that acknowledges how the community wishes a given law to be enforced.
         1. If a law is enforced too harshly, or the community feels it silly to enforce at all, the government will lose control by insisting on its enforcement.
         2. If the community feels strongly about the prosecution and punishment of certain offenders, the government will lose control by refusing to capture and isolate those criminals.
      vi. The government and bodies appointed by the government (like the jury) are charged with determining whether a prescription was violated and by whom.

1. A police officer or a judge decides whether probable cause exists to arrest someone.
2. A prosecutor decides whether to prosecute that person who has been arrested.
3. Juries determine guilt or innocence.
4. Judges impose a sentence.
5. Individuals making the decisions about whether a crime has occurred and who should be held responsible are typically unrelated to the crime itself.
6. The victim does not control the ultimate decision to arrest, prosecute, convict, or sentence.

H. Control is preserved in this system because the decision makers are not the victims; rather, they impartially and neutrally enforce prescriptions.

9. "Stand Your Ground" has turned this system on its head for cases involving the justifiable use of force.
   A. Anyone who fears the threat of imminent death or great bodily harm can use deadly force in self-defense.
      i. Castle/presumption of reasonable fear.
   B. Now: Fear = snap decision to kill; automatic immunity.
   C. Before: Defendant must establish self-defense, prosecution must disprove.
      i. Victim-shooter becomes judge, jury, and executioner.
      ii. No accountability.
      iii. No longer a reasonable expectation of punishment in Florida "Stand Your Ground" cases, this doctrine has created an expediency.
   D. The judicial process should be a check to preserve societal values through recognition of the counter-mores of Duty to Retreat and the traditional castle doctrine; no check under new law.

10. Legislature has effectively undermined its natural goal of preserving power by ceding control to individuals in "Stand Your Ground" cases.
    A. Admitted that its purpose was to empower individuals to protect themselves through acts of violence.
    B. Control relates to the governmental processes that ensure legal prescriptions are enforced consistently.
    C. "Stand Your Ground" has virtually eliminated the police and prosecutor roles in many homicides; legal control has vanished.
    D. In the absence of control, there is no law, just pretended power.
    E. Pretended power creates community instability and unpredictability by both encouraging violence and impeding the investigation of cases involving acts of violence.

ii. The National Rifle Association and the American Legislative Exchange Council. (Roig-Franzia) (NPR) (Mayors against Illegal Guns) (Bender)

(Weinstein) (Achenbach) (McGillis) (http://www.alec.org/about-alec/) (Daly) (Sourcewatch)

1. NRA powerful and wealthy lobby group that drafted language of Stand Your Ground statutes.
    A. Goal: zero gun regulation. *How NRA's True Believers Converted a Marksmanship Group into a Mighty Gun Lobby*
    B. Leverages wealth and power to acquire more of both.
    C. "Elite of influence."
    D. Base value
        i. "Power"?
            1. Increased power in the legislative process = involvement in the power structure.
            2. Assuming power NRA is a pressure group.
                a. Pressure groups engage in "activity specialized to influencing particular decisions by peaceful means."
                b. It leverages so much influence over the legislative process that it often is the effective decision maker.
            3. Collaboration with the American Legislative Exchange Council ("ALEC"). *What is ALEC?*
                a. Forum for legislators, lobbyists, and corporations to work together on drafting legislation and voting on the proposed statutory language so that legislators may return to their home states and propose new laws to the benefit of the participating lobbyists.
                b. Corporate entities and lobby groups primarily fund ALEC.
                c. Claims to be non-partisan, but only one of 104 participating legislators is a Democrat.
                d. Purchase the opportunity to draft legislation to become part of the decision-making process.
                e. Side-by-side collaboration = greater influence over legislatures.
                    i. Values of the ALEC groups tend to be given greater weight because they are presented more often and more systematically to legislatures.
                    ii. Values are likely to be adopted even when they are inconsistent with commonly held community values.
        ii. Wealth?
            1. Well-financed.
            2. Adept at leveraging wealth to command power as a scope value.
            3. Wealth derives from two sources—membership dues and corporate sponsorship from gun manufacturers and related industries.

        4. Campaign contributions to control lawmakers and exert pressure on political and legislative decisions

        5. NRA's ability to deliver votes by creating and then directing large blocs of single-issue voters.

          a. Gun regulation as an assault on every citizen's fundamental rights.

          b. This framing technique taps into community values of respect, rectitude, and well-being.

  2. Examples of leveraging:

    A. Friendship between Marion Hammer and Dennis Baxley. *Meet Dennis Baxley*

    B. Affection scope value.

      i. Hammer drafted substantial portions of the language in the bill and provided it to Representative Baxley and Senator Peaden to propose to the Florida legislature.

      ii. Baxley leveraged the scope value of well-being to convince the legislature that this law, as drafted, was good for the community and would ensure re-election because it coincided with commonly held values.

  3. NRA drafted the language of the legislation and it is evidence of its direct participation in the decision, or power outcome.

  4. Thus, it appears that in leveraging wealth to gain command over power, the NRA might have succeeded, through "Stand Your Ground," in commanding power as a base value.

  5. Problems:

    A. Does not represent the values held by the majority of the community.

      i. Only about 500,000 of Florida's 19.3 million residents are members of the NRA, and only around 800,000 are registered gun owners. *How the NRA Attained Dominance*

      ii. Less than 3 percent of Florida's citizenry has membership in the NRA.

      iii. Vocal opposition from law enforcement and other groups was unorganized and ineffective.

      iv. Post-Trayvon Martin, louder opposition voices have had no influence—NRA has blocked the reconsideration of "Stand Your Ground" laws in Florida.

    B. Disconnect between the legislation and societal values could make legislature lose its authority.

    C. With "Stand Your Ground," the legislature is responding primarily to the NRA, which is a small percentage of the community.

    D. Common interests of many community members are not represented by "Stand Your Ground."

    E. Civil unrest is likely to escalate as citizens express their disagreement with the laws.

iii. Gun control lobby
1. The gun control lobby is comprised of several groups, like the Brady Campaign, Mayors Against Illegal Guns, Moms Demand Action, and others, whose base value is well-being. Gun control lobby did not have to time to respond to the proposals pre-outcome.
2. Post-outcome efforts have effected no change.
3. To achieve its goal of providing for a safer community and increased vitality, the gun control lobby leverages primarily enlightenment to influence power institutions.
  A. Gun-control groups do not have the same type of wealth and corporate support mustered by the NRA.
  B. None of these groups are members of ALEC. *ALEC Corporations*
  C. Their ability to leverage wealth as an influential force with the legislature is limited.
  D. They do not have access to a captive multistate legislative audience.
  E. They have historically relied solely on leveraging enlightenment to promote gun regulation.
4. Enlightenment:
  A. Limited success.
  B. Gun deregulation leads to increased violence competes against the NRA enlightenment message that gun control threatens a fundamental right.
  C. Pre-outcome:
    i. NRA suggested innocent citizens in danger and needed to arm themselves so criminals would be too afraid to attack.
    ii. Couching it as an enlightenment message, the NRA was able to capture public support, with little to no opposition.
  D. Post-outcome:
    i. Gun-control enlightenment message reaches individuals and small groups but not legislatures.
    ii. Lawmakers are minimally influenced by gun control data and reasoning.
    iii. Example:
      1. Jonathan E. Lowy, of the Brady Campaign, testified before the United States Senate Committee on the Judiciary Subcommittee on the Constitution, Civil Rights, and Human Rights.
        a. Relied on at least two studies to support the conclusion that Florida's "Stand Your Ground" legislation has led to "a net increase in homicide, with no evidence of deterrence of other crimes."
5. Well-being was a stated goal—empower individuals to protect themselves against criminals.

A. Justifiable homicides in Florida have increased by roughly 200 percent since 2005.
B. Widely reported killings suggest an increased disregard for human life.
C. Example:
D. Michael Dunn incident.
E. Curtis Reeves incident.
6. Choice is "shoot or be shot"—changes in cultural expectations and personal perspectives, values, and beliefs about what is appropriate in society.
7. Contrary to the NRA's and legislature's enlightenment message that "Stand Your Ground" has made communities safer, the law has clearly had the opposite effect.
8. Gun control lobby's enlightenment message that less gun regulation inherently leads to increased gun violence rings true.
iv. NAACP
1. Most widely recognized civil rights organization in America.
2. Uses base value of enlightenment to leverage power through grassroots and national organizations fighting for equality and against the disenfranchisement of racial minority groups.
A. "Stand Your Ground" is a step backward in the struggle for racial equality.
3. People still notice color, and there is no question that racism, prejudice, and bias exist.
A. For many, racial differences symbolize the "Other," who should be feared.
B. When subjective fear is motivation enough to shoot and kill without question, then inherent biases, prejudices, and racism will necessarily provoke killings.
C. Statistical evidence on the racial impact of "Stand Your Ground" in Florida is mixed.
i. Law seems to be enforced uniformly. *Race Plays Complex Role*
ii. Numbers of black victims are higher overall than white victims.
iii. Black-on-black killings occur at higher rates than interracial killings.
D. Race-based enlightenment message presents a myopic interpretation of the data that is unlikely to influence legislative change.
4. NAACP and Trayvon Martin.
A. Claims
i. Killing itself was racially motivated.
ii. Reticence to investigate and prosecute George Zimmerman resulted from endemic institutional racism in the City of Sanford, Florida.
B. Evidence

    i. Zimmerman had used a racial slur when describing Martin to the 911 operator. However, the audio recording of Zimmerman's call to 911 was unclear and could not be enhanced to show he had used such a term.

    ii. Zimmerman had called the authorities on numerous occasions to report suspicious individuals and each of the reports involved an African American. Evidence supporting the allegation of racial profiling, however, was not forthcoming.

    iii. Additionally, neighbors and friends of Zimmerman claimed he was not racist and that he socialized with people of all races.

    iv. NAACP alleged authorities were hesitant to arrest Zimmerman because the victim was black and the shooter was white. The physical evidence in the case, however, supported the police decision not to arrest Zimmerman. Upon arriving on scene, law enforcement noticed Zimmerman had cuts on the back of his head and a broken nose, which were consistent with his account of being pinned to the ground and punched in the face by Martin.

    v. Several eyewitness accounts confirmed Zimmerman's version of events. Under these facts, it would have been subjectively and objectively reasonable for Zimmerman to believe he was in danger of suffering great bodily harm. In fact, he did suffer great bodily harm. Under "Stand Your Ground," therefore, he would have been entitled to immunity, and the failure to arrest and prosecute Zimmerman would have been lawful under the statute. Additionally, a decision not to prosecute would have been entirely consistent with other, more egregious cases around Florida that have not been prosecuted at all.

C. Despite the tragedy of Martin's death, the evidence and data did not clearly support the theories of racism and enlightenment message was not persuasive.

D. Enlightenment value is functionally the same as that of the gun control lobby and other groups opposed to "Stand Your Ground."

E. Aligning with other groups may give all of them more power to bring a unified message to the legislature.

  v. Media

  vi. Media plays two distinct roles in society: passive "informing role" and an "activating role." *Media Ethics and Media Law*, 18

 vii. Leverages the scope value of enlightenment to achieve goals.

viii. Leverages its knowledge and its reputation in order to gain access to both information and the widest possible audience, with the desired outcome of increasing wealth and, more importantly, gaining respect.

  ix. Steer audience knowledge and activity to increase the power and wealth of the news corporation itself.

  x. News media on the other side is the nefarious actor.

1. "Activating role" regarding "Stand Your Ground."
   A. Journalists who oppose the law will naturally publish stories about its unforeseen ill effects in order to guide public opinion and steel citizens' resolve to change the status quo through activism.
   B. Those who favor the law, on the other hand, take a similar two-pronged approach: First, they publish the sort of "glad-I-had-my-gun" stories that highlight the shooter as victim; second, they portray the law's detractors as the Other, who is not to be trusted.
2. Other entities — like the legislature, NRA, gun control lobby, and NAACP — use the media to enlighten the public and shape values.
3. Competing media messages evidence the tension among these various groups.
4. As its own vehicle, the media also seeks to influence the shaping of community values.
5. At the same time, the media transmits messages about community values to these other groups as well.
6. Media is at the same time a tool of civil engineering and a barometer of community values.
   A. Since Martin's killing, legislature has been unresponsive to the media message.
   B. Many news outlets have reported the failure of "Stand Your Ground" and called for its repeal.
   C. Community support for it in Florida has drastically declined.
   D. Florida legislature has refused to seriously reconsider the legislation.
   E. Governor's task force on "Stand Your Ground" was staffed with four sponsors of the original bill and only two individuals on that team expressed concerns about the law.
   F. Representative Alan Williams introduced a bill to repeal "Stand Your Ground," but Marion Hammer, former president of the NRA, testified in opposition to it before the Florida legislature in November 2013, and it ultimately died in committee.
   G. Considering the emerging enlightenment message that commonly held community values are at odds with existing "Stand Your Ground" legislation, it is perplexing that the legislature would not more seriously reconsider repealing "Stand Your Ground."

xi. Individuals
   1. Difficult because individual personalities influence perspectives and value systems and individual base values change over time. L&D, 350
   2. Individuals are capable of leveraging any of the eight values to achieve goals.
   3. Legislature convinced the populace of the necessity of SYG by tapping into individual fears for safety and well-being.
      A. Legend of the Other and stranger danger.

      i. Unanticipated harm that has come upon the state is the blatant disregard for human life.

      ii. Aggression toward the Other has dramatically increased.

      iii. The legislature has convinced the community that broader access to guns and greater freedoms to shoot and kill the Other makes us all safer.

      iv. The paradoxical effect: greater freedom to kill creates a greater fear of being killed.

      v. Individuals are primarily concerned with personal security.

          1. Us vs. Them mentality — Stand Your Ground is better because it increases individual power while protecting personal well-being.

          2. Community is broad mentality — Stand Your Ground is worse because it creates a danger to individuals who may not be Other after all.

4. Respect and rectitude.

   A. Preservation of personal honor implicates respect.

   B. Example:

      i. Dunn and Reeves

      ii. Two implications

          1. Shooter feels disrespected and entitled to defend his honor. The violence is evidence of leveraging respect to preserve respect.

          2. The second way that respect is implicated is in the lack of respect for the Other. The reason the shooter feels entitled to kill is because the shooter does not value or respect the Other.

          3. Rectitude is also intimately tethered to respect in these scenarios because the shooter believes in the rightness of the decision to shoot.

5. Originally, "Stand Your Ground" was intended to protect the innocent.

   A. Assume dead person is a bad guy.

   B. Dead guy isn't always bad.

   C. Family and friends of dead guy.

   D. Stand Your Ground essentially lifts gun restrictions.

6. Before: Defendant had to prove justification prior to getting a not guilty.

7. Proponents of SYG:

   A. Any Duty to Retreat is an unreasonable infringement on individual rights.

   B. "Stand Your Ground" increases individual power and well-being.

8. Opponents of SYG:

   A. Duty to Retreat is a necessary component of law in a society that values the dignity of human life.

      B. "Stand Your Ground" obviously decreases social well-being, first by increasing access to violent conflict resolution, but worse, by upsetting social balances relating to respect and rectitude.

    9. Hard to determine which values the majority commonly holds.

    10. Majority has little ability to leverage its base values.

        A. Dream Defenders 31-day protest.

        B. NRA response.

VI. CONCLUSION

  a. "Stand Your Ground" has not made the community safer.

  b. Tragedies have continued.

  c. Community is calling out for change.

  d. Accountability is necessary in homicide cases.

  e. Society does not want justifiable uses of force to be an expediency.

  f. Use of force should remain a counter-more that is not necessarily punished harshly.

  g. Florida's "Stand Your Ground" is an expediency.

  h. Inconsistent with commonly held values and expectations

  i. Citizenry will begin to withdraw its consent to being governed.

  j. In a civilized society, the government must be mindful of enacting statutes that will preserve the integrity of human dignity.

  k. "Stand Your Ground" gives individuals the freedom to disregard the sanctity of human life.

  l. By creating such far-reaching protections for individuals who engage in violent behavior, the legislature has effectively ceded control and is now operating with pretended power.

  m. "Stand Your Ground" cannot even be accurately called a law because it has divested the government of control over the people in cases of justifiable use of force.

  n. The need for amendment or repeal of this law is urgent, and the community is now voicing its cry for change, pleading with the legislature to realign with commonly held values to preserve the well-being, respect, and rectitude of the community.

Sample Abstract

An abstract is a short description of the thesis that whets a reader's appetite to read the article in full. Some publishers require an abstract, while others do not. If you are posting your paper on SSRN or another similar database, having an abstract will be helpful in attracting readers to your article. Notice how the abstract is similar to the topic selection essay, but it offers a much more precise explanation of the thesis. As you refine your topic selection essay throughout this process, you should naturally develop a comprehensive yet concise abstract to accompany your final paper.

ABSTRACT

Florida's Stand Your Ground law has stood center stage since the tragic killing of Trayvon Martin. On the one hand, certain sectors of society are calling for its repeal,———1 and on the other, proponents vigorously defended its value and efficacy. Despite the public outcry for reform, every attempt to repeal or change the law has been defeated. This Article examines whether Florida's Stand Your Ground law is inconsistent with commonly held societal values, and if so, what might prompt a change in the law.

To that end, this Article relies on the jurisprudential framework established by Myers S. McDougal and Harold D. Lasswell that identifies the law as an expression of commu-———2 nity interests and a source of authority rooted in community values. The common interests, or values, identified by McDougal and Lasswell are power, enlightenment, wealth, well-being, skill, affection, respect, and rectitude. This Article examines these values in the context of Florida's Stand Your Ground law and analyzes them from competing perspectives to conclude the law is inconsistent with commonly held community values.

---

1 The beginning of the abstract states the question at the center of the article.

2 The second paragraph identifies the framework and briefly states why and how it will be used.

This Article concludes by exposing the legislature's reticence to repeal the statute as a reflection of its entrenched mode of thinking. It calls for opposition voices to collaborate in advancing reform messages aimed at deconstructing the entrenched categories and restructuring them to prompt an amendment to or repeal of Florida's Stand Your Ground statutory scheme.

3

---

3 The final paragraph identifies the central thesis and overall claim of the paper.

APPENDIX IX

Annotated Samples and Examples

Part I: Elizabeth Megale, *A Call for Change: A Contextual-Configurative Analysis of Florida's "Stand Your Ground" Laws,* **68 U. Miami L. Rev. 1052 (2014)**

This article is a good example of a strong analytical framework. You will note that it has been annotated with two purposes in mind. First, some of my notes demonstrate critical reading and note-taking. I have attempted to demonstrate the thought processes you should be engaging in while you are reading your sources. Therefore, you will see comments to the effect of "do I agree with the author's characterization" or "need to pull sources to verify accuracy." In your own research process, you will want to make similar notes and then follow through on pulling the original sources. You will also want to add in the details about why you do or do not agree with the author's characterization as well as notes about how the author's thesis fits into the broader discourse community.

Second, some of my notes highlight the structure and function of the analytical framework. So, you will see comments to the effect of "notice how the definitions support the author's use of the concept in context" or "defining terms is essential to establishing a strong analytical framework." For these comments, pay attention to how the author develops ethos by clearly identifying and explaining the analytical framework before applying it. Take note of how the analytical framework is applied to the specific situation. Finally, use the same techniques when evaluating other scholars' work and developing your own project.

The annotations provided in this article reveal my use of the methods described in Chapters 3, 4, 5, and 6 and follow the checklists suggested by this book. They are intended to be a demonstration of the metacognitive processes necessary for scholarly research and analysis.

1 ———————————A Call for Change:
A Contextual-Configurative Analysis
of Florida's "Stand Your Ground" Laws

ELIZABETH MEGALE

I. INTRODUCTION

3 ——— Public response to the shooting death of Trayvon Martin evidenced a drastic schism in community values. To some, the problem of "Stand Your Ground" represents purely a race issue that not only perpetuates endemic racial tensions amongst members of society,[1] but also generally protects whites more often than blacks.[2] On the other hand, some view the statutory scheme as a non-racist[3] protection of individual liberties that makes the community safer.[4] These two perspectives lie at the opposite ends of the spectrum, and both perspectives tend to oversimplify a complex issue.

In tracking the media coverage, protests, and commentary related to Florida's most recent "Stand Your Ground" cases, it is readily apparent that the various interest groups and individuals weighing in are sharply

[1] Michael H. Cottman, Commentary: Zimmerman Acquittal Says it's Open Season on Black Males, BLACK AM. WEB (July 14, 2013), http://blackamericaweb.com/2013/07/14/zimmerman-acquittal-black-teens/.
[2] Id.
[3] Matt Wilstein, Ted Cruz Tells Trayvon's Mother Why Stand Your Ground Laws Can't Possibly Be 'Racist,' MEDIAITE (Oct. 29, 2013), http://www.mediaite.com/tv/ted-cruz-tells-trayvons-mother-why-stand-your-ground-laws-cant-possibly-be-racist.
[4] Abby Goodnough, Florida Expands Right to Use Deadly Force in Self-Defense, N.Y. TIMES (Apr. 27, 2005), http://www.nytimes.com/2005/04/27/national/27shoot.html.

1051

1 Notice how the title communicates the author's purpose: to change Florida's Stand Your Ground Laws.
2 Section II will explain the framework and Section III will apply it.
3 The author identifies competing points of view and criticizes their oversimplification of a complex issue.

1052   *UNIVERSITY OF MIAMI LAW REVIEW*   [Vol. 68:1051]

divided.[5] This disagreement occurs for two principle reasons. First, the participants embrace fundamentally different value structures, so their acceptance of the legitimacy of Florida's "Stand Your Ground" law will naturally create dissonance. Second, most viewpoints being advanced are far too myopic to account for the multi-faceted issues presented by Florida's version of "Stand Your Ground."

This Article attempts to account for each of the competing viewpoints related to the statutory scheme. This author's position is that in legalizing certain types of homicide by decriminalizing killings and other acts of violence involving self-defense,[6] Florida has exchanged respect for human dignity with cold self-import.[7] To examine the process by which this transformation occurred, this Article relies on a jurisprudential model, created by Yale professors Harold Lasswell and Myres McDougal, for the preservation of human dignity.[8] It is important to note that this theory of legal inquiry was intended to be applicable to both micro and macro analyses,[9] though most scholars have employed it as a tool for studying international law and politics.[10] The peculiar feature of this model, however, is that it also specifically contemplates individuals, making it uniquely suited to the inquiry of any legal system.[11]

As a central premise, it establishes that effective[12] law requires the existence of both authority and control.[13] Authority and control manifest when laws are created consistently with commonly held community values.[14] By the same token, if a law is inconsistent with commonly held values, it may lose its authority, control, or both.[15] In the case of Florida's "Stand Your Ground" statutory scheme, this Article suggests that the turmoil following the shooting death of Trayvon Martin and the continuing media attention of other shooting deaths since that time illustrate the inconsistency between the law and relevant human values.

---

5. Elizabeth Megale, *Disaster Unaverted: Reconciling the Desire for Safe and Secure State with the Grim Realities of Stand Your Ground,* 37 Am. J. Trial Advoc. 255, 282 (2013).

6. *Id.* at 257.

7. *Id.*; Elizabeth Megale, *Deadly Combinations, How Self-Defense Laws Pairing Immunity with a Presumption of Fear Allow Criminals to 'Get Away with Murder,'* 34 Am. J. Trial Advoc. 105 (2010).

8. Harold D. Lasswell & Myres S. McDougal, Jurisprudence For A Free Society (1992).

9. *Id.* at 335; *see also* Winston P. Nagan, Contextual-Configuration Jurisprudence: The Law, Science, and Policies of Human Dignity 3 (2013).

10. Nagan, *supra* note 9, at vi.

11. *Id.* at 1.

12. The Lasswell/McDougal model predates modern legal legitimacy discourse, though it employs similar vocabulary. Modern theories about legitimacy of the law are beyond the scope of this Article.

13. Lasswell & McDougal, *supra* note 8, at 400.

14. *Id.*

15. *Id.* at 401.

---

4 Do you think the author treats the opposing viewpoints fairly? From the introduction, you may not have enough information to know.

5 The author explains that this framework was not created for use in this context, but explains why it is a valid framework for analysis of the questions contemplated by this article. Do you agree?

The legal theory mapped out by Lasswell and McDougal employs a discrete vocabulary attributing particularized meanings to words, which are sometimes inconsistent with common parlance.[16] Throughout this Article, these terms will be defined in the words of the authors and used as intended within the jurisprudential context.[17] The analytical framework creates a launching point with identification of an outcome relevant to a particular value situation.[18] From there, pre- and post-outcomes can be determined.[19] Once outcomes are identified, the community participants must be identified.[20] The value situation is assessed by analyzing the participants, their values, and the strategies used to leverage their values to gain command over others and achieve a specific outcome and effect.[21] Section II provides the background for this normative framework.

Section III applies this jurisprudential framework in the context of Florida's "Stand Your Ground" statutes. It begins the legal analysis by identifying the decision to enact Florida's "Stand Your Ground" as the central outcome giving rise to the present value situation. The pre- and post-outcomes will be analyzed together with the participants, their values, and strategies for leveraging to achieve the desired outcome. The effects will then be identified and interpreted to reach the conclusion that Florida's "Stand Your Ground" law is inconsistent with commonly held community values. Finally, Section IV concludes by examining the implications of the analysis and suggesting reforms for aligning the law with community values.

II. NORMATIVE FRAMEWORK

Jurisprudence for a Free Society[22] is the two-volume magnum opus of Myres McDougal and Harold Lasswell. Labeled contextual-configurative jurisprudence,[23] it is a normative response to the tension cre-

---

16. *Id.* at 391–97 ("It is beyond dispute that new modes of discourse are difficult to grasp and assess. In part, this comes about because the processes of thought and of communication typically receive scant attention during formative years. Although vocabularies are taught, they are seldom examined as phenomena whose fundamental principles ought to be part of the intellectual equipment of every educated member of society. As a result, it is much more difficult than need be for educated persons to master relatively new and systematic modes of discourse.").

17. EMILE DURKHEIM, SUICIDE: A STUDY IN SOCIOLOGY 41 (1951) (providing particularized definitions is not unusual because "words of everyday language, like the concepts they express are always susceptible of more than one meaning, and the scholar employing them in their accepted use without further definition would risk serious misunderstanding").

18. LASSWELL & McDOUGAL, *supra* note 8, at 379.

19. *Id.*

20. *Id.* at 381.

21. *Id.*

22. *Id.*

23. *Id.* at vi.

---

6 The author sets forth a clear and precise roadmap for how the article will explain and utilize the analytical framework to resolve whether Florida's Stand Your Ground laws should be changed.

7 The author is relying on a framework developed by other scholars. If this is a framework you want to adopt, you would need to go to the original source itself and develop your own understanding of it.

1054   *UNIVERSITY OF MIAMI LAW REVIEW*   [Vol. 68:1051

ated by the simplicity[24] of other legal theories like legal formalism and legal realism.[25] McDougal and Lasswell developed this jurisprudence over decades throughout their careers with the purpose of providing a multi-faceted approach to legal analysis taking into account other disciplines that study the nuances of humanity.[26] In particular, "Lasswell's deepest personal commitment was to the creation of a comprehensive theory for inquiry about the individual human being in social process."[27] This interdisciplinary framework provides a workable, albeit complex,[28] method for analyzing the development, implementation, and evolution of the law.[29]

    This Article does not purport to evaluate the validity of the legal theory; rather, accepting the theory at face value, it uses it as a framework to analyze the enactment, effect, and status of Florida's "Stand Your Ground" legislation. This framework offers a ready lens to expose the imbalance of power and conflict in values represented by Florida's "Stand Your Ground" law. To that end, an overview of the legal theory is necessary.

    Essential to the jurisprudence is a basic understanding of the social process itself and the role of the legal process as a part of it.[30] To state it simply, "[w]hen two persons influence one another, the process is social, whether the individuals concerned are aware of one another or not. Wherever there is mutual influencing there is community."[31] The social process involves people pursuing "values through institutions using resources."[32] Because legal processes involve individuals who use institutions and resources[33] to advance values, it would be naïve to consider

---

24. Patricia J. Williams, The Alchemy of Race and Rights 8 (1991) (one characteristic of American jurisprudence is "[t]he hypostatization of exclusive categories and definitional polarities, the drawing of bright lines and clear taxonomies that purport to make life simpler in the face of life's complication: rights/needs, moral/immoral, public/private, white/black").

25. Lasswell & McDougal, *supra* note 8, at xxx (in Lasswell's view, "American legal realists had demonstrated that technical legal rules and concepts are not the only factors affecting decision and had intensely demanded certain heterogeneous and uncoordinated reformist goals, with little indication of how authoritative decision might best be changed to achieve such goals").

26. Nagan, *supra* note 9, at 1.

27. *Id.* at 8.

28. Lasswell & McDougal, *supra* note 8, at xxxvi-xxxvii ("In one perspective much of what had to be done seems obsessively trivial. And yet, unless 'trivia' are dealt with, the reinterpretation of 'tradition' is deferred another generation.").

29. *Id.* at xxxvii.

30. *Id.* at 335 ("The legal process is part of the process of decision which in turn is part of the social process as a whole.").

31. *Id.*

32. *Id.* at 336.

33. *Id.* at 355 ("The term 'resource' is used to designate the physical environment in which social interactions are carried on, and which may be directly involved in an interaction."); *Id.* at

---

8 This framework seems to work well for the author's thesis because the author is interested in studying how the law has impacted society.

9 The author begins to explain the framework by defining specific terms.

2014]   *A CALL FOR CHANGE*   1055

the law in a vacuum without accounting for the surrounding social process and the reciprocal effects.

A. *The Social Process*

Focusing on the broader social process first, human values include power, enlightenment, wealth, wellbeing, skill, affection, respect, and rectitude.[34] Lasswell and McDougal were cautious to define each value with particularity.

> Power is the making of decisions important to the social context as a whole and enforcible against challengers when necessary by the use of severe sanctions. . . . Enlightenment is the gathering and spreading of information. . . . Wealth is the production and distribution of goods and services. . . . Well-being is opportunity for safety, health and comfort. . . . Skill is opportunity to acquire and exercise excellence in a particular operation. . . . Affection is giving and receiving intimacy, friendship and loyalty. . . . Respect is recognition and the reciprocal honoring of freedom of choice. . . . Rectitude refers to responsibility for conduct.[35]

All eight values appear in communities in varying degrees,[36] but the specifics, details, and modalities of how these values are engendered and pursued throughout different communities are widely varied.[37] Moreover, even within communities it might be difficult to reach consensus as to how values ought to be pursued and prioritized, and "it is usual to find many degrees of inequality."[38] Inequalities arise by virtue of the fact that values are distributed unevenly throughout communities.[39] Additionally, discrepancies in defining values, particularly those like "respect" and "well-being," create systems of inequality within and amongst communities.[40] Thus, a class system emerges within any given value with individuals occupying an elite, mid-elite, or rank and file status.[41]

Theoretically, values might be agglutinative,[42] but in practice it does not necessarily hold true that an elite in one value is the elite for all

---

356 (depending on the usefulness of resources for values, the physical environment's role will be affected).
    34. LASSWELL & McDOUGAL, *supra* note 8, at 377.
    35. *Id.* at 337–38.
    36. *Id.* at 339.
    37. *Id.* at 339–40.
    38. *Id.* at 343.
    39. *Id.*
    40. *Id.*
    41. *Id.* at 344.
    42. *Id.* at 345 (in theory, "'values are agglutinative[,]' that is, that the possession of a high position in one value increases the probability that the individual or group will hold a high position in the command of any value").

---

10 Defining terms and using direct quotes here cultivates the author's ethos, or credibility. It also demonstrates compliance with universal intellectual standards of accuracy and precision.

11 Nearly every citation in this section will be to Lasswell & McDougal because this section explains their framework so that it can be applied in the latter part of the article.

1056   *UNIVERSITY OF MIAMI LAW REVIEW*   [Vol. 68:1051

values.[43] Notwithstanding, the initial distribution of values will impact the potential for a given individual or group to successfully leverage them to gain command of other values.[44] For example, an elite in power or wealth generally has more potential to command other values than an elite in well-being or respect, at least in Western cultures.[45]

The potential for a value to be leveraged is related to the perspectives and practices of the individuals in community. "Perspectives" contemplate the "inner life of those who participate in an interaction,"[46] accounting for identity, demands, and expectations.[47] Taking the perspectives along with the behavior, or "operations," of the participants, recurrent patterns ("practices") emerge.[48] Human beings tend to modify their behavior when they interact with each other, but some "relatively stable patterns emerge."[49] These stable patterns are referred to as personality and are separate from the behavior of an individual as affected by the social process.[50] Together, all the perspectives existing in a given institutional context create a "myth,"[51] and the cumulative operations represent "technique."[52] As an extension, cultures emerge when there is a "distinctive and stable pattern of community values and institutions."[53]

— 12

The leveraging of values allows the elite to dominate the sharing and shaping of values throughout the community. To understand how this leveraging is possible, one must first consider the role of base and scope values. To a certain degree, "each category of value is sought as an end or employed as a means."[54] The pursuit of values refers to "scope values," while their utilization implicates base values.[55] Values might be used as a base for augmenting their own scope[56]—consider the adage, "it takes money to make money," as representative of wealth used as a base to expand the scope of wealth. Likewise, a base value can serve as the impetus for increasing the scope of another value—"money is

43. *Id.*
44. *Id.* at 343.
45. *Id.*
46. *Id.* at 347.
47. *Id.* at 350.
48. *Id.* at 347.
49. *Id.* at 349.
50. *Id.* ("By adopting this usage, we separate the purely biological organism from the human being as changed by participation in social process.").
51. *Id.* at 347 (in this context, "myth" is employed as is established in the social sciences and "is intended to express or imply no judgment of approval or disapproval, or of realism or unrealism").
52. *Id.* at 347–48; *id.* at 353 ("myth" refers to the subjective "stable patterns of personal as well as group perspectives"); *id.* at 348 ("[t]echnique" tends to be objectively measurable").
53. *Id.* at 348.
54. *Id.* at 340.
55. *Id.*
56. *Id.* at 340–43.

12   The author begins to show how the complexity of the framework accounts for many facets of law, culture, and society that are not typically considered through the lens of less nuanced frameworks.

13 ———

power' is a notion that represents the use of wealth as a base value to achieve a greater scope of power. To the extent any individual or group commands a particular value, that base may be used to acquire command over other values by shaping and sharing those within the community. Based upon this system of interaction, it would be possible for a dominant minority to define community values for a weaker majority.[57]

Personality plays a significant role in value determination because it is "organized in reference to values and employs practices specialized in varying degree to the shaping and sharing of each value."[58] Consider the following: "[T]he power-centered personality is of special interest to lawyers and legal scholars. Such a political personality diverges in discernible ways from the wealth-centered, respect-centered, or enlightenment-centered person."[59] Additionally, because personality is embedded in culture while simultaneously representing the individual, it is possible to observe collective personality patterns intertwined with personal patterns to create a common context or system.[60] This personality system is comprised of identification, demands, and expectations.[61]

Considering the first of these three components, identification is critical to assessing the participants in a given community, as well as their potential command over the shaping and sharing of values.[62] The symbols used by individuals and groups within a community create a system of identification.[63] The difficulty emerges in identifying the various participants because "'identities' are far more numerous than 'bodies,' and relate the biological individuals to one another in many different ways in the pursuit of value goals in various institutional networks."[64] Emphasizing individuals and organized groups makes it possible to identify "targets of responsibility."[65] Notwithstanding, unorganized groups should not be discounted, as they are useful "in examining factors that help to explain conduct."[66]

The second and third components of personality systems relate to perspectives, or demands and expectations. "The demand system is composed of the values sought, and the practices assumed to embody these

---

57. *Id.*
58. *Id.* at 350.
59. *Id.*
60. *Id.*
61. *Id.*
62. *Id.* at 351 ("It is possible to classify the identification system of any member of a culture for the purpose of ascertaining the degree to which the person is identified within the culture as a whole or with component classes and institutions.").
63. *Id.* at 350–51.
64. *Id.* at 351.
65. *Id.*
66. *Id.*

---

13 Notice the breadth and depth of treatment this author provides. Perhaps because the theory of jurisprudence is somewhat obscure and not typically applied to domestic law, the author is careful to make no assumptions about what the reader may already know.

values."[67] Demands can be placed by the self on the self, or they can be placed by the self on others.[68] Typically, demands evolve into patterns involving a complex amalgamation of values and particularized demands.[69] Intertwined with demands are expectations, which can be either positive or negative and involve the self or others.[70] The following formula[71] illustrates this point:

System of expectations   =   positive[72] expectations concerning demands by self on self

             +

              negative[73] expectations concerning demands by self on self   —— 14

             +

              positive expectations concerning demands by self on others

             +

              negative expectations concerning demands by self on others

             +

              positive and negative expectations concerning demands by others on self

             +

              positive and negative expectations concerning demands by others on others

     Identification, demands, and expectations, both personal[74] and group, eventually stabilize into myths,[75] which can be subcategorized as doctrine, formula, and miranda.[76] Doctrine refers to "abstract propositions that affirm the perspectives of the group."[77] It is typically expressed through symbols of identification coupled with demands and expectations[78] and is often memorialized in canonical documents such as

---

67. *Id.* at 352.
68. *Id.*
69. *Id.*
70. *Id.*
71. *Id.*
72. *Id.* at 352–53 ("In this setting the term 'positive' means a favorable indulgence of the self in the situation referred to.").
73. *Id.* at 353 ("'Negative' refers to deprivations of the self.").
74. *Id.* at 355 ("The aggregate of stabilized perspectives which comprise a person's myth are also divisible into doctrine, formula and miranda (lore). The formula includes the 'shalt' and 'shalt not' components of the self-system.").
75. *Id.*
76. *Id.* at 353.
77. *Id.*
78. *Id.* (doctrinal "propositions make use of the basic symbols of identification, together with the formulation of fundamental goal values and expectations concerning the past, the present, and the future").

---

14 Notice how in this section, the author does not seem to be including her own ideas. Rather, she is acting as a faithful reporter and interpreter of McDougal and Lasswell's work. She is careful not to imply that the framework itself is her own. Rather, she explains the framework as she understands it. In later sections, she will add her own thoughts about the law through the lens of this framework.

the Declaration of Independence or the Magna Carta.[79] To give effect to doctrine, formulas are necessary to develop prescriptions and mechanisms ensuring consistent implementation of doctrine.[80] Miranda facilitates the understanding of doctrine and provides a mode for interpretation of formulas vis-à-vis doctrine.[81] Patterns of myths evolve over time and differ throughout communities.[82] Dominant myths are those advanced by the elite in any given social structure and may be labeled ideology.[83] Counter-ideology is the systematization of discontent within communities and requires an "explicit rejection of the established 'ideology.'"[84]

15

Analysis of each of these elements would be impossible without the outward expression of inward processes through communication and collaboration.[85] "Communication" refers to the signals (including speech and gestures) used to communicate subjective perspectives between various systems.[86] Collaboration, on the other hand, refers to activities bridging competing perspectives.[87]

Of course, consideration of this framework would be pointless without some ability to measure outcomes. Outcomes analysis studies the complex relationships between demands, expectations, and perceptions of identity as well as myths, modes of communication, and value systems.[88] Additionally, "some outcomes deal directly with the formulation of prescriptions,"[89] a component of myth, while others invoke existing prescriptions.[90] The formulation of prescriptions is effectively a normative act sanctioning specific expectations with regard to particular activities.[91] Activities promoting any given prescription are common prior to its adoption, as are intelligence missives including collection

---

79. *Id.* at 353 (examples of doctrinal statements include: "Governments (derive) their just Powers from the Consent of the Governed.") (citing Declaration of Independence (1776)); *see also* Magna Carta Art. 29 ("No freeman shall be taken, imprisoned, disseised, outlawed, banished, or in any way destroyed, nor will We proceed against or prosecute him, except by the lawful judgment of his peers or by the law of the land.").
80. LASSWELL & McDOUGAL, *supra* note 8, at 354.
81. *Id.*
82. *Id.* at 355.
83. *Id.*
84. *Id.* (an example would be "when a communist mass party rejects the ruling 'feudal' or 'capitalistic' doctrine").
85. *Id.* at 357.
86. *Id.*
87. *Id.*
88. *Id.* at 358.
89. *Id.*
90. *Id.* at 359 ("An invocation is a provisional characterization of a concrete situation in terms of an alleged prescription.").
91. *Id.*

---

15 Notice the use of the word "myth" here. Does it fit with your understanding of myth? How does the author define myth?

1060 .   *UNIVERSITY OF MIAMI LAW REVIEW*   [Vol. 68:1051

and analysis of data and planning.[92] Through intelligence and promotion activities, community perspectives can be assessed, measured, and influenced.[93]

Related to the invocation of prescriptions are the notions of application, termination, and appraisal. Invocation of a prescription will include any "initial steps taken to put a prescription into effect."[94] Application refers to the point in time when a prescription is finally (not provisionally) characterized as such.[95] Terminations refer to the point in time when a prescription ceases.[96] Appraisal is the process by which prescriptions are evaluated to assess their functionality vis-à-vis the goals of collective policy and to allocate responsibility for results.[97]

Working together, these apparatuses create policy systems that assist in identifying patterns of future actions by individuals or groups.[98] Interests arise from policies and "refer to events expected to harmonize with value demands."[99] Shared interests are referred to as "common" and other incompatible interests are "special." This dynamic reflects a system of exclusivity such that "[c]ommon interests are 'inclusive' when the events involved are of considerable importance for all; they are 'exclusive' when the relevant events are of very much greater importance to identifiable sub-groups than to the whole."[100]

To return to the beginning, values and outcomes are tethered through the complex interplay of each salient element of the social process. Values are manifested through particular outcomes, as follows:[101]

Value	Outcome	
Power	Decision	
Enlightenment	Knowledge	——————————16
Wealth	Transaction	
Well-being	Vitality	
Skill	Performance	
Affection	Cordiality	
Respect	Prestige	
Rectitude	Rightness	

Moving forward, a working definition of each outcome is necessary. "[A] decision is giving, withholding, rejecting or receiving support

---

92. *Id.*
93. *Id.*
94. *Id.*
95. *Id.*
96. *Id.*
97. *Id.*
98. *Id.* at 360.
99. *Id.*
100. *Id.*
101. *Id.* at 377 (chart is reproduced from *Jurisprudence for a Free Society*).

---

16 Placing information in lists or charts provides a nice break for
the reader and eliminates the proverbial "wall of words."

2014]   *A CALL FOR CHANGE*   1061

in an interaction that affects the entire social context to a significant extent (including the probable use of severe deprivational sanctions against challengers)."[102] Knowledge is "a culminating interaction in which information about the past and present, together with estimates of the future, are made available, withheld, rejected or received."[103] Transactions are "the giving, withholding, rejecting or receiving of claims to processed (or processable) resources."[104] Vitality refers to individual and group health, with an eye toward elongation and preservation of life free from disease, illness, discomfort, or defect.[105] Performance is evidenced through formal examinations and the appraisal of work product.[106] Congeniality is related to loyalty and assessed by examining families and their disruptions, social activities, and clashes between and commitments to one another.[107] Prestige requires a method of "taking note of the culminating circumstances in which recognitions are given or received."[108] Finally, rightness evolves from sequences of affirmations and inquiries that solidify the moral and ethical conscience.[109]

B. *Legal Processes*

Lasswell and McDougal adopted a broad definition of the "law" as "a process of authoritative decision by which the members of a community clarify and implement their common interests."[110] This legal system is also an embedded element within the broader social process.[111] Accordingly, it must be both stable enough and dynamic enough to respond to the various demands and expectations of the community.[112] Thus, it both affects, and is affected by, the social process.

All institutions within a society must strike a balance between competing worlds.[113] Competing worlds can be identified by comparing inclusive and exclusive interests, or by the distribution of base values in a given community.[114] Social order is maintained when stability is flexible enough to provide for change as values and interests evolve.[115]

---

102. *Id.* at 379.
103. *Id.*
104. *Id.*
105. *Id.* at 520–23.
106. *Id.* at 532.
107. *Id.* at 553–54.
108. *Id.* at 566.
109. *Id.* at 588–590.
110. *Id.* at xxx.
111. *Id.*
112. *Id.* at 365.
113. *Id.* at 366.
114. *Id.*
115. *Id.*

---

17 Do you think lawmakers consider these social processes when they create law? Are they unconsciously affecting these processes? Are they affected by these processes? How practical is consideration of these social processes? Is it merely a curiosity question, or is this something relevant and real?

Often, a dominant majority of the collective may define values, but sometimes, like in apartheid, a powerful minority might have sufficient power to define them. Additionally, the boundaries separating the majority from the minority are always shifting such that over time individuals and groups who were traditionally excluded from the collective, the "others," find themselves included in the mainstream.[116] Also, as boundaries shift, those who were once included may become outsiders. These boundaries morph as values and beliefs of the collective evolve. ——————18

Law "refers to the 'power institutions' in a community,"[117] and power is correlated to decision outcomes.[118] In turn, the processes affecting decisions implicate the balance of authority and control.[119] "Control" avers to the "effective impact on the choices being made."[120] "Authority" means the "expectations of permissibility, [and] expectations among community members that decision functions are properly performed."[121]

As a foundational matter, both Lasswell and McDougal assert that to be law, it must possess both authority and control.[122] If either is absent, the rule of "law" is an abuse of power.[123] The absence of control leads to pretended power, and the absence of authority leads to naked power.[124] When authority and control are absent, anarchy and chaos erupt.[125] According to Lasswell and McDougal, authority and control derive from members of society when the law is consistent with their values.[126] ——————19

Furthermore, authority and control are manifested through the enactment of various types of codes. Constitutive codes are the most comprehensive and operate as the formula component of myth to "establish[ ] a process of authoritative decision and [to] allocate[ ] permissible

---

116. Elizabeth Megale, *The Invisible Man: How the Sex Offender Registry Results in Social Death*, 2 J. L. & Soc. Deviance. 92, 96 (2011).

117. Lasswell & McDougal, *supra* note 8, at 379.

118. *Id.* at 377.

119. *Id.* at 362 (though authority and control relate to the broader social process, too, this Article analyzes them through a legal lens and thus explains them through analysis of their role in the legal process).

120. *Id.*

121. *Id.*

122. *Id.* at 400.

123. *Id.*

124. *Id.* (demonstrating in mathematical terms, it appears:
   "+ authority + control = law
   + authority − control = pretended power
   + control − authority = naked power").

125. *See id.*

126. *See id.* at xxx, 362.

---

18 These examples make the abstract concepts easier to understand. Is it becoming obvious how this framework might apply to the author's thesis?

19 This last sentence clearly identifies why the author has chosen this framework. Her thesis is that Florida's Stand Your Ground Laws do not align with societal values. Therefore, the laws are not truly laws; rather, they are an abuse of power.

participations in the decision process."[127] Supervisory codes "refer[ ] to the more general principles for settlement of controversies between private parties."[128] A "'regulative' code refers to the community limits within which private shaping and sharing activities are to be carried on."[129] Finally, the "'sanctioning and corrective' code includes all the activities designed in appropriate contingencies to maintain conformity to the norms of collective policy."[130]

Each code has particular objectives, but only the sanctioning and corrective code is relevant to this Article. The six permissible objectives of the sanctioning and corrective code are deterrence, prevention, restoration, rehabilitation, reconstruction, and correction.[131] Deterrence and prevention "are [both] designed to influence the expectations of potential violators by making the point that compliance is likely to leave one better off than non-compliance."[132] The difference between deterrence and prevention rests in the "scope of the measures adopted to forestall non-compliance."[133] For example, a deterrent measure might use the fear of sanctions to punish certain behavior, while prevention might include an educational campaign aimed at shifting a mindset toward or against a particular activity.[134]

In a similar vein, restoration and rehabilitation share the goal of "putting a stop to acts of violation and as far as possible reinstate the original situation,"[135] but rehabilitation simply takes the additional step of "undo[ing any] deprivations of value occasioned by the impermissible activities."[136] The purpose of reconstruction is to fundamentally alter "prevailing institutions."[137] Finally, corrective measures are intended to achieve "personality changes in offenders (an objective paralleling the reconstruction of a group)."[138]

As a legal institution, the sovereign's decisions are "an outcome of power,"[139] and become authoritative as an outcome of the sovereign's pattern of "established and recognized authoritative practice."[140] Returning to the notion of social order, this pattern factors into percep-

---

127. *Id.* at 362.
128. *Id.*
129. *Id.*
130. *Id.* at 363.
131. *Id.* at 363–4.
132. *Id.* at 363.
133. *Id.*
134. *Id.*
135. *Id.*
136. *Id.*
137. *Id.*
138. *Id.* at 364.
139. NAGAN, *supra* note 9, at 92.
140. *Id.*

---

20 For a legal reader, this paragraph should be familiar. The six permissible objectives defined here align with the purposes of punishment taught in a basic criminal law course. As a society, we tend to agree on these objectives.

1064   *UNIVERSITY OF MIAMI LAW REVIEW*   [Vol. 68:1051]

tions of stability insofar as it employs "'built-in' regulative practices that identify and negatively sanction acts deviating from shared prescriptions."[141] Moreover, the most stable prescriptions are simultaneously authoritative and controlling—these are the most supported by society and which, upon violation, are expected to result in punishment.[142] These prescriptions are known as "mores" and have a tendency to strongly influence societal norms and values.[143] "Counter-mores," on the other hand, are prescriptions that individuals expect to be violated even though the community might strongly support the norms.[144] Violation of a counter-more is not likely to be punished harshly because "it is perceived that violators cannot be entirely stamped out."[145]

———— 21

While, mores, counter-mores, and expediencies are culture traits,[146] only mores and counter-mores create social order because they are the only cultural traits involving prescriptions.[147] Over time, societal norms can evolve such that mores eventually become counter-mores or expediencies.[148] This evolutionary process is reciprocal; expediencies may turn into counter-mores and then mores as societal values change.[149]

An example of the former can be seen in the cultural shifts in norms related to marijuana use. Between 1951 and 1996, every state and federal jurisdiction criminalized the use of marijuana.[150] Initially, the prescription represented a more that was "expected to be countered by negative sanctions"[151] upon violation. Over time however, in many communities, marijuana use evolved into a counter-more. For example, for many years New York City has treated marijuana as an infraction and not a crime.[152] Additionally, over time, individuals have changed their

———— 22

---

141. LASSWELL & McDOUGAL, *supra* note 8, at 366.
142. *Id.*
143. *Id.*
144. *Id.*
145. *Id.*
146. *Id.* ("'Expediencies' are the culture traits which are neither mores nor counter-mores.").
147. *See id.* at 366–67.
148. *Id.* at 366 ("Every culture possesses patterns which are open to change though changes are often mildly disapproved.").
149. *See* Megale, *The Invisible Man*, *supra* note 116, at 95–96.
150. *History of Marijuana as Medicine – 2900 BC to Present*, PROCON.ORG (Aug. 13, 2013, 4:48 PM), http://medicalmarijuana.procon.org/view.timeline.php?timelineID=000026 (stating that Congress passed the Boggs act in 1951, establishing mandatory minimum sentences for simple possession of marijuana, and, in 1996, California became the first state to legalize the drug for medical use).
151. LASSWELL & McDOUGAL, *supra* note 8, at 366.
152. Erik Altieri, *NYC Mayor Bloomberg: Starting Next Month, No Jail for Marijuana Possession*, NORML (Feb. 14, 2013), http://blog.norml.org/2013/02/14/nyc-mayor-bloomberg-starting-next-month-no-jail-for-marijuana-possession/ ("Under current law, possession of marijuana for personal use in private is punishable by a ticket, but possession of marijuana open to public view or being burnt in public is a Class B misdemeanor punishable by a fine of $250 with a

---

21 This section is essentially describing the law-culture-law cycle. Sometimes society and culture demand changes in the law, but sometimes the law must change and force society to catch up.

22 This is an easily understandable example.

expectations about the consequences of marijuana use such that even those opposed do not necessarily expect it to be harshly punished.[153] Currently, the legalization of marijuana in some jurisdictions has prompted evolution of the counter-more into an expediency, because it has ceased to be a prescription.[154]

Expediencies evolve into counter-mores and mores in a similar fashion. Consider the trends of pederasty.[155] Though a common practice in ancient Greek Society,[156] today the idea of grown men engaging young boys in sexual activity is heinous. Since society now expects such acts to be severely punished,[157] the practice has become a more.

Culture traits are influenced by all the salient elements of the social process and the evolutionary quality of culture traits propels the law-culture-law cycle.[158] In this cycle, laws are created through the influence of existing values, institutions, and other elements of the social process. The law comes into existence by aligning with dominant values to achieve authority and control, and as counter-mores emerge in response to evolving value systems, the law risks losing authority and control over the community.[159] Simultaneously, law affects value systems in the way it is administered—"[a]n important key to any social order is the severity or the mildness of the value deprivations employed as negative sanctions against any challenger of established norms."[160]

For example, consider the evolution of adultery laws in the United States. Two hundred years ago, adultery was considered a crime in virtually all jurisdictions.[161] As of 2013, however, only twenty-two states still

maximum sentence of 90 days. This initiative could go a long way towards correcting the draconic policy currently in place in the city, which disproportionately effects [sic] people of color and costs taxpayers about 75 million dollars a year in enforcement and prosecution costs. New York City is the marijuana arrest capitol [sic] of the world, with 50,684 arrests for marijuana offenses in 2011 alone[;] hopefully[,] this action from the mayor will encourage his fellow New Yorkers in Albany to cease the arrest of marijuana consumers across the state.").

153. *See* Lauren McGaughy, *Marijuana Laws in Louisiana Should Be More Lenient, New Poll Results Say*, THE TIMES-PICAYUNE (Sept. 5, 2013, 5:48 PM), http://www.nola.com/politics/index.ssf/2013/09/marijuana_pot_louisiana_poll_p.html.

154. *See* CAL. HEALTH & SAFETY CODE § 11362.5 (2011); COLO. CONST. art. XVIII, § 16; WASH. REV. CODE § 69.51A.005(2) (2011).

155. *See* Francisco Valdes, *Unpacking Hetero-Patriarchy: Tracing the Conflation of Sex, Gender, & Sexual Orientation to Its Origin*, 8 YALE J.L. & HUMAN. 161, 186–87 (1996).

156. *Id.*

157. *See* Megale, *The Invisible Man, supra* note 116, at 146.

158. Megale, *Disaster Unaverted, supra* note 5, at 33–39.

159. LASSWELL & MCDOUGAL, *supra* note 8, at 368.

160. *Id.* at 367.

161. JOANNE SWEENY, HISTORY OF ADULTERY AND FORNICATION CRIMINAL LAWS 1, *available at* http://ssrn.com/abstract=2242473.

23 These systems and cycles take place unconsciously. No one is sitting around thinking about power, authority, and control in such a metacognitive way.

criminalize adultery,[162] and it is rarely prosecuted.[163] Take for example the case of David Patraeus, a four-star general and former director of the CIA, who resigned amidst an adultery scandal.[164] Although both his state of residence, Virginia, and the military criminalize adultery, he has not been prosecuted.[165] Moreover, most Americans would not consider him a criminal simply because he had an extra-marital affair.[166] ————24

Similarly, courts have evolved their interpretation of the significance of adultery.[167] In 1838, Mr. Lash, a married man, was accused in New Jersey of committing the crime of adultery with an unmarried woman.[168] In considering how adultery could be "a crime against society, and not [ ] a mere breach of the marriage vow,"[169] the court sought guidance from the Holy Bible to determine that adultery could only be committed with a married woman.[170] Furthermore, the court commented on the collectively held value that, "where the woman is married, *all* admit that both are guilty of adultery, whether the man be married or single."[171]

Comparatively, in 1992, a court in the same jurisdiction observed a different value system related to adultery.[172] Specifically, in *S.B. v. S.J.B.*, the court reasoned that "it is the function of the court to define terms, based upon the standards of the times so that law may truly reflect the mores of our society."[173] Upon this premise, the court retreated from

---

162. *See* Ala. Code § 13A-13-2(c) (2014); Ariz. Rev. Stat. § 13-1408(A) (2013); Fla. Stat. § 798.01 (2013); Ga. Code § 16-6-19 (2013); Idaho Code § 18-6601 (2014); 720 Ill. Comp. Stat. 5 / 11-35(b) (2014); Kan. Stat. § 21-5511(b) (2013); Md. Code § 10-501(b) (2014); Mass. Gen. Laws 272 § 14 (2014); Mich. Comp. Laws § 750.30 (2014); Minn. Stat. § 609.36; Miss. Code § 97-21-1 (2013); N.H. Rev. Stat. § 645:3 (2014); N.Y. Adultery Law § 255.17 (McKinney 2014); N.D. Cent. Code § 12.1-20-09(1) (2013); Okla. Stat. § 872 (2013); R.I. Gen. Laws § 11-6-2 (2013); S.C. Code § 16-15-60 (2013); Va. Code § 18.2-365 (2013); W. Va. Code § 62-9-20 (2014); Wis. Stat. § 944.16 (2013).
163. Tim Murphy, *Map: Is Adultery Illegal?*, Mother Jones (Nov. 29, 2011, 2:20 PM), http://www.motherjones.com/mojo/2011/11/is-adultery-illegal-map ("State-level adultery provisions are rarely if ever enforced.").
164. Ethan, Bronner, *Adultery, an Ancient Crime That Remains on Many Books*, N.Y. Times, Nov. 15, 2012, http://www.nytimes.com/2012/11/15/us/adultery-an-ancient-crime-still-on-many-books.html?_r=1&.
165. *Id.*
166. *Id.* ("When David H. Petraeus resigned as director of the C.I.A. because of adultery he was widely understood to be acknowledging a misdeed, not a crime. Yet in his state of residence, Virginia, as in 22 others, adultery remains a criminal act, a vestige of the way American law has anchored legitimate sexual activity within marriage.").
167. *See* State v. Lash, 16 N.J.L. 380, 381 (1838); *see also* S.B. v. S.J.B., 609 A.2d 124, 126 (N.J. Ch. 1992).
168. *Lash*, 16 N.J.L. at 380.
169. *Lash*, 16 N.J.L. at 381.
170. *Id.* at 382.
171. *Id.* at 383 (emphasis added).
172. S.J.B., A.2d at 126.
173. *Id.*

---

24 The variety of examples accompanied by intricate detail evidences the author's diligence and care at supporting her thesis. It also demonstrates empathy for the reader who will likely be unfamiliar with the abstract concepts supporting the thesis.

A CALL FOR CHANGE   1067

the definition of adultery as articulated in *Lash* to hold "that adultery exists when one spouse rejects the other by entering into a personal intimate sexual relationship with any other person, irrespective of the specific sexual acts performed, the marital status, or the gender of the third party."[174]

Returning to the challenge of balancing stability and innovation in society, Lasswell and McDougal employed the maximization postulate which affirms "that policies are chosen which are expected to yield net value advantages."[175] Appearing simple at first glance, the maximization postulate in-fact reveals a complex decision-making process.[176] "Degrees of unfreedom and freedom [must be distinguished] according to the variety of alternatives open to the responder, and the magnitudes of value indulgence or deprivation involved."[177] Outcomes cannot be characterized as "either/or" options, but rather "more or less."[178]

In the context of social order, the maximization postulate allows some predictability, particularly with regard to habitual behavior.[179] Additionally, the maximization postulate optimalizes by balancing value indulgences against deprivations to achieve maximum advantages.[180] As it relates to the use of base values to expand scope values, framing goals to portray optimalization is essential to garnering community support for policies and preserving social order.[181] Given the type of institution, policies might be formed by the elite without any input from the mid-elite or rank and file, while in other systems, contribution of the mid-elite and rank and file are essential to the success of the policy and preservation of social order.[182]

The maximization postulate is not only backward-looking toward the explanation of past behaviors, but it is also forward-looking and relevant to the identification of goals.[183] The challenge of the law is to advance goals that will maximize desired values.[184] Policies will generally guide goal formation and value optimalization for legal institu-

---

174. *Id.* at 127.
175. LASSWELL & McDOUGAL, *supra* note 8, at 368–69.
176. *Id.* at 369 ("We generally take it for granted that people will try to choose the course of conduct that leaves them better off than the alternatives they reject. . . . [But m]any policy outcomes are not genuine choices.").
177. *Id.*
178. *Id.*
179. *Id.* at 370 ("Habitual behavior typically conforms to the maximization postulate without arousing perception of conflicting impulses.").
180. *Id.*
181. *See id.*
182. *Id.* at 371.
183. *Id.* at 370.
184. *Id.* at 371 (stating that "the goal question is: 'What ought I to want?'").

---

25 Good example of a court recognizing evolving mores.
26 Do all cultures and societies act consistently with this theory? Is this exclusive to observations of western cultures?

27 Does it matter that most actors are not thinking so deliberately about their actions?
28 How are goals set? Who gets to do it?

tions.[185] Certainly, social change is a result of legal action because of its interconnectivity with culture traits (mores, counter-mores, and expediencies). Stability can be maintained by minimizing the nature and degree of changes at any given time.

Changes can be classified in one of two ways: Functional or structural.[186] Functional changes alter the way the salient elements of the social process interact with each other. Structural changes, on the other hand, "are exhibited in the pattern of value shaping and sharing (changes in priorities, or from wide to narrow distribution, or the reverse), or in basic institutions (in myth or technique)."[187] Past changes can be studied to predict pathways of future change, and they can also be used as models for achieving desired change.[188]

C. *Schematic for Analytical Framework*

Returning to Florida's "Stand Your Ground" laws, this Article will examine the value situation surrounding Florida's enactment of a "Stand Your Ground" statutory scheme. The normative analytical framework requires a methodological approach to analyzing the relevant value situation by taking into account the participants, perspectives, base values, strategies, outcomes, and effects.[189] A value situation can be described as a "value shaping and sharing sequence."[190]

Lasswell and McDougal counsel that "identification of outcome events is the critical step both in value and institution analysis."[191] The identification of a given outcome permits the analysis of the surrounding events, including pre- and post-outcomes.[192] Furthermore, it also facilitates the identification of base and scope values.[193] Moreover, the characterization of value outcomes facilitates the identification and description of institutional practices in any context.[194] The eight-value model, in Section II A, is the instrument of choice for "search[ing] for situations that are relatively specialized to the shaping and sharing of each value, and whose detailed patterns comprise each institution."[195] Identifying the boundaries of a value situation is critical to correctly

----

185. *Id.* at 370–71.
186. *Id.* at 372.
187. *Id.*
188. *Id.* at 373.
189. *Id.* at 381.
190. *Id.* at 384.
191. *Id.* at 379.
192. *Id.*
193. *Id.*
194. *Id.* at 379–380.
195. *Id.* at 380.

29 With a complicated framework, explicitly describing how it will be used is helpful.

identifying the participants and their roles.[196]

Participants include those individuals and groups that shape and share values both formally[197] and informally.[198] Perspectives include the demands and expectations of the participants.[199] Base values are values that any given participant possesses that can be used to achieve power and other values.[200] Strategies are the methods the participants employ to leverage base values.[201] Outcomes include both the resulting concrete events and the general prescriptions.[202] The effects "implicate all values, especially those critical to power, decision making, and organizing formalized authority, which will then affect the production and distribution of all values other than power."[203]

By studying the participants and their perspectives, strategic patterns of leveraging base values to achieve particular outcomes and effects can be observed. Through this study, the evolution of culture traits and law can be identified, analyzed, and critiqued. Additionally, measuring outcomes "in units of interaction" is critical to assessing the value situation,[204] as different units of measure apply to different outcomes.[205] For example, power outcomes (decisions) are measured by votes,[206] wealth outcomes (transactions) are measured by prices,[207] enlightenment outcomes (knowledge) are measured by "informativeness,"[208] well-being outcomes (vitality) are measured by "salubrity,"[209] skill outcomes (performance) are measured by "craftsmanship,"[210] affection outcomes (cordiality) are measured by "friendliness,"[211] respect outcomes (prestige) are measured by "distinction,"[212] and rectitude out-

---

196. *Id.* ("For scientific purposes it is expedient to set minimum limits on the frequency of the interactions that must take place before a marginal territory or a pluralistic group is regarded as part of a given value situation (at the pre-outcome, outcome, or post-outcome stage). The 'critical frequency' would be selected in order to reveal the presence of at least minimum recognition that the social context is one in which particular outcomes are influenced and achieved.").

197. *Id.* at 382.

198. *Id.*

199. *Id.* at 350.

200. *Id.* at 340.

201. *Id.* (stating that "[t]he management of base values to achieve scope values is 'strategy'").

202. *Id.* at 357–58.

203. NAGAN, *supra* note 9, at 91.

204. LASSWELL & McDOUGAL, *supra* note 8, at 394.

205. *Id.*

206. *Id.*

207. *Id.*

208. LASSWELL & McDOUGAL, *supra* note 8, at 385–86. ("Informativeness" refers to the number of informative reports in a given period).

209. *Id.* ("Salubrity" includes non-signs regarding health, safety and comfort).

210. *Id.* ("Craftsmanship" refers to levels of operational excellence).

211. *Id.*

212. *Id.*

30 How will the author define the participants? Is everyone in a society included in participants?

31 Who decides what is the desired outcome?

comes (rightness) are measured by "morality" or "responsibility."[213]

This schema is useful for the methodological study of a value situation because it guards against overlooking a value that may be only minimally involved. Mapping the study consistently with this framework will "call[ ] attention to connections that might otherwise be overlooked."[214] Additionally, general categorizations will not be sufficiently nuanced to validate the study.[215] In other words, businesses are not always wealth institutions and power institutions are not always governmental.[216] In this regard, particularized word choice and labels promote precision in analysis.[217]

III.   FLORIDA'S "STAND YOUR GROUND" STATUTES

A.   *Outcome at Issue*

To begin our inquiry, we must identify the outcome giving rise to the value situation. For the purposes of this Article, the enactment of Florida's "Stand Your Ground" statutes is the outcome because the statutes are a result of legislative decisionmaking. Recall, "decision" is the outcome related to power.[218] The remainder of the analysis will be organized by participants because each pre- and post-effect, base value, and strategy is particular to a given participant.[219]

Florida's "Stand Your Ground" statutes took effect October 1, 2005.[220] Prior to the enactment, justifiable use of force was a limited defense that required proof of retreat to the wall, except in "castle" cases.[221] Pre-enactment, the "castle" included the home and workplace, and individuals were not required to retreat to the wall before justifiably using deadly force to prevent an attack likely to cause death or great bodily harm.[222] Before 2005, "duty to retreat" was the majority rule in most states.[223]

Three key changes to the statute were implemented with the transi-

---

213. *Id.* at 386.
214. *Id.* ("The theoretical image acts as a prod and a guide to the focus of attention in considering the value significance of a specific detail.").
215. *See id.* at 389.
216. *Id.*
217. *See id.*
218. *Id.* at 377.
219. *Id.* at 381.
220. Megale, *Deadly Combinations, supra* note 7, at 113–14; Daniel Michael, *Florida's Protection of Persons Bill*, 43 HARV. J. ON LEGIS. 199, 200 (2006).
221. Megale, *Deadly Combinations, supra* note 7, at 111–12. At common law, the castle doctrine was a "privilege that allow[ed] a person attacked within his dwelling to stand his ground." Michael, *supra* note 220, at 201.
222. Megale, *Deadly Combinations, supra* note 7, at 112–13.
223. *See id.* at 112.

---

32 Author clearly identifies one particular outcome and states the analysis will be focused around the participants to explain how the outcome occurred and the lingering effects.

33 Historical analysis is helpful, but notice author cites herself. Should verify original sources in her previous articles and determine whether her articles have been cited.

34

tion to "Stand Your Ground."[224] First, the duty to retreat was eliminated, as codified by Section 776.012, Florida Statutes.[225] That meant that wherever anyone had a right to be, that person would be justified in using deadly force to prevent the likelihood of death or great bodily harm.[226] The effect was to expand the historical notion of castle to anywhere a person has a right to be, even a public place.[227] The second change, as codified in Section 776.013, expanded the concept of castle in Florida to include vehicles as well as homes, but the workplace was eliminated from the definition of castle.[228] Additionally, the legislature created a presumption of reasonable fear for any castle cases involving the justifiable use of force.[229] The third change created immunity for anyone using force as permitted under Section 776.012 or Section 776.013.[230] Immunity under Section 776.032 is broad-based and prohibits the punishment of an individual claiming self-defense, punishment including detention, arrest, prosecution, or civil liability.

Though not limited to cases of homicide, immunity is most easily asserted in homicide cases because rarely is there evidence to contradict

---

224. *Id.* at 113–14.

225. FLA. STAT. § 776.012 (2005) ("A person is justified in using force, except deadly force, against another when and to the extent that the person reasonably believes that such conduct is necessary to defend himself or herself or another against the other's imminent use of unlawful force. However, a person is justified in the use of deadly force and does not have a duty to retreat if: (1) He or she reasonably believes that such force is necessary to prevent imminent death or great bodily harm to himself or herself or another or to prevent the imminent commission of a forcible felony; or (2) Under those circumstances permitted pursuant to s. 776.013.").

226. *Id.*

227. *See* Megale, *Deadly Combinations, supra* note 7, at 115, 117–18.

228. FLA. STAT. § 776.013 ("(1) A person is presumed to have held a reasonable fear of imminent peril of death or great bodily harm to himself or herself or another when using defensive force that is intended or likely to cause death or great bodily harm to another if: (a) The person against whom the defensive force was used was in the process of unlawfully and forcefully entering, or had unlawfully and forcibly entered, a dwelling, residence, or occupied vehicle, or if that person had removed or was attempting to remove another against that person's will from the dwelling, residence, or occupied vehicle.").

229. *Id.*

230. FLA. STAT. § 776.032 ("(1) A person who uses force as permitted in s. 776.012, s. 776.013, or s. 776.031 is justified in using such force and is immune from criminal prosecution and civil action for the use of such force, unless the person against whom force was used is a law enforcement officer, as defined in s. 943.10(14), who was acting in the performance of his or her official duties and the officer identified himself or herself in accordance with any applicable law or the person using force knew or reasonably should have known that the person was a law enforcement officer. As used in this subsection, the term 'criminal prosecution' includes arresting, detaining in custody, and charging or prosecuting the defendant. (2) A law enforcement agency may use standard procedures for investigating the use of force as described in subsection (1), but the agency may not arrest the person for using force unless it determines that there is probable cause that the force that was used was unlawful. (3) The court shall award reasonable attorney's fees, court costs, compensation for loss of income, and all expenses incurred by the defendant in defense of any civil action brought by a plaintiff if the court finds that the defendant is immune from prosecution as provided in subsection (1).").

---

34 The plain language of the statutes seems to support this explanation.

UNIVERSITY OF MIAMI LAW REVIEW [Vol. 68:1051

the defendant's claim of reasonable fear.[231] Since 2005, the number of justifiable homicides in Florida has risen dramatically.[232] Additionally, the statutes have been liberally interpreted to employ a subjective standard regarding reasonable fear.[233] So, rather than determining whether a reasonable man would have feared death or great bodily harm, the courts question whether the defendant, in the defendant's circumstances and with the defendant's knowledge, formed a reasonable belief that death or great bodily harm was imminent.[234] In multiple ways, therefore, "getting away with murder" has become easier in Florida.[235]

Until 2012, Florida's "Stand Your Ground" law had not received much attention, even though homicide rates began rising.[236] This began to change when Trayvon Martin was shot and killed by George Zimmerman and the media descended upon Sanford, Florida.[237] The circumstances of the shooting itself and the ensuing prosecution and acquittal are not relevant to this inquiry.[238] What is relevant is *that* was the ————35 moment the public began to question "Stand Your Ground."[239] Since then, media attention has not subsided in the state of Florida. Florida shooting deaths grab national attention because people wonder whether and to what extent the shooter will be punished.[240] The claims of reasonable fear grow increasingly preposterous,[241] and it would seem to the critical observer that many individuals in Florida feel entitled to shoot and kill for any reason at all.

The national conversation that began in 2012 evidences a clash in cultural values—in other words, a value situation. This clash has arisen ————36 because "Stand Your Ground" was promulgated to advance the interests

231. Megale, *Disaster Unaverted, supra* note 5, at 14.
232. Tim Murphy, *Justifiable Homicides up 200 Percent in Florida Post-Stand Your Ground,* Mother Jones (Sept. 16, 2013), http://www.motherjones.com/mojo/2013/09/stand-your-ground-justifiable-homicide-increase.
233. Megale, *Disaster Unaverted, supra* note 5, at 45.
234. *Id.* at 46.
235. *See* Megale, *Deadly Combinations, supra* note 7, at 134.
236. Quanic Fullard, *A License to Kill?,* Chic. Policy Rev. (Feb. 20, 2013), http://chicagopolicyreview.org/2013/02/20/a-license-to-kill/.
237. *See* Jerry Lanson, *In Trayvon Martin Case, Media Need to Examine Their Own Role,* Huffington Post (Apr. 2, 2012), http://www.huffingtonpost.com/jerry-lanson/critique-of-trayvon-martin-coverage_b_1393453.html.
238. For a full discussion of the prosecution, trial, and acquittal of George Zimmerman, see generally Megale, *Disaster Unaverted, supra* note 5, at 38–60.
239. *See id.* at 40–60.
240. *See, e.g.,* Jack Maddox, *Florida Teen Dead After Row that Began with Loud-Music Complaint, Suspect Jailed,* CNN (Nov. 27, 2012), http://www.cnn.com/2012/11/26/us/florida-music-shooting/; Steve Almasy, *Dad's Texting to Daughter Sparks Argument, Fatal Shooting in Movie Theater,* CNN (Jan. 13, 2014), http://www.cnn.com/2014/01/13/justice/florida-movie-theater-shooting/.
241. *See, e.g.,* Maddox, *supra* note 240; Almasy, *supra* note 240.

35 Is it accurate to use media evidence to document the moment public sentiment changed? Was public sentiment really ever in favor? Did the public know anything before?

36 Clash in values clearly fits with the framework described earlier in the article.

of certain groups, but because of careless drafting, the law has had far-reaching detrimental impacts in other communities.[242] Despite strong public outcry for amending the statutes, Florida has not changed the "Stand Your Ground" laws to better represent commonly held values. To analyze this value situation, the following Sections examine the participants, their base values, and strategies for achieving desired outcomes.

B. *Participants*

1. THE FLORIDA LEGISLATURE

The Florida Legislature is the participant at the center of the value situation presented by Florida's "Stand Your Ground" statutory scheme. As an organization, it is stable and specializes in the shaping and sharing of human values by making decisions to create prescriptions with an "expectation that severe deprivations will be, or are being, imposed on the challengers of policy and that high indulgences will be, or are being, granted to supporters of policy."[243] As the state legislative decision-maker, this body politic made the decision to pass Florida's "Stand Your Ground" law in 2005.[244]

Prior to 2005, pre-outcome, Florida was a duty to retreat[245] and traditional castle doctrine[246] state, which meant that anyone claiming to act in self-defense was required to make a prima facie showing of reasonable fear of death or great bodily harm.[247] Once that initial threshold was established, the prosecutor was tasked with disproving, beyond a reasonable doubt, the claim of self-defense.[248] If the prosecutor could not both prove guilt beyond a reasonable doubt and disprove self-defense beyond a reasonable doubt, the defendant was entitled to an acquittal.[249] Although duty to retreat and traditional castle doctrine were still the norm in most states at the time, Florida deviated by adopting "Stand Your Ground" in 2005.[250]

Duty to retreat and the traditional castle doctrine represented an

242. See Megale, *Deadly Combinations, supra* note 7, at 117–19; Alex Altman, *Beyond Trayvon: How "Stand Your Ground" Laws Spread from Florida to Half the U.S.*, TIME (Mar. 28, 2012), http://swampland.time.com/2012/03/28/beyond-trayvon-how-stand-your-ground-laws-spread-from-florida-to-half-the-u-s/.
243. LASSWELL & MCDOUGAL, *supra* note 8, at 399 (it is generally accepted that governmental bodies, including state legislatures, employ power as their base value).
244. Megale, *Deadly Combinations, supra* note 7, at 113–14.
245. Michael, *supra* note 220, at 200.
246. *See id.* at 201.
247. *See* Megale, *Deadly Combinations, supra* note 7, at 114–15.
248. *See id.* at 112–13, n.43.
249. *See id* at 112–13.
250. *See id.*

37 Was the drafting really careless? Or was it intentional?   38 Does this description of this participant seem accurate?

evolved counter-more with regard to homicide.[251] In medieval times, the notion of excuse or justification in homicide cases was not recognized at all.[252] Any killing, regardless of the reason, was punished as a capital crime.[253] In other words, homicide was a more, strongly opposed by society, and one that members of the community would expect to be punished harshly. Moving into the modern age, courts in England began to recognize the desire for excusing or justifying certain types of killings.[254] Excusable homicide and justifiable homicide emerged, then, as evolutions from the more of the draconian medieval law to the counter-more of modern law. As a counter-more, society continued to embrace the prohibition against homicide, but under certain circumstances the offense was not expected to be punished harshly.[255] Thus, the principles of duty to retreat and the castle doctrine are counter-mores.

    When the Florida Legislature began to consider adopting "Stand Your Ground," it was essentially evolving the counter-mores of duty to retreat and castle doctrine in the direction of an expediency. Importantly, not all jurisdictions with "Stand Your Ground" legislation have created an expediency; however, all have at least created a more expansive counter-more than duty to retreat. The particular combination of laws encompassed in Florida's "Stand Your Ground" legislation essentially legalized homicide in many circumstances.[256] As a result, it converted self-defense into an expediency by eliminating the expectation of any punishment with regard to the justifiable use of force.[257]

    To achieve this evolutionary result of normalizing homicide related to self-defense, the legislature was primarily influenced by two core values: power and wealth. Of course, individual legislators are motivated by the desire to retain office,[258] so they must also promulgate laws that

---

251. *See* LASSWELL & McDOUGAL, *supra* note 8, at 366.
252. *See* Joseph H. Beale, Jr., *Retreat From a Murderous Assault*, 16 HARV. L. REV. 567, 567 (1903).
253. *See id.* at 567–68.
254. *Id.* at 572–73.
255. *Id.* at 573, 579.
256. *See* Megale, *Disaster Unaverted*, *supra* note 5, at 257.
257. *See* FLA. STAT. § 776.032 (2005); LASSWELL & McDOUGAL, *supra* note 8, at 366.
258. *See, e.g.*, Janie Campbell & Amanda McCorquodale, *8 Florida Republicans Who Helped Pass 'Stand Your Groud' or Worked to Keep it on the Books*, HUFFINGTON POST (July 15, 2013, 6:12 PM), http://www.huffingtonpost.com/2013/07/15/florida-republicans-stand-your-ground_n_ 3600017.html ("In 2005, all 20 votes against the Stand Your Ground law were cast by House Democrats. 'In a few years, you will be back trying to fix this bill,' said Rep. Ken Gottlieb (D-Hollywood) during a floor debate, according to the Tampa Bay Times. And he was right. But when Gov. Rick Scott (R) set up a task force to review the law following Martin's death, it was mostly stocked with members unlikely to find fault with the legislation—including the bill's sponsor and three co-sponsors. (A 'shining example of cynical political window dressing,' as South Florida Sun-Sentinel editorial cartoonist Chan Lowe put it)."); Luimbe Domingos, *Why Florida Senate Democrats Voted with Republicans on "Stand Your Ground" Law*, LUIMBE.COM

---

39 Situating the current law against the history is helpful to understand the evolution of Stand Your Ground.
40 Why would society shift from a more to counter-more?

41 In light of the framework, this conclusion seems logical.

42 ———

at least appear consistent with commonly held values to maintain author-ity and control and ensure re-election.[259] The legislative history preced-ing enactment of "Stand Your Ground" reveals why power and wealth were the two values central to the legislature's decision,[260] and how the legislature reconciled them with commonly held community values.[261]

In 2005, Florida became the first state to adopt "Stand Your Ground" legislation as drafted and proposed by the National Rifle Asso-ciation ("NRA").[262] At the time, the NRA boasted that Florida's adop-tion of the law was the "first step of a multi-state strategy."[263] As explained more fully below, the NRA is a powerful and wealthy lobby-ing organization that exercises great legislative influence, in part through its participation in the American Legislative Exchange Council ("ALEC").[264] Though law enforcement and other groups voiced opposi-tion to the proposed bill,[265] Florida, through the leadership of Represen-

---

(Mar 23. 2012), http://www.luimbe.com/blog/2012/03/23/why-florida-senate-democrats-voted-with-republicans-on-stand-your-ground-law-wed-be-seen-as-democrats-soft-on-crime/ ("So the logic here for Florida Senate Dems: We didn't want to seem like soft on crime, so we let ourselves get punked into a bad law that even the Police and Prosecutors said would make crime worse and remove the ability to seek justice in violent crimes.").

259. David Westin, *Divided We Stand (But How Divided Are We Really?)*, HUFFINGTON POST (Nov 10, 2012, 9:53 AM), http://www.huffingtonpost.com/david-westin/election-media-politics_b_2109093.html.

260. *See* Josh Israel, *How the NRA Fueled Florida's 'Stand Your Ground' Law*, THINKPROGRESS (Mar. 22, 2012, 5:20 PM), http://thinkprogress.org/justice/2012/03/22/449961/how-nra-fueled-floridas-stand-your-ground-law/.

261. *See* Andy Kroll, *The Money Trail Behind Florida's Notorious Gun Law*, MOTHER JONES, (Mar 29, 2012, 3:00 AM), http://www.motherjones.com/politics/2012/03/NRA-stand-your-ground-trayvon-martin.

262. *See* Megale, *Deadly Combinations, supra* note 7, at 114–15.

263. Manuel Roig-Franzia, *Fla. Gun Law to Expand Leeway for Self-Defense*, WASH. POST (Apr 26 2005), http://www.washingtonpost.com/wp-dyn/content/article/2005/04/25/AR2005042501553.html ("NRA Executive Vice President Wayne LaPierre said in an interview that the Florida measure is the 'first step of a multi-state strategy' that he hopes can capitalize on a political climate dominated by conservative opponents of gun control at the state and national levels 'There's a big tailwind we have, moving from state legislature to state legislature,' LaPierre said. 'The South, the Midwest, everything they call 'flyover land'—if John Kerry held a shotgun in that state, we can pass this law in that state.'").

264. Joel Achenbach, Scott Higham, & Sari Horwitz, *How NRA's True Believers Converted a Marksmanship Group into a Mighty Gun Lobby*, WASH. POST (Jan. 12, 2013), http://www.washingtonpost.com/politics/how-nras-true-believers-converted-a-marksmanship-group-into-a-mighty-gun-lobby/2013/01/12/51c62288-59b9-11e2-88d0-c4cf65c3ad15_story.html; Adam Weinstein, *How the NRA and its Allies Helped Spread a Radical Gun Law Nationwide*, MOTHER JONES (June 7, 2012, 3:10 AM), http://www.motherjones.com/politics/2012/06/nra-alec-stand-your-ground.

265. John F. Timoney, Op-Ed., *Florida's Disastrous Self-Defense Law*, N.Y. TIMES, Mar. 23, 2012 http://www.nytimes.com/2012/03/24/opinion/floridas-disastrous-self-defense-law.html; Goodnough *supra* note 4; Michael Mayo, *How Did Stand Your Ground Pass Florida Senate 39-0?*, SUN SENTINEL (Mar. 24, 2012), http://articles.sun-sentinel.com/2012-03-24/news/fl-trayvon-mayocol b032512-20120324_1_flawed-law-shooting-death-deadly-force; Michael Daly, *Hammer Is the Woman Behind Stand Your Ground*, DAILY BEAST (Mar. 28, 2012), http://www.thedailybeast.com/articles/2012/03/28/marion-hammer-woman-behind-stand-your-ground.html ("Hammer

---

42 The author is using the media to prove these assertions. Are these reliable sources? Are there counter-stories that would suggest a different conclusion?

tative Dennis Baxley in the House and Senator Durrell Peaden in the Senate, rapidly pushed the legislation through.[266] The lobby was so swift, in fact, that gun-control groups were unable to craft a response prior to the legislature's vote.[267]

    The proposed bill received overwhelming support in the legislature and was passed unanimously in the Senate and by a vast majority of the House.[268] These results were due in large part to the anecdotal legends of "stranger danger" and rampant violence that arguably necessitated empowering the public to defend itself.[269] Particularly, the legislature advanced the story of James Workman, who shot and killed an intruder shortly after Hurricane Ivan.[270] In the legislature's version of the story, Workman lived in legal limbo for a number of months and spent substantial funds on legal fees to ensure his exoneration.[271] In fact, Workman was never even arrested for shooting the intruder, and after a short, three-month investigation, the prosecutor's office declined to press charges.[272] Nevertheless, the legislators identified with this tale, sympathizing with the fear of the "Other" and the violence the "Other" represented.[273] The "Stand Your Ground" laws were supposed to prevent

---

was manifestly untroubled that the legislation was opposed by every significant voice in Florida law enforcement, notably including such actual defenders of freedom as Miami police chief John Timoney. 'You're encouraging people to possibly use deadly physical force where it shouldn't be used,' he was quoted saying. At the time, Timoney was finding it challenging enough to reduce the use of deadly physical force by the officers of his department. And here was a law proposing to give civilians with no training or experience even greater leeway than cops to blaze away.").

266. *See* Altman, *supra* note 242; Weinstein, *supra* note 264.

267. Roig-Franzia, *supra* note 263 (in 2005, *The Washington Post* reported "[t]he overwhelming vote margins and bipartisan support for the Florida gun bill—it passed unanimously in the state Senate and was approved 94 to 20 in the state House, with nearly a dozen Democratic co-sponsors—have alarmed some national gun-control advocates, who say a measure that made headlines in Florida slipped beneath their radar. 'I am in absolute shock,' Sarah Brady, chair of the Brady Center to Prevent Gun Violence, said in an interview. 'If I had known about it, I would have been down there'"); *see also* Mayo, *supra* note 265; Michael, *supra* note 220, at 199.

268. *See SB 436 - Protection of Persons/Use of Force*, FLA. H.R., http://www.myfloridahouse.gov/Sections/Bills/billsdetail.aspx?BillId=15498 (last visited Mar. 20, 2014).

269. *See* Megale, *Disaster Unaverted*, *supra* note 5, at 6; Daly, *supra* note 265 ("But Hammer knew how to sell the bill in a way that a great majority of legislators would find politically irresistible. 'No one knows what is in the twisted mind of a violent criminal,' she testified before the legislature. 'You can't expect a victim to wait before taking action to protect herself and say: 'Excuse me, Mr. Criminal, did you drag me into this alley to rape and kill me or do you just want to beat me up and steal my purse?' She dismissed such objections from the most seasoned experts as 'nothing but emotional hysterics.' She termed those who opposed the bill as a 'bleeding heart criminal coddlers,' which most Florida politicians seemed to consider a synonym for 'unelected.'").

270. Megale, *Disaster Unaverted*, *supra* note 5, at 6.

271. *Id.*

272. For a more detailed discussion of the mistaken beliefs various legislators held regarding Mr. Workman's case, see *id.* at 29–32.

273. *Id.* at 35.

---

43 Is the legislature compromised? How would other voices have been heard?

44 Why would the legislature have manipulated the truth of this story? What advantage did it have?

innocent people acting in self-defense from having to defend themselves or worry about being prosecuted and having to pay exorbitant legal fees.[274] In other words, the legislature intended to empower individuals in the community to take matters into their own hands.[275]

Applying Lasswell and McDougal's framework in the context of "Stand Your Ground," two main goals (desired outcomes) are apparent. First, the legislature wished to retain its power by ensuring authority and control over constituents. Second, to maintain authority and control, the legislature wished to increase the sense of security and well-being of its constituents. These two goals implicate two values: power and well-being. Power is the base value because a governmental agency is involved.[276] By tapping into a community value such as well-being, the government was attempting to gain command over a scope value to build and ensure its own power.

As first stated in Section II.B, "law" is "a process of authoritative decision by which the members of a community clarify and implement their common interests."[277] Individual legislators are generally concerned with preserving their positions of power through re-election, and when laws coincide with community interests, citizens are more likely to re-elect legislators. Through voting, citizens express their consent to governance and vest authority in the legislature. The legislature exercises control by creating prescriptions, in the form of laws that are then enforced by other legitimate agencies, including the executive and judicial branches. Recall that law exists when both authority and control manifest; if either is missing, pretended or naked power exists, but there is no law.[278]

The enforcement of laws ensures continued effective control by the government.[279] With regard to criminal laws, it simply means that law enforcement agencies will arrest individuals who commit crimes and state attorneys will prosecute those crimes. The judicial branch will provide a forum for the prosecution, and upon a showing of guilt, the offender will be punished. The concept of mores and counter-mores informs us that some crimes will not be prosecuted as readily or pun-

---

274. *Id.* at 5–6.
275. *Id.* at 6 ("According to Baxley, the purpose of the law was to let 'citizens . . . know that if they are attacked, the presumption will be with them.'") (alteration in original) (quoting Ben Montgomery, *Florida's 'Stand Your Ground' Law Was Born of 2004 Case, But Story Has Been Distorted*, TAMPA BAY TIMES (Apr. 14, 2012), http://www.tampabay.com/news/publicsafety/floridas-stand-your-ground-law-was-born-of-2004-case-but-story-has-been/1225164).
276. *See* LASSWELL & McDOUGAL, *supra* note 8, at 399.
277. *Id.* at xxx.
278. *Id.*
279. *See id.* at 363.

45 If the general public does not support a law, it compromises the legislature's ability to govern.

ished as harshly as other crimes.[280] The decision to prosecute and punish is thus intimately tied with maintaining control over the constituency. Depending on community values, the government will gain control by prosecuting and punishing in a manner that acknowledges how the community wishes a given law to be enforced.[281] If a law is enforced too harshly, or the community feels it silly to enforce at all, the government will lose control by insisting on its enforcement.[282] By the same token, if the community feels strongly about the prosecution and punishment of certain offenders, the government will lose control by refusing to capture and isolate those criminals.[283]

———46

Under any circumstance, the government or other bodies appointed by the government (like the jury) are charged with determining whether a prescription was violated and by whom. A police officer or a judge decides whether probable cause exists to arrest someone. A prosecutor decides whether to prosecute that person who has been arrested. If the accused elects a trial, a jury of at least six individuals determines guilt or innocence. After verdict, a judge imposes a sentence. Throughout this process, the individuals making the decisions about whether a crime has occurred and who should be held responsible are typically unrelated to the crime itself. In other words, the victim—while preserving some influence[284]—does not control the ultimate decision to arrest, prosecute, convict, or sentence. Control is preserved in this system because the decision makers are not the victims; rather, they impartially and neutrally enforce prescriptions.

In the post-outcome, "Stand Your Ground" has turned this system on its head for cases involving the justifiable use of force. The statutes permit anyone who fears the threat of imminent death or great bodily harm to use deadly force in self-defense.[285] Within the castle, a pre-

———47

---

280. *See id.* at 366.

281. *See id.*

282. *See id.*

283. *See id.*

284. Thirty-three states now have Victims' Bills of Rights or other constitutional protections to provide a voice to victims of crimes. *See* ALA. CONST. art. I, § 6.01; ALASKA CONST. art. I, § 24; ARIZ. CONST. art. II, § 2.1; CAL. CONST. art. I, § 28; COLO. CONST. art. II, § 16a; CONN. CONST. art. I, § 8; FLA. CONST. art. I, § 16; IDAHO CONST. art. I, § 22; ILL. CONST. art. I, § 8.1; IND. CONST. art. I, § 13(b); KAN. CONST. art. 15, § 15; LA. CONST. art. I, § 25; MD. CONST. art. 47; MICH. CONST. art. I, § 24; MISS. CONST. art. III, § 26A; MO. CONST. art. I, § 32; MONT. CONST. art. II, § 28; N.C. CONST. art. I, § 37; NEB. CONST. art. I, § 28; NEV. CONST. art. I, § 8; N.J. CONST. art. I, ¶ 22; N.M. CONST. art II, § 24; OHIO CONST. art. I, § 10a; OKLA. CONST. art. II, § 34; OR. CONST. art. I, § 42; R.I. CONST. art. I, § 23; S.C. CONST. art. I, § 24; TENN. CONST. art. I, § 35; TEX. CONST. art. I, § 30; UTAH CONST. art. I, § 28; VA. CONST. art. I, § 8-A; WASH. CONST. art. I, § 35; WIS. CONST. art. I, § 9m.

285. FLA. STAT. § 776.012 (2005).

---

46 This description seems accurate.

47 If this statement is true, then the potential danger is truly grave.

sumption of reasonable fear arises in cases of justifiable use of force.[286] What this means is that anyone who claims to fear another can make a snap decision to kill that other person under certain circumstances.[287] Pre-outcome, before 2005, the person shooting would have had to make a claim of self-defense, which the prosecution would have had to disprove beyond a reasonable doubt.[288] The judicial process acted as a check to preserve societal values through recognition of the countermores of duty to retreat and the traditional castle doctrine. Post-outcome, however, that same shooter would likely not even be arrested because of the immunity protections of Section 776.032, Florida Statutes.[289] In effect, the victim-shooter becomes judge, jury, and executioner and is not held accountable or required to justify the killing. Because there is no longer a reasonable expectation of punishment in Florida "Stand Your Ground" cases, this doctrine has created an expediency.[290]

Furthermore, the legislature has effectively undermined its natural goal of preserving power by ceding control to individuals in "Stand Your Ground" cases. In fact, the legislature as much admitted that its purpose was to empower individuals to protect themselves through acts of violence.[291] Control relates to the governmental processes that ensure legal prescriptions are enforced consistently.[292] Because "Stand Your Ground" has virtually eliminated the police and prosecutor roles in many homicides,[293] legal control has vanished. In the absence of control, there is no law, just pretended power.[294] In the context of "Stand Your Ground," this pretended power creates community instability and unpredictability by both encouraging violence and impeding the investigation of cases involving acts of violence.

2. THE NRA AND ALEC

As alluded to in the previous section, the NRA was the most enthusiastic proponent of "Stand Your Ground."[295] In fact, Marion Hammer,

---

286. FLA. STAT. § 776.013.
287. Megale, *Disaster Unaverted, supra* note 5, at 36.
288. *Id.* at 16–17.
289. *See* FLA. STAT. § 776.032.
290. *See* LASSWELL & McDOUGAL, *supra* note 8, at 366.
291. Roig-Franzia, *supra* note 263 (shortly after enacting "Stand Your Ground," Baxley commented, "[d]isorder and chaos are always held in check by the law-abiding citizen"); *see also Examining the Foundation of 'Stand Your Ground' Laws*, NPR (July 20, 2013, 3:00 PM), http://www.npr.org/templates/story/story.php?storyId=204013757; Mayo, *supra* note 265.
292. *See* LASSWELL & McDOUGAL, *supra* note 8, at 362–63.
293. Mayors Against Illegal Guns, et al., *Shoot First: 'Stand Your Ground' Laws and Their Effect on Violent Crime and the Criminal Justice System* 5 (Sept. 2013), http://libcloud.s3.amazonaws.com/9/2e/3/2126/ShootFirstReport.pdf.
294. *Id.* at 400.
295. Michael C. Bender, *Pistol-Packing Grandma Pushes NRA Laws Across U.S.*, BLOOMBERG

---

48 This seems risky. 49 Do people realize the legislature has ceded power?

1080   *UNIVERSITY OF MIAMI LAW REVIEW*   [Vol. 68:1051

former president of the NRA, drafted key parts of the legislation as it was ultimately adopted.[296] Although it was once a hunters' and sportsmen's organization that supported moderate gun control, since the 1970s, the NRA appears to have whittled its mission down to a single goal: Zero gun regulation.[297] It works toward that goal by leveraging its wealth and power in order to acquire more of both.[298] Because of the great influence it exacts, the NRA is an "elite of influence."[299]   —50

Determining the NRA's base value presents a challenge. One contender is "power" because the NRA has, at least since the 1970s, gained increasing power in the legislative process.[300] Thus, it certainly is involved in the power structure.[301] Assuming for the moment that power is the base value of the NRA, the NRA is best described as a pressure group.[302] Pressure groups engage in "activity specialized to influencing particular decisions by peaceful means."[303] Even though it does not make final decisions about legal prescriptions because it is not a legislative body, it leverages so much influence over the legislative process that it often is the effective decision-maker.[304]   —51

BusinessWeek (May 11, 2012), http://www.businessweek.com/videos/2012-05-11/pistol-packing-grandma-pushes-nra-laws-across-u-dot-s-dot ("Florida Governor Rick Scott, a Republican, talks with Bloomberg's Michael C. Bender about Marion Hammer, the top lobbyist for the National Rifle Association in the state. Hammer is responsible for such pro-gun legislation as the "Stand Your Ground" law allowing deadly force in self-defense, a model concealed-carry measure and a statute blocking doctors from asking about guns in the home.").

296. Weinstein, *supra* note 264 ("Baxley says he and Peaden lifted the law's language from a proposal crafted by Marion Hammer, a former NRA president and founder of the Unified Sportsmen of Florida, a local NRA affiliate.").

297. Achenbach, *supra* note 264.

298. *See* Alec MacGillis, *This Is How the NRA Ends: A Bigger, Richer, Meaner Gun-Control Movement Has Arrived*, New Republic (May 28, 2013), http://www.newrepublic.com/node/113292/.

299. Lasswell & McDougal, *supra* note 8, at 414–15 ("[W]e speak of someone as a member of the elite of influence when he is among the few who control the most power, wealth, respect, and other values.").

300. Achenbach, *supra* note 264.

301. Lasswell & McDougal, *supra* note 8, at 423 ("[A]ll groups . . . are involved in some degree in politics[, though all] . . . are not specialized to the power value.").

302. *Id.* at 422.

303. *Id.*

304. *Id.* at 413–414; "The American Legislative Exchange Council works to advance limited government, free markets, and federalism at the state level through a nonpartisan public-private partnership of America's state legislators, members of the private sector and the general public." ALEC.orghttp://www.alec.org/about-alec/ (last visited June 1, 2014). Corporate members, like the NRA, participate in drafting legislation and informing social policy to advance their own corporate interests. Because of the limited membership, all members of society do not enjoy a seat at the table, and the conversation does not necessarily consider all community values. Hammer used her influence through ALEC and the Florida legislature to advance the NRA's agenda. Consider this quote: "But do not call her simply a lobbyist. To do so drastically underestimates her while equally overestimating the state legislature. Hammer does not so much lobby as orchestrate the legislature to do her bidding and therefore the bidding of the NRA, where she formerly served

---

50 This sounds like a bit of a conspiracy theory. How is Stand Your Ground directly related to gun regulation? What would the NRA want to accomplish?

51 This description seems to make sense.

One way that the NRA influences decision-making is through its collaboration with ALEC.[305] ALEC provides a forum whereby legislators, lobbyists, and corporations work together on drafting legislation and vote on the proposed statutory language so that legislators may return to their home states and propose new laws to the benefit of the participating lobbyists.[306] Corporate entities and lobby groups primarily fund ALEC, and, though it claims to be non-partisan, only one of 104 participating legislators is a Democrat.[307] By purchasing the opportunity to draft legislation, large entities like the NRA are able to participate in the decision-making process. Moreover, the legislature is more easily influenced by the groups who participate in ALEC because ALEC provides a forum for side-by-side collaboration and drafting of new legislation.[308] The effect is that the values of the ALEC groups tend to be given greater weight because they are presented more often and more systematically to legislatures, and those values are likely to be adopted even when they are inconsistent with commonly held community values.

The other likely contender for base value with regard to the NRA is wealth.[309] As an organization, the NRA is extremely well-financed and is adept at leveraging its wealth to command power as a scope value.[310] This wealth comes from two sources—membership dues and corporate sponsorship from gun manufacturers and related industries.[311] As a strategic leveraging mechanism, the organization makes campaign contributions in an effort to control lawmakers and exert pressure on political and legislative decisions,[312] but exerting pressure on politicians is only one strategic method employed by the NRA. Recall that the legislature's power depends upon the ability to exercise authority and control over the constituency through the passage of laws that reflect commonly held values.[313] In this way, the polity's consent to being governed is

---

for three years, as its first woman president. She continued to serve as a consultant and lobbyist known for standing her own ground. The NRA credits her with being the propelling force behind the Stand Your Ground Law." Daly, *supra* note 265.

305. *See National Rifle Association*, SOURCEWATCH, http://www.sourcewatch.org/index.php/NRA

306. The Center for Media and Democracy, *What is ALEC?*, ALEC EXPOSED, http://alecexposed.org/wiki/What_is_ALEC%3F (last visited May 22, 2014).

307. *Id.*

308. *See What is ALEC?, supra* note 306.

309. Achenbach, *supra* note 264; Wilson Andrews et al., *How the NRA Exerts Influence over Congress* WASH. POST (Jan. 15, 2013), http://www.washingtonpost.com/wp-srv/special/politics/nra-congress/.

310. Achenbach, *supra* note 264; Andrews et al., *supra* note 309.

311. *See* MacGillis, *supra* note 298.

312. *Id.*

313. LASSWELL & McDOUGAL, *supra* note 8, at 400.

---

52 So, legislatures effectively empower pressure groups to draft legislation.

53 Does it matter whether its base value is wealth or power?

1082   *UNIVERSITY OF MIAMI LAW REVIEW*   [Vol. 68:1051

expressed in the form of votes.[314] Another component of the NRA's influence, then, rests in its ability (whether real or perceived) to deliver elections by creating and then directing large blocs of single-issue voters.[315] The NRA's success in harvesting community support is likely the result of its ability to frame gun regulation as an assault on every citizen's fundamental rights.[316] This framing technique taps into community values of respect, rectitude, and well-being.[317]

In the context of "Stand Your Ground," Marion Hammer was able to leverage her friendship with Representative Dennis Baxley and other members of the Florida legislature to advance the NRA's agenda.[318] ——54
Using the scope value of affection as a leveraging tool, Hammer drafted substantial portions of the language in the bill and provided it to Representative Baxley and Senator Peaden to propose to the Florida legislature.[319] Baxley in turn, on behalf of the NRA, leveraged the scope value of well-being to convince the legislature that this law, as drafted, was good for the community and would ensure re-election because it coincided with commonly held values.[320] With this strategy, the NRA was

---

314. *Id.* at 353.

315. Scott Medlock, *NRA=No Rational Argument? How the National Rifle Association Exploits Public Irrationality*, 11 TEX. J. C.L. & C.R. 39, 42 (2005).

316. *See* Michael C. Dorf, *Identity Politics and the Second Amendment*, 73 FORDHAM L. REV. 549, 552, 568 (2004).

317. *See* LASSWELL & McDOUGAL, *supra* note 8, at 342.

318. Steve Bousquet, *Meet Dennis Baxley, The Lawmaker Who Always Stands His Ground*, TAMPA BAY TIMES (Apr. 1, 2012, 9:02 PM), http://www.tampabay.com/news/courts/meet-dennis-baxley-the-lawmaker-who-always-stands-his-ground/1226327 ("A lifelong National Rifle Association member who's been known to sip his coffee from an NRA mug, Baxley has sponsored numerous gun laws in a career marked by his close friendship with the tenacious gun lobbyist Marion Hammer, whom he calls 'awesome.'"); Michael C. Bender, *Marion Hammer, the NRA's Most Powerful Weapon*, BLOOMBERG BUS. WK. (May 17, 2012), http://www. businessweek.com/articles/2012-05-17/marion-hammer-the-nras-most-powerful-weapon ("'There is no single individual responsible for enacting more pro-gun legislation in the states than Marion Hammer,' says Richard Feldman, a former political organizer for the NRA."); *see also* Ann O'Neill, *NRA's Marion Hammer Stands Her Ground*, CNN (Apr. 15, 2012, 9:20 AM), http:// www.cnn.com/2012/04/15/us/marion-hammer-profile/.

319. Daly, *supra* note 265 ("[Hammer] has acknowledged having a hand in actually drafting the enabling Stand Your Ground legislation back in 2004. She introduced it through a proxy, State Sen. Dennis Baxley, whom she had previously arranged to receive the NRA's 2004 Defender of Freedom Award."); Weinstein, *supra* note 264 ("Baxley says he and Peaden lifted the law's language from a proposal crafted by Marion Hammer, a former NRA president and founder of the Unified Sportsmen of Florida, a local NRA affiliate."); Joe Strupp, *Former NRA President: We Helped Draft Florida's "Stand Your Ground" Law*, MEDIA MATTERS (Mar. 27, 2012, 11:15 AM), http://mediamatters.org/blog/2012/03/27/former-nra-president-we-helped-draft-floridas-s/185254 ("'The NRA participated in drafting the Castle Doctrine and supporting it through the process,' Marion Hammer told Media Matters. Hammer was president of the NRA from 1995 to 1998, remains a member of its board, and is a longtime Florida lobbyist for the group.").

320. Daly, *supra* note 265 ("But Hammer knew how to sell the bill in a way that a great majority of legislators would find politically irresistible. . . . She termed those who opposed the bill as a[sic] 'bleeding heart criminal coddlers,' which most Florida politicians seemed to consider

---

54 Is affection truly that powerful?

able to achieve its goal and launch its multi-state campaign to enact "Stand Your Ground" legislation. Success in this campaign is directly attributable to the legislative and special interest collaboration made possible through ALEC.[321]

Returning to the question of whether the NRA's base value is wealth or power, the pre-outcome events surrounding the enactment of "Stand Your Ground" in Florida are telling. The NRA is certainly capable of exercising pressure on the body politic. With respect to "Stand Your Ground," it appears the NRA was responsible for the ultimate decision to enact the legislation as well; the fact that a representative of the NRA drafted the language of the legislation evidences its direct participation in the decision, or power outcome.[322] Thus, it appears that in leveraging wealth to gain command over power, the NRA might have succeeded, through "Stand Your Ground," in commanding power as a base value.

A troubling aspect of the NRA's legislative influence is the fact that it does not necessarily represent the values held by the majority of the community. Only about 500,000[323] of Florida's 19.3 million residents are members of the NRA, and only around 800,000[324] are registered gun owners. In other words, less than three percent of Florida's citizenry has membership in the NRA. Nevertheless, the NRA has succeeded in passing a bill that specifically furthers its own interest in gun deregulation, not necessarily the commonly held values of the

a synonym for 'unelected.' The bill came to a vote in early 2005, passing the state senate by 39-0 and the house by 92-20. Every single state senator voted in favor of a measure that every responsible figure in law enforcement opposed. The legislators seem to have been not so much lobbied by Hammer as directed."); Mayo, *supra* note 265 ("'I have a clear conscience,' said former state Sen. Steve Geller, a Broward Democrat. 'I tried to take the bad parts out, but my amendment was defeated. I sounded warnings about it.' So why did he and the entire South Florida Senate delegation (except for absent Fort Lauderdale Democrat Mandy Dawson) end up voting yes? Geller said it was going to pass anyway in the face of powerful National Rifle Association support, and he was afraid a no vote would be used against him in later campaigns, since the bill included reasonable parts protecting police officers. 'It would have been like voting against apple pie or motherhood,' Geller told me last week. How's that for a profile in political courage?").

321. Weinstein, *supra* note 264.

322. Matt Gertz, *ALEC Has Pushed the NRA's "Stand Your Ground" Law Across the Nation*, MEDIA MATTERS (Mar. 21, 2012), http://mediamatters.org/blog/2012/03/21/alec-has-pushed-the-nras-stand-your-ground-law/186459; Dana Milbank, *ALEC Stands its Ground*, WASH. POST (Dec. 4, 2013), http://www.washingtonpost.com/opinions/dana-milbank-alec-stands-its-ground/2013/12/04/ad593320-5d2c-11e3-bc56-c6ca94801fac_story.html.

323. Dara Kam, *How the NRA Attained Dominance in the "Gunshine State,"* PALM BEACH POST (Apr. 6, 2012), http://www.palmbeachpost.com/news/news/crime-law/how-the-nra-attained-dominance-in-the-gunshine-sta/nN2yY/ (Florida has approximately 900,000 gun owners, but approximately 100,000 reside out-of-state).

324. *Id.*

55 To what end is the NRA interested in power?

56 How much support does the NRA have in Florida? Is this an accurate assessment?

community.[325]

  When "Stand Your Ground" was being considered, the vocal opposition from law enforcement and other groups was unorganized and ineffective.[326] After the shooting death of Trayvon Martin, however, louder opposition voices, like Attorney General Eric Holder, the Dream Defenders, the NAACP, and others, are being heard.[327] Nevertheless, post-outcome, the NRA continues to exact influence over the legislative process and has blocked the reconsideration of "Stand Your Ground" laws in Florida.[328] Disconnect between the legislation and societal values creates a circumstance whereby the legislature could lose its authority. The law is "a process of authoritative decision by which the members of a community clarify and implement their common interests."[329] Currently, with "Stand Your Ground," the legislature is responding primarily to the NRA, which is a small percentage of the community. Since the common interests of many community members are not represented by "Stand Your Ground," civil unrest is likely to escalate as citizens express their disagreement with the laws.

—57

---

325. *Most Americans Favor 'Stand Your Ground' Laws: Poll*, REUTERS (Aug. 2, 2013, 4:46 PM), http://www.reuters.com/article/2013/08/02/us-usa-florida-law-poll-idUSBRE97115F2013 0802 (Quinnipiac "poll found that a strong majority of white voters and men support the laws, while black voters generally oppose them and women are almost evenly divided"); *Majority of Floridians Accept Zimmerman Trial Verdict, Support "Stand Your Ground" Law*, VIEWPOINT FLA. (July 13, 2013), http://viewpointflorida.org/index.php/site/article/majority_of_floridians_accept_zimmerman_trial_verdict_support_stand_yo/ (poll by Viewpoint Florida reporting that "50% said ["Stand Your Ground"] is fine the way it is, while 31% of voters thought the law needed to be changed or limited, and just 13% thought that 'Stand Your Ground' should be repealed entirely"). Both of these polls used registered voters to measure public opinion. Even assuming that polls measuring the opinions of registered voters can holistically measure community values, at best only about half of the community's values align with the existing law. For the other half, the law is inconsistent with their value systems.
326. *See* Timoney, *supra* note 265 (opinion article written by a former Miami Police Chief); *"Stand Your Ground" Laws*, COALITION TO STOP GUN VIOLENCE, http://csgv.org/issues/shoot-first-laws/ (last visited May 10, 2014).
327. *See, e.g.*, Dexter Mullins, *Florida Sit-In Against "Stand Your Ground" Law Continues*, AL JAZEERA AMERICA (Aug. 11, 2013, 11:30 PM), http://america.aljazeera.com/articles/2013/8/11/-dream-defendersholdsitinoverstandyourground.html (discussing the many voices that have involved themselves in the discussion opposing Florida's "Stand Your Ground" law, including U.S. Attorney General Eric Holder, Ebony Magazine, actor Boris Kodjoe, basketball player Dwayne Wade, and director Spike Lee).
328. *See* Joe Saunders, *Fla. House Committee Rejects "Stand Your Ground" Repeal Effort*, BIZPAC REVIEW (Nov. 8, 2013), http://www.bizpacreview.com/2013/11/08/fla-house-committee-rejects-stand-your-ground-repeal-effort-86732; Marion P. Hammer, *ALERT! Florida's Stand Your Ground Law Stood its Ground Against Attack*, NRA-ILA (Nov. 8, 2013), http://www.nraila.org/legislation/state-legislation/2013/11/alert!-floridas-stand-your-ground-law-stood-its-ground-against-attack.aspx.
329. LASSWELL & McDOUGAL, *supra* note 8, at xxx.

---

57 Are supporters of the NRA opposed to Stand Your Ground? What is the NRA's interest in pushing this agenda?

3. GUN CONTROL LOBBY

One of the criticisms to the swift passage of "Stand Your Ground" in Florida was that the gun-control lobby did not have to time to respond to the proposals pre-outcome.[330] Notably, the post-outcome efforts of the gun-control lobby have effected no change in Florida's Stand Your Ground legislation either. The gun-control lobby is comprised of several groups, like the Brady Campaign, Mayors Against Illegal Guns, Moms Demand Action, and others, whose base value is well-being.[331] A unifying feature is that these groups have formed largely in reaction to tragedies involving guns.[332] To achieve its goal of providing for a safer community and increased vitality, the gun-control lobby leverages primarily enlightenment to influence power institutions.[333]

To date, these gun-control groups have not successfully garnered the same type of wealth and corporate support mustered by the NRA. Furthermore, none of these groups are members of ALEC.[334] Therefore, their ability to leverage wealth as an influential force with the legislature is limited,[335] and they do not have access to a captive multistate legislative audience. Instead, they have relied solely on leveraging enlightenment to promote gun regulation.[336]

The enlightenment message has had imperfect success. The general gun-control message that gun deregulation leads to increased violence has always competed against the NRA enlightenment message that gun control threatens a fundamental right.[337] Pre-outcome, the NRA suggested that innocent citizens were at great risk of violence by criminals and therefore needed to arm themselves.[338] The theory was that if innocent citizens armed themselves, criminals would be too afraid to attack.

---

330. Michael, *supra* note 220, at 212.

331. *About Moms Demand Action For Gun Sense in America*, MOMS DEMAND ACTION, http://momsdemandaction.org/about/ (last visited May 10, 2014); *Coalition History*, MAYORS AGAINST ILLEGAL GUNS, http://www.mayorsagainstillegalguns.org/html/about/history.shtml (last visited Mar. 19, 2014); *Our History*, BRADY CAMPAIGN TO PREVENT GUN VIOLENCE, http://www.bradycampaign.org/?q=our-history (last visited May 10, 2014).

332. *About Moms Demand Action For Gun Sense in America*, *supra* note 331; *Our History*, *supra* note 331.

333. *See About Moms Demand Action For Gun Sense in America*, *supra* note 331.

334. *ALEC Corporations*, COMMON CAUSE, http://www.commoncause.org/site/pp.asp?c=dkLNK1MQIwG&b=8078765 (last visited May 10, 2014).

335. Seth Cline, *Firepower: Gun Control Opponents Outspend Opposition 25-to-1*, U.S. NEWS & WORLD REP. (July 24, 2012), http://www.usnews.com/news/articles/2012/07/24/firepower-gun-control-opponents-outspend-opposition-25-to-1.

336. MacGillis, *supra* note 298.

337. Medlock, *supra* note 315, at 59.

338. Ann O'Neill, *supra* note 318 (consider Marion Hammer's argument: "I could have been killed or raped, but I had a gun so I wasn't," she said. "If the government takes away my gun, what's going to happen next time?").

---

58 Why have they been unsuccessful in being heard?

59 Would these groups be heard if they joined ALEC?

60 This juxtaposition seems to make sense. Need to consult footnote sources to verify.

1086　　　　　*UNIVERSITY OF MIAMI LAW REVIEW*　　　[Vol. 68:1051]

By arming themselves, citizens also exercise their fundamental right to bear arms. Couching it as an enlightenment message, the NRA was able to capture public support, with little to no opposition, for its legislative agenda. Even the gun-control lobby failed to vocalize significant opposition to passage of the "Stand Your Ground" legislation pre-outcome.

Post-outcome, the gun-control enlightenment message has been more effective at mobilizing individuals and small groups, but it continues to have limited impact on the legislature. To date, lawmakers seem to be minimally influenced by gun-control data and reasoning—especially when pitted against the NRA's wealth. For example, in October 2013, Jonathan E. Lowy, of the Brady Campaign, testified before the United States Senate Committee on the Judiciary Subcommittee on the Constitution, Civil Rights, and Human Rights.[339] He spoke out against "Stand Your Ground," specifically as it related to Florida's lax concealed carry laws,[340] and relied on at least two studies to support the conclusion that Florida's "Stand Your Ground" legislation has led to "a net increase in homicide, with no evidence of deterrence of other crimes."[341]

As explained in Section III(B)(1) above, one goal of "Stand Your Ground" was to achieve well-being by empowering individuals to protect themselves against criminals; however, the data would suggest that the law has failed. Justifiable homicides in Florida have increased by roughly 200% since 2005.[342] Moreover, since the shooting of Trayvon Martin and ultimate acquittal of George Zimmerman, widely reported killings seem to suggest an increased disregard for human life.[343] For example, Michael Dunn shot and killed Jordan Davis, a teenage passenger in a vehicle.[344] What motivated Dunn to shoot Davis? The teens, who had pulled into the gas station where Dunn was parked, refused to turn down their music when he ordered them to do so.[345] Similarly, Curtis Reeves shot and killed Chad Oulson at a movie theater following a disagreement about cell phone use.[346] During a verbal argument, Oulson threw his popcorn at Reeves, and Reeves responded by shooting and

---

339. *See generally Testimony of Jonathan E. Lowy, "Stand Your Ground" Laws: Civil Rights and Public Safety Implications of the Expanded Use of Deadly Force, Before the S. Judiciary Subcomm. on the Constitution, Civil Rights, and Human Rights* (Oct. 29, 2013).

340. *Id.* at 2–4.

341. *Id.* at 4.

342. Michael George, *I-Team: Justifiable Homicides Double Since "Stand Your Ground,"* ABC Action News (Mar. 27, 2012, 7:48 PM), http://www.abcactionnews.com/dpp/news/local_news/investigations/i-team-justifiable-homicides-double-since-stand-your-ground.

343. Almasy, *supra* note 240; Maddox, *supra* note 240.

344. Maddox, *supra* note 240.

345. *Id.*

346. Almasy, *supra* note 240.

---

61 Is the NRA deliberately thinking about power and wealth? Does this make sense?

62 How would the NRA have preserved power if the public's well-being is not preserved?

killing Oulson.[347]

These are just two examples of the multiple cases evidencing a total disregard for human life. Because Florida's "Stand Your Ground" laws empower a shooter to be judge, jury, and executioner for any perceived transgression, shooters—of course—feel safer making the decision to shoot and kill someone else. To some, the choice appears to be "shoot or be shot."[348] These incidents illustrate how changes in laws begin to cause changes in cultural expectations and personal perspectives, values, and beliefs about what is appropriate in society.

Contrary to the NRA's and legislature's enlightenment message that "Stand Your Ground" has made communities safer, the law has clearly had the opposite effect, at least as measured by the net increase in homicides. At the same time, the gun-control lobby's enlightenment message that less gun regulation inherently leads to increased gun violence rings true.[349] As alluded to earlier, pre-outcome this message was heard against the backdrop of stranger danger and fear of the Other. To the general public, it could easily have seemed like "Stand Your Ground" was in fact necessary to make the community safer. Nearly ten years later, however, the data has been consistent with the gun-control groups' predictions, and as explained more completely in Section III(B)(b) below, it would appear the community has begun to see through the fallacies of the stranger-danger message promulgated by the NRA and the legislature. It remains to be seen, however, whether the legislature will be persuaded by enlightenment.

4. NAACP

Another participant in this value situation emerged prominently during the George Zimmerman case: The NAACP. This group is the most widely recognized civil rights organization in America.[350] For decades, the NAACP has leveraged its base value of enlightenment to

---

347. *Id.*

348. *See* Maddox, *supra* note 240.

349. BRIAN J. SIEBEL, NO CHECK. NO GUN. WHY BRADY BACKGROUND CHECKS SHOULD BE REQUIRED FOR ALL GUN SALES 5 (April 2009), *available at* http://bradycampaign.org/sites/default/files/no-check-no-gun-report.pdf ("[T]the Brady background check system . . . requires background checks only for gun sales by licensed dealers, [so] criminals can obtain guns with no questions asked from unlicensed sellers, as they are allowed to sell guns without conducting a check in most states. . . . In effect, we have two gun markets: A regulated one, where buyers are checked to see if they can legally buy guns, and an unregulated one, where they are not. . . . By requiring background checks on only about [sixty percent] of gun sales, with the rest almost completely unregulated, we make it too easy for dangerous people to obtain dangerous weapons. This leads to senseless gun violence harming tens of thousands of people, year after year.").

350. *NAACP: 100 Years of History,* NAACP, http://www.naacp.org/pages/naacp-history (last visited May 10, 2014).

---

63 According to the framework, negative consequences like these are not enough to fuel legislative change.

leverage power through grassroots and national organizations fighting for equality and against the disenfranchisement of racial minority groups.[351]

The NAACP became vocal in the Zimmerman case during the period of time when it appeared Zimmerman would not be prosecuted for killing the teenager, Trayvon Martin.[352] The NAACP's enlightenment message is that "Stand Your Ground" is a step backward in the struggle for racial equality.[353] Insofar as "Stand Your Ground" promotes disregard for human life, the NAACP's position is logical. People still notice color, and there is no question that racism, prejudice, and bias exist. For many, racial differences symbolize the "Other" who should be feared.[354] When subjective fear is motivation enough to shoot and kill without question, then inherent biases, prejudices, and racism will necessarily provoke killings.

Post-outcome statistical evidence on the racial impact of "Stand Your Ground" in Florida is mixed. For the most part, the statistics would support a conclusion that the law is being enforced uniformly and that there is no bias in application.[355] Nevertheless, the evidence also suggests that numbers of black victims are higher overall than white victims.[356] At the same time, however, black-on-black killings occur at ———— 64 higher rates than interracial killings.[357] As far as the potential to use this information in support of the NAACP's overall purpose of enlightening the public to overcome racism, the statistics do not seem to offer enough leverage for the NAACP to command sufficient support toward accomplishing its goal. Similarly, a race-based enlightenment message presents a myopic interpretation of the data that is unlikely to influence legislative change.

With regard to the shooting of Trayvon Martin, the NAACP advanced two distinct arguments regarding race. First, the NAACP argued the killing itself was racially motivated.[358] Second, it argued that

---

351. *Id.*
352. *Statement by the NAACP on Charges Filed Against George Zimmerman*, NAACP, http://www.naacp.org/news/entry/statement-by-the-naacp-on-charges-filed-against-george-zimmerman (last visited May 10, 2014).
353. *Testimony of Hilary O. Shelton, "Stand Your Ground" Laws: Civil Rights and Public Safety Implications of the Expanded Use of Deadly Force, Before the S. Judiciary Subcomm. on the Constitution, Civil Rights, and Human Rights*, 4–5 (Sept. 17, 2013).
354. SETHA LOW, BEHIND THE GATES: LIFE, SECURITY, AND THE PURSUIT OF HAPPINESS IN FORTRESS AMERICA 137–40 (2003).
355. Susan Taylor Martin et al., *Race Plays Complex Role in Florida's "Stand Your Ground" Law*, TAMPA BAY TIMES, June 2, 2012, http://www.tampabay.com/news/courts/criminal/race-plays-complex-role-in-floridas-stand-your-ground-law/1233152.
356. *Id.*
357. *Id.*
358. Carol Cratty & Tom Cohen, *Despite Outrage, Federal Charges Uncertain in Zimmerman*

---

64 The reporting of this data seems accurate. What is the significance?

the reticence to investigate and prosecute George Zimmerman resulted from endemic institutional racism in the City of Sanford, Florida.[359] However, the evidence surrounding the case undermined the NAACP's arguments against "Stand Your Ground."[360]

With regard to racial motivations, the evidence against Zimmerman was sparse. The NAACP claimed Zimmerman had used a racial slur when describing Martin to the 911 operator.[361] However, the audio recording of Zimmerman's call to 911 was unclear and could not be enhanced to show he had used such a term.[362] There were other allegations that Zimmerman had called the authorities on numerous occasions to report suspicious individuals and that each of the reports involved an African-American.[363] Evidence supporting the allegation of racial profiling, however, was not forthcoming.[364] Additionally, neighbors and friends of Zimmerman claimed he was not racist and that he socialized with people of all races.[365]

With regard to the investigation and prosecution, the NAACP alleged authorities were hesitant to arrest Zimmerman because the victim was black and the shooter was white.[366] The physical evidence in the case, however, supported the police decision not to arrest Zimmerman. Upon arriving on scene, law enforcement noticed Zimmerman had cuts on the back of his head and a broken nose, which were consistent with his account of being pinned to the ground and punched in the face by Martin.[367] Furthermore, several eyewitness accounts confirmed Zimmerman's version of events.[368] Under these facts, it would have been subjectively and objectively reasonable for Zimmerman to believe he was in danger of suffering great bodily harm. In fact, he did suffer great bodily

---

Case, CNN (July 23, 2015, 8:13 PM), http://www.cnn.com/2013/07/15/politics/zimmerman-federal-charges/.

359. *Statement by the NAACP on Charges Filed Against George Zimmerman, supra* note 352.

360. Cratty & Cohen, *supra* note 358.

361. Matt Hadro, *Contrary to CNN's First Assumption, Prosecutors Say Zimmerman Didn't Use Racial Slur,* MEDIA RESEARCH CENTER, (Apr. 13, 2012, 5:25 PM), http://www.mrc.org/biasalerts/contrary-cnns-first-assumption-prosecutors-say-zimmerman-didnt-use-racial-slur.

362. *Id.*

363. Matthew DeLuca, *George Zimmerman's History of 911 Calls: A Complete Log,* DAILY BEAST (Mar. 22, 2012), http://www.thedailybeast.com/articles/2012/03/22/george-zimmerman-s-history-of-911-calls-a-complete-log.html.

364. Cratty & Cohen, *supra* note 358.

365. *George Zimmerman's Friends Speak out, Deny Shooter Was Racist,* INQUISITR (Mar. 26, 2012), http://www.inquisitr.com/211441/george-zimmermans-friends-speak-out-deny-shooter-was-racist/; *see also Dr. Phil: A Dr. Phil Exclusive: Friends of George Zimmerman—"The Most Hated Man in America"—Speak out,* (CBS television broadcast Sept. 11, 2012), *available at* http://www.drphil.com/shows/show/1866.

366. *Testimony of Hilary O. Shelton, supra* note 353, at 5–7.

367. Megale, *Disaster Unaverted, supra* note 5, at 39.

368. *Id.* at 49–50.

---

65 Are the sources cited in the footnotes accurate and reliable?

harm.[369] Under "Stand Your Ground," therefore, he would have been entitled to immunity, and the failure to arrest and prosecute Zimmerman would have been lawful under the statute. Additionally, a decision not to prosecute would have been entirely consistent with other, more egregious cases around Florida that have not been prosecuted at all.[370]

So, despite the tragedy of Martin's death, this case was probably not the best one for the NAACP to use to advance its goals of building enlightenment about the racial impact of "Stand Your Ground." Because the evidence and data did not clearly support the theories of racism, the enlightenment message was not as persuasive as it needed to be to harness changes to "Stand Your Ground." ————66

The NAACP's enlightenment value, though unique in substance, is the same in function as the enlightenment message of the gun-control lobby and other groups opposed to "Stand Your Ground." Although from an analytical perspective its values might not align squarely with these other groups, the similarities in approach to leveraging base value would suggest a potential for effecting positive legislative change if the NAACP aligns with these other groups opposed to "Stand Your Ground." In bringing a unified message to the legislature, these groups together could express a broader enlightenment message and more readily appear to represent commonly held community values. In this way, all groups could leverage value in a way that the legislature might be inclined to accept under the theory that legislators need the approval and consent of the governed to retain their power.

5. MEDIA

Another enlightenment group is the media. In his 1992 law review article on media ethics and the law, Robert Dreschel describes the media as playing two distinct roles in society.[371] In their passive "informing role," news outlets set out to give an account of current events, provide a forum for differing viewpoints, act as "a watchdog over the behavior of government and government officials," and provide other similar functions.[372] In their "activating role," news outlets actually guide and affect ————67 public discourse by acting as "opinion leaders who help people play active roles in community controversies."[373] In this way, the media leverages the scope value of enlightenment to achieve goals.

In both roles, the news media leverages its knowledge and its repu-

---

369. *Id.* at 49.
370. *Id.* at 47–48.
371. Robert E. Dreschel, *Media Ethics and Media Law: The Transformation of Moral Obligation into Legal Principle*, 6 NOTRE DAME J.L. ETHICS & PUB. POL'Y 5, 18 (1992).
372. *Id.* at 18 tbl.1.
373. *Id.* at 18–19.

---

66 Did it detract for the NAACP to become involved?

67 Have news outlets also become pure entertainment? Do they still serve these roles?

APPENDIX IX | Annotated Samples and Examples

2014]   *A CALL FOR CHANGE*   1091

tation in order to gain access to both information and the widest possible audience, with the desired outcome of increasing wealth and, more importantly, gaining respect.

While many news outlets view the prestige of being the fourth estate as a solemn reminder of their duty to report fairly and guide responsibly, many others leverage that prestige by first capturing an audience and then steering that audience's knowledge (and, hence, activity) to increase the power and wealth of the news corporation itself.[374] The trouble with distinguishing the two is that, from the viewpoint of either, the news media on the other side is the nefarious actor.[375]

This trend is especially relevant in the context of the media's "activating role" regarding "Stand Your Ground" because journalists who oppose the law will naturally publish stories about its unforeseen ill effects in order to guide public opinion and steel citizens' resolve to change the status quo through activism.[376] Those who favor the law, on the other hand, take a similar two-pronged approach: First, they publish the sort of "glad-I-had-my-gun" stories that highlight the shooter as victim;[377] second, they portray the law's detractors as the Other, who is not to be trusted.[378] While neither side may be characterized as entirely disingenuous, their ability to control public perception and action through selective reporting and authoritative opining cannot be understated.

Within the jurisprudential framework, the media plays an obviously critical role. Other entities—like the legislature, NRA, gun-control lobby, and NAACP—use the media to enlighten the public and shape values. Competing media messages evidence the tension amongst these various groups. As its own vehicle, the media also seeks to influence the shaping of community values. At the same time, the media transmits messages about community values to these other groups as well. As all these pieces are in constant motion, the media is at the same time a tool of civil engineering and a barometer of community values.

68

---

374. Westin, *supra* note 259.

375. Frank Rich, *Stop Beating a Dead Fox*, N.Y. MAG. (Jan. 26, 2014), http://nymag.com/news/frank-rich/fox-news-2014-2/#; Larry Womack, *The Real Problem with Media Today? The Audience*, HUFFINGTON POST (Jan. 17, 2012, 5:28 PM), http://www.huffingtonpost.com/larry-womack/the-real-problem-with-the_1_b_1207888.html.

376. *See* Walker Bragman, *The Culture of Guns and Misinformation*, HUFFINGTON POST (Jan. 25, 2013, 4:15 PM), http://www.huffingtonpost.com/walker-bragman/guns-misinformation_b_2553021.html.

377. Kurt Nimmo, *Stand Your Ground Upheld in Florida Despite Efforts of Obama's DOJ*, DAILY DRUDGE REPORT (Nov. 8, 2013), http://thedailydrudgereport.com/2013/11/03/mainstream-mixup/stand-your-ground-upheld-in-florida-despite-efforts-of-obamas-doj/.

378. Brian Walsh, *Liberal Media Shrug at Bloomberg's Big Ad Buy*, U.S. NEWS & WORLD REP. (Mar. 28, 2013), http://www.usnews.com/opinion/blogs/brian-walsh/2013/03/28/the-hypocrisy-of-liberal-medias-silence-on-bloombergs-gun-blitz.

---

68 Is it believable that the media is a manipulator with an ulterior purpose?

194

What has been surprising since the shooting death of Trayvon Martin and the other tragic deaths that have continued is that the legislature has been largely unresponsive to the media message. Many news outlets have reported the failure of "Stand Your Ground" and called for its repeal.[379] A number of other states are reconsidering "Stand Your Ground," and community support for it in Florida has drastically declined.[380] Nevertheless, the Florida legislature has refused to seriously reconsider the legislation. Although Governor Rick Scott formed a task force on "Stand Your Ground," it was staffed with four sponsors of the original bill[381] and only two individuals on that team expressed concerns about the law.[382] The task force recommended that no changes be made to "Stand Your Ground."[383] Additionally, in August 2013 when Representative Alan Williams introduced a bill to repeal "Stand Your Ground,"[384] Marion Hammer, former president of the NRA, testified in opposition to it before the Florida legislature in November 2013, and it ultimately died in committee.[385] Considering the emerging enlightenment message that commonly held community values are at odds with existing "Stand Your Ground" legislation, it is perplexing that the legislature would not more seriously reconsider repealing "Stand Your Ground."

6. INDIVIDUALS

Assessing the base value interests of individuals is the most difficult task because individuals within a community possess individual per-

379. Kris Hundley et al., *Florida "Stand Your Ground" Law Yields Some Shocking Outcomes Depending on How Law Is Applied*, TAMPA BAY TIMES (June 1, 2012), http://www.tampabay.com/news/publicsafety/crime/florida-stand-your-ground-law-yields-some-shocking-outcomes-depending-on/1233133; Joy Lawson, *Young People Standing Our Ground to End "Stand Your Ground" Laws*, HUFFINGTON POST (July 17, 2013, 5:30 PM), http://www.huffingtonpost.com/joy-lawson/young-people-standing-our_b_3613108.html.
380. Derek Smith, *States Consider Changes to Stand Your Ground*, BILL TRACK 50 (Apr. 2012), http://www.billtrack50.com/blog/in-the-news/states-consider-changes-to-stand-your-ground/.
381. Campbell & McCorquodale, *supra* note 258 ("But when Gov. Rick Scott (R) set up a task force to review the law following Martin's death, it was mostly stocked with members unlikely to find fault with the legislation—including the bill's sponsor and three co-sponsors. (A 'shining example of cynical political window dressing,' as South Florida Sun-Sentinel editorial cartoonist Chan Lowe put it).").
382. REPORT OF THE GOVERNOR'S TASK FORCE ON CITIZEN SAFETY AND PROTECTION, TASK FORCE ON CITIZEN SAFETY AND PROTECTION, app. E (Feb.21, 2013), http://www.flgov.com/wp-content/uploads/2013/02/Citizen-Safety-and-Protection-Task-Force-Report-FINAL.pdf (opposition voices include Katherine Fernandez Rundle and Rev. Dr. R.B. Holmes, Jr.).
383. *See id.* at 5–8.
384. Hammer, *supra* note 328.
385. *Bill History*, FLORIDA SENATE, http://www.flsenate.gov/Session/Bill/2014/4003 (last visited May 10, 2014).

69 Why would the legislature be unresponsive? Does it not care that it may be losing power? Does it not believe it is using power?

sonalities that influence perspectives and value systems.[386] What is more, individual base values may change over time depending on the circumstance.[387] One constant, though, is that individuals are capable of leveraging any of the eight values to achieve goals.[388]

With regard to "Stand Your Ground," the legislature convinced the populace of the necessity for its enactment by tapping into individual fears for safety and well-being.[389] By advancing the myth of the Other and stranger danger,[390] the legislature succeeded in passing the "Stand Your Ground" legislation with little opposition.[391] In fact, the only expressed fears at the time of its passage were with regard to projected racial disparities in enforcement.[392] This particular fear has not come to fruition, at least not in any way obviously supported by reported data.[393] The unanticipated harm that has come upon the state is the blatant disregard for human life.

Especially since the shooting death of Trayvon Martin, aggression toward the Other has dramatically increased. The legislature has convinced the community that broader access to guns and greater freedoms

---

386 *See* LASSWELL & McDOUGAL, *supra* note 8, at 350.

387 *See id.* at 349–55.

388 *See id.*

389 *Florida Lawmakers Expand Law to Kill in Self Defense*, DEMOCRACY NOW! (Apr. 6, 2005), http://www.democracynow.org/2005/4/6/florida_lawmakers_expand_law_to_kill ("The importance of this bill is to put things back the way they are supposed to be. The courts have manipulated the law into a position where the law favors criminals rather than victims and law abiding citizens because the law, as it was before the bill passed yesterday, said that inside your home, if someone breaks in in the middle of the night, you can only meet force with force, and then only if you reasonably believe it is necessary to prevent death or great bodily harm. Well, in the middle of the night how are you supposed to know the intent of the intruder or what manner of force the intruder intends to use? You can't say, 'Wait a minute, intruder? Are you here to rape and murder me, or are you just here to beat me up and steal my TV set?' You have put the homeowner, who wants to protect himself and his family, in a distinct disadvantage. You are protecting criminals. That's wrong. Out on the street, the courts have imposed a duty to retreat. That basically says if you are attacked, you have to try to turn around and run before defending yourself. When you turn your back on a criminal, you make yourself infinitely more vulnerable. If a rapist tries to drag you into an alley, if you are prepared to fight back and defend yourself, that's your right. The bill we passed yesterday will allow you to decide whether or not you can get away or whether or not you're safer if you stand your ground and fight. Taking away the rights of law-abiding people and putting them in jeopardy of being prosecuted and then sued by criminals who were injured when they were committing crimes against victims is wrong. This bill fixes all of that. It puts back the castle doctrine law with regard to your home, and it gives you the right to protect yourself and your family. And that's all this bill does.").

390 Megale, *Disaster Unaverted*, *supra* note 5, at 35.

391 Michael, *supra* note 220, at 212; Daly, *supra* note 265.

392 *The Black & White of Stand Your Ground*, TOP CRIMINAL JUSTICE DEGREES, http://www.topcriminaljusticedegrees.org/stand-your-ground/ (last visited June 1, 2014).

393 Hundley et al., *supra* note 379 ("Cases with similar facts show surprising—sometimes shocking—differences in outcomes. If you claim 'stand your ground' as the reason you shot someone, what happens to you can depend less on the merits of the case than on who you are, whom you kill and where your case is decided.").

---

70 Fear is a powerful motivator. Has public perception changed at all?

to shoot and kill the Other makes us all safer.[394] The paradoxical effect, however, is that greater freedom to kill creates a greater fear of being killed. In the context of "Stand Your Ground," one of the individual's primary concerns is obviously well-being in the form of security. For most, then, the deciding factor in how a person takes a side on this issue will be which policy—"Stand Your Ground" or "Duty To Retreat"—is more likely to increase well-being—both personal and social.[395] One whose parochial universe is smaller (few of Us but many of Them)[396] is more likely to favor "Stand Your Ground" because it seemingly increases individual power while protecting personal well-being. Those who perceive their own community as being wider-ranging and less clearly bound, however, are likely to oppose it because it creates a danger to individuals who may not be Other after all. 71

Two other values also dominantly emerge in the context of "Stand Your Ground": Respect and rectitude. Because "Stand Your Ground" is tethered to the value of preservation of personal honor, it necessarily implicates respect. This value is also obviously connected to many of the decisions to kill in Florida since 2005. Consider two of the examples mentioned previously. Both Dunn and Reeves clearly felt disrespected by the Other. Dunn's order to turn down music was "rudely" disobeyed. Reeves's order to stop texting in the theater was "rudely" disobeyed. Within minutes of the disobedience, Dunn and Reeves shot the offender without hesitation. Never mind that neither had any authority to bark orders at the Other. 72

Respect is implicated in two ways in these scenarios. First, the shooter feels disrespected and entitled to defend his honor. The violence is evidence of leveraging respect to preserve respect. The second way that respect is implicated is in the lack of respect for the Other. The

394. Megale, *Disaster Unaverted*, *supra* note 5, at 35.
395. *Id.* at 35 n.173.
396. Lasswell & McDougal, *supra* note 8, at 2. ("Under the discipline of tens of thousands of years of primitive living, human beings developed a patchwork of tiny, distinctive, parallel cultures. They acquired three perspectives of enduring significance: identification with a parochial self (the band or tribe); the expectation that inter-band conflicts, especially when strangers are involved, would be settled by violence; and the demand by the self upon the self (and band mates) to sacrifice for the parochial identity. This is the syndrome of parochialism. . . . Clearly we are living in the early stages of exposure to a complex social environment to which human beings are gradually more painfully becoming accustomed. The pre-civilized inheritance of man shadows his future, since the syndrome of parochialism—including the expectation of violence and the morals of parochial sacrifice—continues to characterize the human condition. . . . Since the emergence of cities and the consolidation on a new prototype for human life-ways, history has been characterized by conflicting examples of the prototype, and by clashes or accommodations between civilizations and pre-civilized societies." However, because "[w]hat changes is culture, not the brain," the conflict in SYG is not between disparate cultures, but between the (real or perceived) needs of modern civilization and the mind's reflexive tendency to follow the old paradigm).

71 If individuals understood the reality that they aren't safer, would their position change?

72 Is there a hierarchy of who deserves respect?

reason the shooter feels entitled to kill is because the shooter does not value or respect the Other. Rectitude is also intimately tethered to respect in these scenarios because the shooter believes in the rightness of the decision to shoot.

The converse of these positions is often measurable by examining the victims in these cases. Originally, "Stand Your Ground" was intended to protect the innocent,[397] so the assumption that the dead person is a criminal or otherwise a bad or dangerous person is natural. But often, the victim is a person who is not committing a crime, like Trayvon Martin, Jordan Davis, and Chad Oulson. What is more, "victims" of "Stand Your Ground" are not just those who have died. The group includes anyone who has been negatively impacted by "Stand Your Ground," like the friends and families of the deceased. For victims, it is natural to interpret "Stand Your Ground" as much more than a self-defense statute—it is the lifting of gun restrictions.

Historically, Duty to Retreat was a restriction on gun use that required proof of a justification prior to exoneration for killing another.[398] Advocates of "Stand Your Ground" advance two positions: (1) any duty to retreat is an unreasonable infringement on individual rights; and (2) "Stand Your Ground" increases individual power and well-being.[399] Victims, on the other hand, understand Duty to Retreat to be a necessary component of law in a society that values the dignity of human life.[400] To victims, "Stand Your Ground" obviously decreases social wellbeing, first by increasing access to violent conflict resolution, but worse, by upsetting social balances relating to respect and rectitude.

However, there is difficulty in determining which values the majority commonly holds. Even assessing the members of the majority is nearly impossible. Moreover, to the extent the majority has little ability to leverage its base values, it will necessarily exercise little influence over legislative decision-making. Still, at least one group of individuals, the Dream Defenders, has protested at the Florida Capitol and achieved marginal results. After a thirty-one-day protest against "Stand Your Ground," Governor Rick Scott called a special legislative session to con-

---

397. Campbell & McCorquodale, *supra* note 258 ("The reason for reform was simple. News articles discussed the confusion in Florida's law that required an innocent victim to flee when attacked by a criminal. Imagine a woman being required to flee when attacked in a parking lot, having to turn her back to the attacker, and then likely being run down and raped. Shouldn't she have the option to stand her ground to protect herself? Florida's Stand Your Ground law is a good, common-sense solution to the competing issues that exist in this area of the law.").

398. Elizabeth Chuck, *Mothers of Victims Plead for Changes to Stand-Your-Ground Laws*, NBC News (Oct. 29, 2013, 1:47 PM), http://usnews.nbcnews.com/_news/2013/10/29/21231481-mothers-of-victims-plead-for-changes-to-stand-your-ground-laws.

399. Campbell & McCorquodale, *supra* note 258.

400. *See* Beale, *supra* note 252, at 575.

---

73 Do the powerful care that some groups may not be presumed innocent?

74 What was the harm in requiring a shooter to prove self-defense

sider House Bill 4003 that proposed repeal of Florida's "Stand Your Ground."[401] Not surprisingly, however, the NRA exacted stronger influence and the proposal ultimately died in committee.[402] Nevertheless, the fact that the legislature responded at all might be evidence that it is beginning to heed the post-outcome disconnect between commonly held community values and "Stand Your Ground." If so, steps toward reconciling the law with commonly held values could be forthcoming.

Regardless of which group commands the majority, any civilized society ought to promote the policy that protects well-being, salubrity, and the dignity of human life.

IV. Conclusion

Trayvon Martin's death marked a turning point for Florida because it put a proverbial mirror up to the face of the community. For the first time, individuals were confronted with the stark reality that "Stand Your Ground" was not making the community safer. Since then, tragedies have continued, but the community is calling out for change. Prosecutions in homicide cases seem to be more readily forthcoming and groups opposed to "Stand Your Ground" seem to be mobilizing.

A major theme from the opposition is that some level of accountability is necessary in homicide cases. If so, that means that, as a whole, society does not want justifiable uses of force to be an expediency. Rather, the use of force should remain a counter-more that is not necessarily punished harshly. As it stands now, however, Florida's "Stand Your Ground" is an expediency. Because it is an expediency, it is inconsistent with commonly held values and expectations, and the legislature must find a way to reconcile the law and values. If it does not, the citizenry will begin to withdraw its consent to being governed.

In adopting "Stand Your Ground," the legislature for a time convinced the public that the law was consistent with commonly held values of safety and well-being. Since 2012, however, that myth has been seriously called into question, if not debunked entirely. At this stage, the most appropriate way to reconcile the law and values is to either repeal or amend "Stand Your Ground" to reinstate some level of accountability when citizens use deadly force in self-defense. In other words, the legislature must revert the expediency to a counter-more. It is unlikely that the community will continue to be convinced by conciliatory messages

---

401. See Sascha Cordner, *House Panel Rejects Proposal to Repeal Florida's Stand Your Ground Law*, WFSU (Nov. 7, 2013, 10:33 PM), http://news.wfsu.org/post/house-panel-rejects-proposal-repeal-floridas-stand-your-ground-law.
402. *Id.*; Marion P. Hammer, *supra* note 328.

75 Is this conclusion truly supported by the article, or is this the author's hope?

76 Does the public understand that its safety and well-being is compromised?

that "Stand Your Ground" is good legislation advancing commonly held community values, absent a significant change to the statutory scheme.

In a civilized society, the government must be mindful to enact statutes that will preserve the integrity of human dignity. "Stand Your Ground" gives individuals the freedom to disregard the sanctity of human life. By creating such far-reaching protections for individuals who engage in violent behavior, the legislature has effectively ceded control and is now operating with pretended power. In fact, "Stand Your Ground" cannot even be accurately called a law because it has divested the government of control over the people in cases of justifiable use of force. The need for amendment or repeal of this law is urgent, and the community is now voicing its cry for change, pleading with the legislature to realign with commonly held values to preserve the well-being, respect, and rectitude of the community.

Part II: Anna Stearns, *Patch by Patch: North Carolina's Crazy Quilt of Campaign Finance Regulation,* 40 Campbell L. Rev. 669 (2018)

This article is a good example of a student comment. You will note that it has been annotated with two purposes in mind. First, some of my notes demonstrate critical reading and note-taking. I have attempted to demonstrate the thought processes you should be engaging in while you are reading your sources. So, you will see comments to the effect of "do I agree with the author's characterization" or "need to pull sources to verify accuracy." In your own research process, you will want to make similar notes and then follow through on pulling the original sources. You will also want to add in the details about why you do or do not agree with the author's characterization as well as notes about how the author's thesis fits into the broader discourse community.

Second, some of my notes highlight the structure and function of the analytical framework. So, you will see comments to the effect of "notice how the definitions support the author's use of the concept in context" or "defining terms is essential to establishing a strong analytical framework." For these comments, pay attention to how the author develops ethos by clearly identifying and explaining the analytical framework before applying. Take note of how the analytical framework is applied to the specific situation. Finally, use the same techniques when evaluating other scholars' work and developing your own project.

The annotations provided in this article reveal my use of the methods described in Chapters 3, 4, 5, and 6 and follow the checklists suggested by this book. They are intended to be a demonstration of the metacognitive processes necessary for scholarly research and analysis.

Patch by Patch: North Carolina's Crazy Quilt of Campaign Finance Regulations

ABSTRACT

After more than a decade of judicial intervention and legislative reforms, North Carolina's campaign finance laws resemble a crazy quilt— a patchwork of provisions pieced together from remnants and scraps. The law is a dizzying array of proscriptions, requirements, and exceptions, sometimes based on speaker identity and sometimes based on the content or context of the political message. This quilt is what remained after the Fourth Circuit's strained and confusing decision in North Carolina Right to Life, Inc. v. Leake, *decided in 2008, immediately following the Supreme Court's landmark decision in* McConnell v. FEC. *This Comment evaluates and summarizes North Carolina's existing campaign finance regulations, provides a critical analysis of both the state of the law and of the Fourth Circuit's decision in* North Carolina Right to Life, Inc. v. Leake, *and offers a suggested analytical framework for future judicial review of campaign finance regulations.*

———77

———78

669

---

77 In the abstract, the author clearly states that she will be problematizing the existing framework for campaign finance and will offer a new framework. As the reader, you can expect she will identify problems, explain why they are problematic, and then offer a solution to address the problems she has identified.

78 The table of contents lists the problems the author will be exploring in this comment.

INTRODUCTION

Modern political campaigns are dominated by political ads and the money required to produce and air them. Candidates and Political Action Committees break new fundraising records every election cycle.[1] By July 31, 2016, Hillary Clinton and Donald Trump, along with their Super PACs and party committees, raised over $1 billion for the 2016 presidential contest.[2] Here in North Carolina in the same period, candidates for state and local races raised more than $38 million.[3] Independent political groups spent another $33.1 million, with more than $16 million spent on the gubernatorial race alone.[4]

Campaign finance regulations seek to ensure that candidates raising such large sums of money are not doing so in exchange for political favors, and if they are, that the public has sufficient information available to hold them accountable. These regulations pose a tricky balancing act for the federal and state governments. Political speech is vital to our democracy and has been the bedrock of our nation's history.[5] Citizens expect the

---

1. Paul Blumenthal, *Get Ready for the Most Expensive Senate Races of All Time*, HUFFINGTON POST (Sept. 30, 2016, 4:11 AM), https://perma.cc/A85U-4ZWQ.

2. Anu Narayanswamy, Darla Cameron & Matea Gold, *Campaign 2016: Money Raised as of July 31*, WASH. POST (July 31, 2016), https://perma.cc/VB3Y-TF7Q.

3. Ctr. for Responsive Politics, *North Carolina, State Summary, 2016 Cycle*, OPENSECRETS.ORG, https://perma.cc/A6G7-K2EW.

4. Alex Kotch, *North Carolina's 2016 State Elections Smashed Outside Spending Records*, FACING SOUTH (Feb. 22, 2017), https://perma.cc/T8VK-63ZE.

5. Whitney v. California, 274 U.S. 357, 375 (1927) (Brandeis, J., concurring). The Founders

> believed that freedom to think as you will and to speak as you think are means indispensable to the discovery and spread of political truth . . . . They knew . . . that it is hazardous to discourage thought, hope and imagination; that fear breeds repression; that repression breeds hate; that hate menaces stable government; that

---

79 The introduction begins by broadly identifying the two competing interests that have led to the problem of campaign finance.

greatest freedom when they engage in political speech. But, for the last century, free-flowing political discourse has had to yield to protections against the threat of corruption. As candidates continue to appeal to anonymous donors who pour millions of dollars into state and national campaigns, the public is apt to suspect that political favors will be exchanged for those donations. When the public perceives corruption in the political process, distrust of government often follows, and that can be as damaging to our system of government as the constraint of speech.

                                                     —80

    As a result, federal and state governments have sought to carefully thread the needle—permitting the broadest free speech possible while also ensuring that campaign contributions do not result in corruption or seriously undermine the public's confidence in our electoral system. That struggle has resulted in a set of regulations and exceptions so confusing that an average citizen could easily run afoul of the law without ever intending to do so.[6] As the Fourth Circuit noted:

> It is no unfounded fear that one day the regulation of elections may resemble the Internal Revenue Code, and that impossible complexity may take root in the very area where freedom from intrusive governmental oversight should matter most."[7]

If we have not yet reached that day, it is fast approaching.

                                                     —81

    For more than a decade, North Carolina has made piecemeal revisions to its campaign finance laws, amending, repealing, or replacing sections of the law in response to court orders.[8] The result is a code that has lost its original purpose. It is a quilt stitched together without a pattern. The average citizen is left unsure what the law is, with his speech chilled by the threat of criminal sanction if he fails to adequately understand how to comply with the law. In its current form, North Carolina's campaign

---

the path of safety lies in the opportunity to discuss freely supposed grievances and proposed remedies; and that the fitting remedy for evil counsels is good ones.

Id.

    6. *See* Citizens United v. FEC, 558 U.S. 310, 335–36 (2010) (holding that the Federal Election Commission's two-part, eleven-factor balancing test amounted to a prior restraint on speech because an average speaker who desired to avoid criminal liability would need to ask the government whether his speech was regulated).

    7. N.C. Right to Life, Inc. v. Leake (*NCRL III*), 525 F.3d 274, 296 (4th Cir. 2008).

    8. *See* Act of May 4, 1999, no. 31, 1999 N.C. Sess. Laws 34 (revising the definition of "political committee" in response to the holding in N.C. Right to Life, Inc. v. Bartlett, 168 F.3d 705, 712–13 (4th Cir. 1999); Act of Aug. 19, 2007, no. 391, § 3, 2007 N.C. Sess. Laws 1150, 1152 (repealing the $3,000 rebuttable presumption that had previously been used to classify issue advocacy after the test was held unconstitutional in N.C. Right to Life, Inc. v. Leake, 344 F.3d 418, 430 (4th Cir. 2003)); Act of Aug. 2, 2008, no. 150, 2008 N.C. Sess. Laws 605 (titled in part as "An Act . . . to Respond to the Decision of the 4th Circuit U.S. Court of Appeals in North Carolina Right to Life v. Leake").

---

80 Here the author hearkens to deeply-held values dear to the American people. She is providing a broad context and clearly stating the significance and importance of what she is saying.
81 The author is essentially saying that the reason the law has become such a mess is that there has not been a systematic approach. Piecemeal legislation is the antithesis of an analytical framework—it is ineffective to try to solve legal problems without a systematic method of inquiry. In other words, an analytical framework is essential.

672   CAMPBELL LAW REVIEW   [Vol. 40:2

finance regulations fail to accomplish the government's goals of encouraging political participation while limiting the possibility and perception of corruption.

This Comment will begin by providing an overview of North Carolina's campaign finance regime, explaining which individuals and organizations are subject to regulation and which types of speech are subject to regulation. It will also explain how the North Carolina Board of Elections[9] uses disclosure reporting requirements along with civil and criminal penalties to fulfill its duty to regulate campaign finance.

Part II offers a critique of the Fourth Circuit Court of Appeals' decision in *North Carolina Right to Life, Inc. v. Leake*,[10] which struck two provisions of North Carolina's campaign finance laws as facially unconstitutional. Rather than analyzing the law's ability to achieve a governmental interest without burdening constitutionally protected speech, the court subjected the law to bright-line tests that it incorrectly adopted and applied.

Part III proposes a framework for future review of challenges to campaign finance regulations. This framework suggests that the court proceed by (1) identifying the type of burden imposed by the regulation, (2) selecting the appropriate level of constitutional scrutiny, (3) determining whether the method of regulation chosen is capable of achieving that stated purpose, and (4) determining whether the law incidentally burdens protected speech that the government need not regulate in order to accomplish its purpose. Finally, the court should assess the law for vagueness under both the First and Fourteenth Amendments.

This Comment concludes by asserting that what remains of North Carolina's campaign finance regime is incapable of achieving the

---

9. On December 16, 2016, the Bi-Partisan Ethics, Elections and Court Reform Act was enacted and signed by outgoing Governor Pat McCrory. S. 4, 2016 Gen. Assemb., 4th Extra Sess. (N.C. 2016). The Act combined the North Carolina Board of Elections and the North Carolina Ethics Commission into a new board designated The North Carolina Bipartisan State Board of Elections and Ethics Enforcement. The incoming Governor, Roy Cooper, challenged the new act and a preliminary injunction was issued blocking all portions of the law from taking effect. Cooper v. Berger, No. 16 CVS 15636, 2017 WL 1433242 (N.C. Super. Ct. Jan. 6, 2017). The Act was repealed and replaced by the Bipartisan Board of Elections and Ethics Enforcement Act five months later. S. 68, 2017 Gen. Assemb., Reg. Sess. (N.C. 2017). The portions of the Act which provided for the composition of the new board were found unconstitutional by the North Carolina Supreme Court. Cooper v. Berger, 809 S.E.2d 98 (N.C. 2018). The legislature again sought to combine the board and commission immediately following the court's holding. H.B. 90, 2018 Gen. Assemb., Reg. Sess. (N.C. 2018). For the sake of clarity, throughout this Article the board is referred to as the Board of Elections.

10. *NCRL III*, 525 F.3d 274.

---

82 The author explicitly states what she will be criticizing and how she will criticize it. Her thesis is clearly stated: the court erred when it failed to "analyz[e] the law's ability to achieve a governmental interest without burdening constitutionally protected speech" and instead "subjected the law to bright-line tests that it incorrectly adopted and applied."

83 The framework proposed by the author identifies a multi-step process to ensure integrity and soundness of decision-making when campaign finance issues arise.

governmental interest that is purportedly the justification for its existence. Instead, the law unconstitutionally chills free speech. The resulting patchwork of regulation is so complex that an average citizen cannot understand it and, without the assistance of an attorney, could face criminal penalties for innocently violating the law through the simple act of collectively associating and advocating for a candidate. —84

I. NORTH CAROLINA'S CAMPAIGN FINANCE SCHEME

North Carolina's statutory scheme for regulating campaign finance restricts political speech in three primary ways. It imposes restrictions on the basis of the speaker's identity; it imposes restrictions on the basis of the content of certain messages; and it imposes disclosure requirements on certain speakers and messages. The statute uses civil and criminal penalties to enforce the law. The following sections will summarize those restrictions, requirements, and penalties. —85

A. Restrictions Imposed on the Basis of Speaker Identity

North Carolina's statutes identify seven types of speakers subject to regulation: (1) individuals,[11] (2) candidates,[12] (3) for-profit corporations,[13] (4) non-profit corporations,[14] (5) segregated funds created by corporations or labor unions,[15] (6) political parties and their affiliated party committees,[16] and (7) any other organization which has "the major purpose to support or oppose" the nomination, election, or defeat of a candidate (political action committees, colloquially known as PACs).[17] The regulations impose different burdens on the different types of speakers, —86

---

11. *See generally* N.C. GEN. STAT. §§ 163A-1410 to -1505 (2017) ("Regulating Contributions and Expenditures in Political Campaigns"). Registered lobbyists are subject to more stringent regulations. *Id* § 163A-1427. Discussion of the constitutionality of these restrictions is beyond the scope of this Comment; however, for a more thorough discussion on the constitutionality of these restrictions, see *N.C. Right to Life, Inc. v. Bartlett*, 3 F. Supp. 2d 675 (E.D.N.C. 1998).
12. §§ 163A-1411(9), -1475(2).
13. *Id* §§ 163A-1411(24), -1436.
14. *Id* § 163A-1436(h).
15. *Id* § 163A-1436(g); *see also id* § 163A-1436(d).
16. *Id* §§ 163A-1411(76), -1416 to -1417.
17. *Id* § 163A-1411(74)(d). The statute defines a political committee as "a combination of two or more individuals . . . that makes . . . contributions or expenditures and has . . . the major purpose to support or oppose the nomination or election of one or more clearly identified candidates." *Id* § 163A-1411(74).

---

84 The author concludes by emphasizing the significance of the problem subject of this comment.
85 Good, precise introduction for the reader to know exactly what to expect in this section.
86 Need to read the statute itself to determine whether this summary is accurate. The footnotes conveniently provide precise subsections to make that easy to do.

674   CAMPBELL LAW REVIEW   [Vol. 40:2

with some subject to very stringent regulation and others provided great latitude to raise and spend funds to further their political messages.

Individual donors may not contribute more than $5,200 per election cycle to any candidate or political committee.[18] Because the statutes treat "coordinated expenditures" (purchases that are made in concert or agreement with the candidate) as donations, individuals who collaborate with a candidate to make purchases, as opposed to direct donations, must treat those expenditures as donations subject to the contribution limit.[19]

For-profit corporations are prohibited from making campaign contributions,[20] but this does not mean they are prohibited from participating in the political process. They may encourage their employees, stockholders, or members to register and vote,[21] and they may advocate for or against a candidate so long as the expenditure is not coordinated with the campaign.[22] They may also directly support candidates by establishing "a separate segregated fund to be utilized for political purposes."[23] The segregated fund can make contributions to candidates or other political committees and engage in electioneering.[24] The restrictions on corporate contributions do not apply to non-profit corporations,[25] which are free to make contributions to candidates and political committees, subject to the $5,200 cap per election cycle.[26]

The statutes also regulate political committees and require that every candidate must establish and register a "political committee" with the

---

18. *Id.* § 163A-1425(a). The limit is adjusted for inflation every two years. *Id.* § 163A-1425(b).

19. *Id.* § 163A-1411(20). "'[C]oordinated expenditure' means an expenditure that is made in concert or cooperation with, or at the request or suggestion of, a candidate . . . ." *Id.* The precise level of coordination required has yet to be established in North Carolina courts, but federal courts have held coordination in the context of federal campaign finance laws to mean "the candidate or her agents can exercise control over, or where there has been substantial discussion or negotiation between the campaign and the spender over, a communication's: (1) contents; (2) timing; (3) location, mode, or intended audience . . . ; or (4) 'volume.'" FEC v. Christian Coal., 52 F. Supp. 2d 45, 92 (D.D.C. 1999).

20. § 163A-1436(a).

21. *Id.* § 163A-1436(d).

22. *See id.* § 163A-1436. While corporations are prohibited from making contributions, the definition of "contribution" expressly excepts independent expenditures. *Id.* § 163A-1411(13).

23. *Id.* § 163A-1436(d).

24. *Id.* The corporation may provide administrative support to its segregated fund but must report the value of that support, as well as a portion of the salary of any officer or employee who works for the segregated fund, as a contribution from the parent corporation. *Id.* § 163A-1436(g).

25. *Id.* § 163A-1436(h).

26. *Id.* § 163A-1425(a).

---

87   This looks like it could be author opinion - need to make sure she backs this claim up through the analysis.

88   How strict is this rule? Is it a total prohibition?

89   Need to read the footnotes and consult those sources carefully to ensure this summary is accurate and that the claims are completely understood.

state.[27] Once registered, the political committee is subject to several special requirements. It must:

(1) appoint a treasurer,[28]

(2) disclose the location and account information of all bank accounts and loans,[29]

(3) file periodic detailed accountings of receipts and expenditures,[30]

(4) abide by certain fundraising and expenditure limitations,[31] and

(5) not receive or solicit donations of more than $5,200 per election from any donor.[32]

— 90

Political parties, their affiliated party committees, and other committees controlled by them are exempted from many of North Carolina's campaign finance regulations.[33] Political parties are not subject to the donation cap[34] and can make contributions to or expenditures on behalf of candidates in unlimited amounts; they can also receive donations in unlimited amounts.[35] Political parties are also authorized to establish separate "headquarters building funds" to be used for the purchase and maintenance of physical office space.[36] Donations to the "building fund do

---

27. *Id.* §§ 163A-1411(74), -1418(a)(1).

28. *Id.* § 163A-1412(a).

29. *Id.* §§ 163A-1412(b)(8), -1422.

30. *See id.* § 163A-1414(a) (requiring detailed accounts current within seven days); *id.* § 163A-1418 (establishing reporting periods for various election cycles); *id.* § 163A-1422 (setting out information that must be included in periodic reports).

31. *Id.* § 163A-1425.

32. *Id.* §§ 163A-1425(a), (c). This cap is waived for the candidate and his or her spouse, who can contribute unlimited funds to the campaign. *Id.* § 163A-1425(d).

33. *Id.* § 163A-1411(76). The definition of "political committee" includes the "political party or [its] executive committee," as well as any committee controlled by it. *Id.* § 163A-1411(74)(b). This includes the state, county, and congressional district committees of each party, as well as the caucuses of each party (e.g., the Democratic Women or the Young Republicans) and the affiliated committees, (e.g., the Senate Democrats, the Republican Council of State), which are referred to collectively throughout this Comment as "political parties."

34. *Id.* § 163A-1425(h).

35. The political parties are subject to federal contribution limits. Federal Elections Campaign Act of 1971, 52 U.S.C. § 30116(a)(1)(D) (Supp. IV 2017). No person may contribute in excess of $10,000 "to a political committee established and maintained by a State committee of a political party in any calendar year." *Id.* The parties may, however, separate their finances into a federal fund and a state fund, and the state fund may accept donations above the federal donation limit. *See* 11 C.F.R. § 106.6 (2018).

36. N.C. GEN. STAT. § 163A-1438.

---

90 Why are the laws set up this way?

CAMPBELL LAW REVIEW [Vol. 40:2

not constitute contributions or expenditures" and therefore are not subject to any contribution regulations, including the ban on corporate giving.[37]

Finally, the statutes regulate a "catch-all" category of political speakers: those who engage in electoral advocacy but are not controlled by candidates or political parties—PACs. Understanding this category of regulated speakers requires a more detailed breakdown of the definition of "political committee."

The statute defines "political committee" as any combination of two or more people, business entities, or organizations "that makes . . . contributions or expenditures and has . . . the major purpose to support or oppose the nomination or election of one or more clearly identified candidates."[38] "Contribution" and "expenditure" are defined to include anything of value given to, or made in coordination with, a candidate, political committee, or political party "to support or oppose the nomination or election of one or more clearly identified candidates."[39] The phrase "to support or oppose" is a term of art, which appears throughout the statutory scheme.[40] The statute provides a list of particular words and phrases that show "an individual or other entity acted 'to support or oppose the nomination or election of one or more clearly identified candidates.'"[41]

In short, a "political committee" is a combination of individuals or entities whose major purpose is to either: (1) make contributions to candidates or political committees, (2) make expenditures that are coordinated with a candidate or political committee, or (3) engage in electoral advocacy by communicating messages to the public that, in

---

37. *Id.* The statute provides that if the party (1) establishes a "separate segregated bank account," (2) informs donors that funds will be used exclusively for the headquarters building, and (3) ensures all donations are designated for the building fund, its receipts and expenses are not deemed "contributions" or "expenditures." *Id.* §§ 163A-1438(2)–(3). Notwithstanding that exemption, the party is required to report donations to and spending by the building fund to the Board of Elections. *Id.* § 163A-1438(5).

38. *Id.* § 163A-1411(74). The statute also provides that a candidate who serves as his own treasurer, and is therefore a committee of one, is still subject to regulation as a "political committee." *Id.*

39. *Id.* § 163A-1411(13), (51). The definition of "expenditure" includes a slight variation from the language used to define "contribution." That definition encompasses "anything of value . . . to support or oppose the nomination, election, or passage of one or more clearly identified candidates, or ballot measure." *Id.* § 163A-1411(51).

40. *See id.* §§ 163A-1410 to -1505.

41. *Id.* § 163A-1429(a). The list is an adaptation of the list originally supplied by the Supreme Court in its landmark decision, *Buckley v. Valeo*, and includes "vote for," "reelect," "support," "vote against," "defeat," etc. *Id.*; Buckley v. Valeo, 424 U.S. 1, 44 n.52 (1976) (per curiam).

---

91 Seems like a very broad definition. Is it too broad? What is the purpose of regulating these groups? Is the law accomplishing that purpose?

express terms, advocate for the election or defeat of a candidate.[42] Classification as a political committee subjects the organization to each of the requirements enumerated above for candidates' political committees and means that all financial information will become public record, including the names, addresses, occupations, and employers of all supporters.[43]

The statutes provide an exception for a special subset of these committees, called independent expenditure political committees, because they "do[] not . . . make contributions, directly or indirectly, to candidates or to political committees that make contributions to candidates."[44] These special committees must adhere to all of the reporting and disclosure requirements for other political committees but are exempt from campaign contribution limits.[45] In exchange for giving up the right to make contributions to candidates or coordinate their expenditures with candidates, they can raise funds in unlimited amounts from individuals, non-profit corporations, or political parties.

An example may be helpful in illustrating the difference in the two types of political committees. Imagine a group of neighbors who want to work together to support Ben Franklin in his run for the North Carolina Senate. They could form a PAC: Citizens for Ben. This PAC would be regulated as a political committee, and the neighbors would have to comply with all of the provisions of Article 22A of the North Carolina General Statutes. If they tell Ben they plan to mail flyers that say "Vote for Ben!" to all of the scientists in his district, the money spent on the flyers would be treated as a donation to Ben because his knowledge of the mailer has value to him. It was coordinated. He now knows that he can shift campaign funds away from contacting the scientists in his district and can use those resources in other areas. This "coordinated expenditure" would have to be reported by Ben as an in-kind donation from the PAC. Because it is considered a donation, it is subject to the $5,200 contribution limitation, meaning the PAC would have to spend less than $5,200 to design, print and mail the flyer. If, however, the neighbors send the mailer without consulting Ben, the same flyer is treated as an "independent expenditure," which is by definition not a donation and therefore not subject to the

42. §§ 163A-1411(74), -1429. To satisfy this prong, the communication *must* include one of the words or phrases listed in section 163A-1429.

43. *See id.* §§ 163A-1412, -1414, -1425.

44. *Id.* § 163A-1425(j); *see also id.* § 163A-1411(13) (exempting independent expenditures from the definition of contribution); *id.* § 163A-1411(53) (defining independent expenditure). An expenditure is "independent" if it is made without coordinating with the candidate, generally without his or her direction or input. *Id.*

45. *Id.* § 163A-1425(j).

9

92 What are the implications of exempting these from contribution limits?

678   CAMPBELL LAW REVIEW   [Vol. 40:2

93 ——

contribution limit. If the neighbors decide at the outset to never collaborate with Ben or make any donations to candidates, their PAC is an "independent expenditure political action committee"—a Super PAC—that can raise and spend unlimited money for their effort.

To recap, candidates may not accept more than $5,200 from a single donor in a given election cycle and cannot accept donations from for-profit corporations. Political parties may solicit and accept unlimited donations from individuals but may only solicit or accept contributions from for-profit corporations if those funds are used solely for a "building fund." While for-profit corporations may not contribute to candidates or PACs (other than political party building funds), they may establish segregated funds to do so and may provide administrative support and staff to the segregated fund. Non-profit corporations may make contributions to candidates and other political committees. Any other group whose "major purpose" is expressly advocating for the election or defeat of a candidate must register as a political committee and comport with all attendant regulatory requirements, including the limitation on contributions. If a political committee certifies that it will not make contributions to candidates, it is exempt from the contribution limits and may raise unlimited funds from its donors.

B.   *Restrictions Imposed on the Basis of Message Content*

North Carolina also imposes restrictions based on the content of political messages.[46] Political communications can be classified along a spectrum, with "express advocacy" at one end, "issue advocacy" at the other, and the "functional equivalent" of express advocacy occupying some amount of space in the middle.[47] Messages that clearly call for a vote for or against a particular candidate are express advocacy, while those that seek to inform or persuade the public about a particular policy are issue advocacy.[48]

Early regulatory schemes classified express advocacy as those messages that used certain "magic words." The list was first formulated in the landmark *Buckley v. Valeo* decision and included words like "vote for,"

---

46. *See id.* §§ 163A-1410 to -1505.

47. *See* McConnell v. FEC, 540 U.S. 93, 126 (2003) (explaining how the sharp distinction between express and issue advocacy led to the rise of communications that eschewed the use of "magic words" while still advocating the election or defeat of a candidate), *overruled in part on other grounds by* Citizens United v. FEC, 558 U.S. 310 (2010).

48. *Id.*

---

93 This seems to leave a lot of room for abuse. Is there a way to control that?

"support," "vote against," or "defeat."[49] The use of such a finite list made it easy for political advertisers to disguise their express advocacy as issue advocacy and thereby avoid regulation.[50] Courts have come to refer to ads that skirt regulation by avoiding the listed magic words as the functional equivalent of express advocacy.[51]

For instance, the Citizens for Ben PAC might purchase advertising space on a billboard that says "Vote for Ben!" That message would be a clear example of express advocacy. A billboard that read "Ben supports fewer restrictions on kites" would lie at the other end of the spectrum and be categorized as issue advocacy. While the speaker might intend to support Ben by appealing to kiting enthusiasts, the objective purpose is to inform the public about Ben's position on kiting restrictions. But, what if the PAC ran a television ad the week before the election that showed Ben braving a storm, kite in hand, while a voiceover proclaims "Ben Franklin, the only candidate willing to brave storms to make our state better"? The language of the ad avoids the magic words but is clearly intended to support the candidate. In North Carolina, this ad would only be subject to regulation if it qualifies as an "electioneering communication"—North Carolina's analogue for the functional equivalent of express advocacy.[52]

A message is an electioneering communication under North Carolina's statute only if it:

(1) does not contain express advocacy;[53]

(2) is a broadcast, cable or satellite communication, mass mailing, or telephone bank;[54]

———————————————————————————————————— 94

---

49. Buckley v. Valeo, 424 U.S. 1, 44, n.52 (1976) (per curiam). The *Buckley* Court narrowed the application of a federal statute such that it would only apply "to communications containing express words of advocacy of election or defeat, such as 'vote for,' 'elect,' 'support,' 'cast your ballot for,' 'Smith for Congress,' 'vote against,' 'defeat,' 'reject.'" *Id.* These were quickly adopted in both federal and state law as a clear means of regulating campaign messages. *See McConnell*, 540 U.S. at 126–29.

50. *McConnell*, 540 U.S. at 126–29.

51. *Id.*; *see e.g.*, Vt. Right to Life Comm. v. Sorrell, 758 F.3d 118, 132 (2d Cir. 2014) (explaining that disclosure requirements need not "be limited to speech that is the functional equivalent of express advocacy" (quoting *Citizens United*, 558 U.S. at 369)); Nat'l Org. for Marriage v. McKee, 649 F.3d 34, 68 (1st Cir. 2011) (discussing *McConnell*'s functional equivalent test).

52. N.C. GEN. STAT. § 163A-1411(41) (2017).

53. *Id.* § 163A-1411(43)(b). "[C]ommunication[s] that constitute[] an expenditure or independent expenditure" are specifically exempted from the definition. *Id.*

54. *Id.* § 163A-1411(41). The definition identifies four modes of communication: radio, television, mass mailings, and telephone banks. *Id.* The enumeration of certain modes of communication necessarily precludes its application to others—*expressio unius est exclusio alterius*. Consequently, Internet communications are left wholly unregulated

---

94 Clear detail re: legal standard

680   CAMPBELL LAW REVIEW   [Vol. 40:2

(3) which refers to a clearly identified candidate;[55]
(4) is transmitted during the specified time period;[56]
(5) is received by the requisite number of people or households;[57] and
(6) does not fall within the list of enumerated exceptions.[58]

So, if the Citizens for Ben PAC were to run its ad on local television the week before the election, it would be regulated as an electioneering communication if it reached at least 7,500 people, despite the fact that it is not express advocacy and is not coordinated with the campaign. That same ad appearing on television in August would not be subject to regulation.

A message that is not an "electioneering communication" is regulated only if it contains words of express advocacy. When the production or distribution of such an ad is coordinated with a candidate, it is treated as a contribution to the candidate and is subject to contribution limits.[59] If the communication contains express advocacy but is not coordinated with the candidate, it is an "independent expenditure" and is not subject to contribution limits.[60] Any political message that does not contain express

---

during the electioneering window. *Id.* § 163A-1429(b)(3). In fact, the word "Internet" only appears one time in the entire chapter, in an exception to the definition of express advocacy—"a communication shall not be subject to regulation . . . if it: . . . [i]s distributed . . . through the Internet." *Id.* The definition also fails to include billboard and print media advertising and further expressly excludes telephone banks when calls are made by volunteers. *Id.* § 163A-1411(93).

55. *Id.* § 163A-1411(41)(a).
56. *Id.* § 163A-1411(41)(b).
57. *Id.* § 163A-1411(41). Advertisements for candidates for statewide office made by broadcast, cable, or satellite transmission must be received by at least 50,000 individuals to meet the requirement. *Id.* Ads distributed by mass mailing or telephone bank for candidates for statewide office must be received by 20,000 households. *Id.* Advertisements for candidates for local office transmitted by broadcast, cable, or satellite must be received by at least 7,500 individuals, or 2,500 households if distributed by mass mailing or telephone bank. *Id.*
58. *Id.* § 163A-1411(43). The statute exempts the following:
   1. News, commentary, or editorials distributed by a broadcasting station not owned by a political party, political committee or candidate;
   2. Printed news stories;
   3. Debates and promotions of debates;
   4. Ads calling on the public to lobby a representative to support or oppose specific legislation pending before the general assembly while it is in session;
   5. Commercial ads that do not mention the election and do not take a position on a candidate's character; and
   6. Public opinion polls.
Id.
59. *Id.* § 163A-1411(20); *see supra* text accompanying note 19.
60. § 163A-1411(53).

---

95 Is this a workable or fair standard? Considering reach seems reasonable. Looking at content alone may not be the fairest way to think about it because the impact of the message is just as important as the content.

advocacy and is not an "electioneering communication" is not subject to ⎯⎯⎯⎯ 96
regulation or disclosure, even if coordinated with a candidate or political
committee.[61]

C. Disclosure Requirements Imposed on Certain Speakers

The purposes of North Carolina's campaign finance statutes are
accomplished in large part through the reporting requirements. All political
committees are required to file periodic reports with the Board of
Elections.[62] These reports must include detailed information about each
receipt and expenditure.[63] The statute also imposes disclosure requirements
for anyone who makes independent expenditures that exceed $100[64] or

---

61. 30 N.C. Reg. 721 (Oct. 1, 2015) (advisory opinion of Kim Strach, Executive Director of the North Carolina State Board of Elections). The Executive Director of North Carolina's State Board of Elections confirmed that entities other than political committees can coordinate issue advocacy with candidates, provided that those communications do not constitute electioneering communications. Id. "[P]ayments for those communications cannot be deemed 'coordinated expenditures' or 'contributions.'" Id. at 722. Because the request for the opinion was limited to organizations that are not political committees, the opinion was also limited. Id. There is, however, no reason to believe the same opinion would not apply to political committees or individuals when they engage in activity that constitutes only the coordination of issue advocacy. Id.; see also Tom Bullock, Open the Floodgates? NC Political Candidates, Outside Groups Can Coordinate, WFAE (Nov. 27, 2015), https://perma.cc/R9FL-2377.

62. § 163A-1418. The frequency of reports varies depending on whether the filing is done in the year of the general election or in the year of the municipal elections. Id. Certain candidates are required to file reports with County Boards of Election rather than the State Board of Elections. Id. §§ 163A-1495 to -1500. Candidates for certain offices who certify they will not raise or spend more than $1,000 are exempt from reporting requirements. Id. § 163A-1421. The statute further provides that "[t]he exemption . . . applies to political party committees and affiliated party committees under the same terms as for candidates." Id. § 163A-1421(b).

63. Id. § 163A-1422(a). The statute requires that the report identify the name, address, profession, and employer of each contributor, as well as the date and amount of the donation. Id. § 163A-1422(a)(1). Additionally, the report must include the name and address of the payee and purpose of each expenditure, as well as the amount and date that the expense was paid or incurred. Id. § 163A-1422(a)(2). For donations under fifty dollars, there is no requirement to disclose the name, address, and occupation of the donor. Id. § 163A-1422(b).

64. Id. § 163A-1423(a). The report is due within thirty days of the date it surpasses the $100 threshold or ten days before the election, whichever first occurs. Id. § 163A-1423(d). Once the initial report is filed, subsequent reports must be filed according to the schedule for political committees. Id. § 163A-1423(e). Expenditures of more than $5,000 made between the last required filing and election day must be disclosed within forty-eight hours. Id.

---

96 This is the loophole.

spends more than $5,000 for the production or airing of electioneering communications.[65]

Electioneering communication reports must include significantly more information than independent expenditures reports.[66] The electioneering communication report must, in addition to disclosing the amount paid and to whom, disclose the filer's principal place of business and identify who incurred the expense, who directs the activities of the filer, and who keeps the books and accounts.[67] Additionally, the disclosure must include the name of any candidate(s) identified in the communication and the election to which it pertains.[68] Finally, it must identify anyone who donated more than $1,000 to further the electioneering communication.[69]

Whether a particular expenditure must be disclosed depends on the identity of the purchaser, the content of the message, and whether that message is coordinated with a candidate or political committee. The following table helps summarize these different reporting requirements for expenditures by different speakers for various types of messages:

---

65. *Id.* § 163A-1424.
66. *See id.* § 163A-1424(a).
67. *Id.* §§ 163A-1424(a)(1)–(3).
68. *Id.* § 163A-1424(a)(4).
69. *Id.* § 163A-1424(a)(5).

2018]   PATCH BY PATCH   683

	Express Advocacy		Issue Advocacy	
	Coordinated	Independent	Coordinated	Electioneering Communication
Non-political speakers	Reported as donation	One-time disclosure report	Unreported	One-time disclosure
Party	Reported as donation	███	Required periodic filing	Required periodic filing
Candidate	Reported as donation	███	Required periodic filing	Required periodic filing
Non-Major Purpose PAC	Reported as donation	One-time disclosure report	Unreported	One-time disclosure
Major-Purpose PAC	Reported as donation	Required periodic filing	Required periodic filing	Required periodic filing
Super PAC	Prohibited	Required periodic filing	Unreported	Required periodic filing

These disclosures are accomplished through a dizzying array of forms.[70] A complete periodic disclosure filing can sometimes comprise nearly a dozen separate forms. The cover sheet has its own form.[71] The reconciliation page is a separate form.[72] Contributions from individuals are

---

70. *Required NC Campaign Reporting Forms*, N.C. ST. BOARD OF ELECTIONS & ETHICS ENFORCEMENT, https://perma.cc/ESD2-TP27. Forms are available in both PDF and Microsoft Word format. *See id.* Notably, the forms do not make use of either software's ability to incorporate mathematical functions to eliminate the risk of human mathematical errors. As an example of a reporting form that does make use of such mathematical functions, see Form AOC-E-506, created by the Administrative Office of the Courts for use in estate accountings. *Account*, AOC, https://perma.cc/Y8TF-BDYF.

71. *Disclosure Report Cover*, N.C. ST. BOARD OF ELECTIONS, https://perma.cc/WMD5-J7XE.

72. *Detailed Summary*, N.C. ST. BOARD OF ELECTIONS, https://perma.cc/P37K-U26S.

97 Why is this blacked out?

684   CAMPBELL LAW REVIEW   [Vol. 40:2

reported on a different form than contributions from another campaign committee, as are contributions from political parties.[73] In-kind contributions are reported separately from cash contributions.[74] Loans obtained, repaid, and forgiven each require separate forms.[75] Every form must be independently totaled and reconciled by hand. It is possible to submit a report whose receipts and expenditures do not balance with the committee's reported cash on hand.[76] No verifying information is required unless the committee is selected for an audit. All of this complexity in reporting serves to undermine the government's efforts to ensure that its campaign finance laws are being followed and that voters are being provided with accurate information about the funding of campaigns.

The efficacy of this disclosure system is further undermined by the fact that it is decentralized. Candidates for local races file their reports with county boards of election rather than with the State Board of Elections, meaning that there are 101 separate repositories of campaign finance data in the state.[77] What's more, there is no vertical integration of that data. Campaign finance reports filed at the county level stay there.[78] The data is not forwarded to the State Board of Elections to be included in its existing, searchable database. The result is that a voter who wants access to the complete campaign contribution information for a given PAC or individual would need to separately search all 101 repositories—a cumbersome process that virtually prevents the free flow of information that the law seeks to put in the hands of the electorate.

---

73. *Contributions from Individuals*, N.C. ST. BOARD OF ELECTIONS, https://perma.cc/R6QJ-EPL9; *Contributions from Political Party Committees*, N.C. ST. BOARD OF ELECTIONS, https://perma.cc/CK5C-5KZQ; *Contributions from Other Political Committees*, N.C. ST. BOARD OF ELECTIONS, https://perma.cc/T889-KUWC.

74. *In-Kind Contributions*, N.C. ST. BOARD OF ELECTIONS, https://perma.cc/BX4E-M7Z8.

75. *Loan Proceeds*, N.C. ST. BOARD OF ELECTIONS, https://perma.cc/F25M-YR33; *Loan Repayments*, N.C. ST. BOARD OF ELECTIONS, https://perma.cc/6F36-M7YL; *Forgiven Loans*, N.C. ST. BOARD OF ELECTIONS, https://perma.cc/P48M-UQ3E.

76. *See supra* note 70 for a discussion of the lack of mathematical functions in the State Board of Election's computerized forms.

77. *See* N.C. GEN. STAT. §§ 163A-1495 to -1500 (2017); *see also supra* text accompanying note 62 discussing the disclosure and filing requirements for candidates for local offices.

78. *See, e.g.*, Bd. of Elections, *Campaign Finance Reports*, WAKEGOV, http://www.wakegov.com/elections/candidates/pages/reports.aspx [https://perma.cc/E9ZE-6CB2] (last updated Jan. 19, 2018).

---

98 This process seems quite cumbersome. What are the consequences of non-compliance? Are individuals held accountable in the same way that corporations or other experts in the field would be?

D. The Danger of Noncompliance

Compliance with the statutory and regulatory framework is compelled under penalty of both civil and criminal punishment. Any filing submitted late or without required information is subject to fines of $250 per day, up to a total of $10,000.[79] The board is also authorized to assess civil penalties against any person who accepts a contribution or makes an expenditure in violation of the law.[80] Before assessing such a penalty, the board is required to "notify and consult with the district attorney" about possible criminal prosecution for the violation.[81]

— 99

Intentional violations of benign provisions of the scheme are punishable as Class 2 misdemeanors, while offenses that more directly impede the ability of the Board of Elections to trace the flow of money are punishable as felonies.[82] So, intentionally failing to appoint a treasurer or report the closure of the campaign committee is a Class 2 misdemeanor.[83] Knowingly reporting false information to the Board of Elections is a Class I felony,[84] as is intentionally accepting anonymous contributions or contributions from for-profit corporations.[85]

These intentional or knowing violations of the law are appropriately punished with criminal sanctions. But, can the same be said of violations that are neither intentional nor knowing? The statute provides that the Board of Elections "*shall*" report any violation to the appropriate district attorney who "*shall*" prosecute the violation.[86] The statute does not appear to provide for the exercise of discretion on the part of the Board of Elections or the district attorney, and there is no *mens rea* requirement.[87]

— 100

The product of this incredibly intricate system, stitched together by legislators, regulators, and the courts, is not an electoral system free from the influence of big donors; it is an electoral system that silences everyday

---

79. § 160A-1451(a). The statute provides for civil penalties in the amount of $250 per day for statewide races or $50 per day for any other race. *Id.* The Board of Elections is given the authority to "waive a late penalty if it determines there is good cause for the waiver." *Id.*

80. *Id.* § 160A-1451(b).

81. *Id.* § 160A-1451(f).

82. *Id.* §§ 160A-1445(a)–(c).

83. *Id.* § 160A-1445(a).

84. *Id.* § 160A-1445(b).

85. *Id.* § 160A-1445(c).

86. *Id.* §§ 160A-1445(d)–(e) (emphasis added). If the district attorney has not initiated a prosecution within forty-five days, any voter in the district may petition the court for appointment of a special prosecutor to investigate and prosecute the allegation. *Id.* § 160A-1446(b).

87. *See id.* § 160A-1445.

---

99 How often are crimes prosecuted?   100 Is there a constitutionality argument here because of the lack of *mens rea* requirement?

686   CAMPBELL LAW REVIEW   [Vol. 40:2

citizens who are unwilling to risk criminal punishment to participate in a
system they do not fully understand, while leaving them without adequate
information about the origins of campaign cash flowing through the state.

II. *NORTH CAROLINA RIGHT TO LIFE, INC. V. LEAKE*: DEFICIENCIES IN THE
FOURTH CIRCUIT'S ANALYSIS

As written, North Carolina's campaign finance laws impose
significant burdens on political speech without accomplishing the
government's goals of limiting corruption and preventing circumvention of
the laws. Both the statutes and the disclosure system need to be pulled into
the twenty-first century. When such changes are made, they are likely to
face legal challenges. Unfortunately, the legal framework established by
the Fourth Circuit Court of Appeals' decision in *North Carolina Right to
Life, Inc. v. Leake (NCRL III)*[88] is fraught with errors that would inhibit an
effective judicial review.

A.   *The Challenges Brought by North Carolina Right to Life, Inc.*

The sweeping decision was handed down by the Fourth Circuit after a
non-profit organization and its affiliated PACs brought facial and as-
applied challenges to a number of North Carolina's campaign finance
statutes.[89] The organizations argued they should not come within the ambit
of the law because their activities were not regulable.[90]

North Carolina Right to Life, Inc. (NCRL) asserted that it was not a
political committee and challenged the definition of "political committee"
on two bases.   First, it alleged the definition was vague because it
incorporated a subjective test that employed contextual factors open to a
broad range of interpretations.[91]   Second, NCRL alleged the definition was
overbroad and would impose regulations on "organizations not primarily
focused on nominating and electing political candidates"[92] because the
definition applied to organizations that had electioneering as "*a* major
purpose" rather than as "*the* major purpose."[93]   The court agreed and held
both provisions facially unconstitutional.[94]

---

88. *NCRL III*, 525 F.3d 274 (4th Cir. 2008).
89. *Id.* at 278–79.
90. *Id.*
91. *Id.* at 281.
92. *Id.* at 279.
93. *Id.* at 286–87.
94. *Id.* at 308.

---

101 Marketplace is effectively excluding certain voices.

102 Read the opinion to ensure full understanding of court's
rationale.

The court's analysis was flawed. It failed to identify any sufficiently important governmental interest, articulate a standard of review, or analyze the burdens on unregulated speech. It chose instead to read the Supreme Court's narrowing constructions of federal statutes as bright-line tests to be applied to all campaign finance regulations.[95] Judge Michael's dissenting opinion was sharply critical of this approach and correctly noted that the court employed the tests without properly balancing the burden imposed by the law against the strength of the government's interest.[96]   — 103

B.   *Failure to Articulate the Standard of Scrutiny*

Departing from the familiar structure of constitutional analysis, the court did not begin by identifying the burden imposed by the regulation on free speech—whether the definition was used to restrict expenditures or contributions or to require disclosures. Because it did not begin by identifying the burden, it also failed to articulate the applicable standard of — 104 scrutiny. This failure set the court on a course that avoided the typical balancing of the government's interest and the burden on speech and instead proceeded with application of bright-line tests.

A proper review would have begun by identifying that the definition of "political committee" imposed both disclosure requirements (compelling the speaker to divulge information that would otherwise be kept private) and contribution limits (which constrain expressive association). The former is subject to exacting judicial scrutiny while the latter is subject to heightened scrutiny.[97]   While the court agreed that the state had an

95 *Id.* at 282–83 (stating tests for the constitutional boundary of legislation in the realm of campaign finance).

96 *Id.* at 316 (Michael, J., dissenting) (criticizing the majority's adoption of "test[s] without . . . a proper overbreadth analysis [which] considers the burden on First Amendment rights as balanced against the strength of the governmental interest"). The majority responded, "According to the dissent, the burdens imposed on political speech and the state's interests may vary by the type of regulation. . . . The dissent would thus have us uphold [the law] in full and wait to consider the constitutionality of each of its applications in an as-applied fashion." *Id.* at 299–300 (majority opinion). The majority mischaracterized the dissent's position, which was that the court "must examine the degree to which the regulation burdens First Amendment rights and evaluate whether the governmental interests are sufficient to justify that burden." *Id.* at 310 (Michael, J., dissenting).

97 Citizens United v. FEC, 558 U.S. 310, 366–67 (2010). "Disclaimer and disclosure requirements may burden the ability to speak, but they 'impose no ceiling on campaign-related activities' and 'do not prevent anyone from speaking.'" *Id.* at 366 (internal citation omitted) (first quoting Buckley v. Valeo, 424 U.S. 1, 64 (1976) (per curiam); then quoting McConnell v. FEC, 540 U.S. 93, 201 (2003), *overruled in part on other grounds by Citizens United*, 558 U.S. 310). The requirements are therefore subject "to 'exacting scrutiny,' which requires a 'substantial relation' between the disclosure requirement and a 'sufficiently

103 Is this accurate? When reading the opinion, can the important governmental interest be discerned?

104 Good detail on how author believes the court's analysis got off track.

"important governmental interest" in "limit[ing] the actuality and appearance of corruption," it did not take the next step to determine whether the statutes were either closely drawn to achieve that interest or at least bore a substantial relation to it.[98] The result following the opinion was considerable confusion as to what level of scrutiny should be applied in such cases within the circuit.[99]

The court should have framed the questions at issue as: (1) whether the definition of political committee, when used to impose contribution limits, was closely drawn to achieve the substantially important governmental interest of preventing corruption or the appearance of corruption, and (2) whether the definition, when used only to determine who must register and file disclosures, bore a substantial relation to the government's interest in providing information to the electorate and preventing the circumvention of the law.

The court's overbreadth and vagueness analysis should then have been framed within that context. Rather than proceeding through this type of constitutional analysis, the court favored application of bright-line tests when reviewing the statute's definition of express advocacy and its use of a "major purpose" test.

C. Erroneously Applying a Bright-Line Test to the Definition of Express Advocacy

Classification as a "political committee" under the law was premised on an organization engaging in express advocacy.[100] Consequently, the court began by reviewing the state's attempt to define express advocacy through the use of contextual factors.[101] The definition at the time provided that when a communication's "essential nature" was unclear, regulators could consider contextual factors like the language, timing, distribution, and cost of the ad to determine "whether the action urged could only be

---

important' governmental interest." *Id.* at 366–67 (citing *Buckley*, 424 U.S. at 64, 66). "When the Government burdens the right to contribute, we apply heightened scrutiny," which is met when the government demonstrates that the statute is "'closely drawn' to match a 'sufficiently important interest.'" *McConnell*, 540 U.S. at 231–32 (quoting FEC v. Beaumont, 539 U.S. 146, 162 (2003)).

98. *NCRL III*, 525 F.3d at 281 (alteration in original) (quoting *Buckley*, 424 U.S. at 26).

99. Hillary Kies, Note, Preston v. Leake: *Applying the Appropriate Standard of Review to North Carolina's Campaign Contributions Ban*, 47 WAKE FOREST L. REV. 875, 886–87 (2012).

100. N.C. GEN. STAT. § 163-278.14A (2007) (amended and transferred to § 163A-1429 (2017)); *see supra* discussion in Section I.B.

101. *NCRL III*, 525 F.3d at 283. North Carolina's "context prong" allowed for a communication to be evaluated in light of its timing, content, reach, and cost. *Id.* at 283–84.

---

105 The court defined the question incorrectly—do I agree?

106 Why is the new frame superior to the one the court used? Did the court take the easy way out?

interpreted by a reasonable person as advocating the nomination, election, or defeat of that candidate."[102]

The court held that the statute was facially unconstitutional not because it was overbroad in light of the government's interests but because it did not match *exactly* the FEC's definition of "electioneering communication."[103]   That definition had recently been upheld by the Supreme Court in *FEC v. Wisconsin Right to Life, Inc. (WRTL II)*.[104]   The *WRTL II* Court considered an as-applied challenge to a federal regulation that prohibited corporations from producing electioneering communications.[105]   The plaintiffs in that case had run a television ad that urged voters to "[c]ontact Senators Feingold and Kohl and tell them to oppose the filibuster" of several judicial nominees.[106]   The ad was aired within thirty days of the election and therefore fell within the ambit of a federal law that regulated "electioneering communications."[107]   The Court determined that the purpose of the statute was to regulate communications that were the functional equivalent of express advocacy, those that were "susceptible of no reasonable interpretation other than as an appeal to vote for or against a specific candidate."[108]   The Court held that the ads produced by the plaintiff were not the "functional equivalent of express advocacy" within the meaning of the statute and that the statute had been improperly applied to those communications.[109]

In reaching this conclusion, the Court, in dicta, stressed that while courts may consider background information "to put an ad in context," they should avoid using "contextual factors" in the judicial inquiry to ensure that such challenges do not "become an excuse for discovery or a broader inquiry."[110]   The Court was not suggesting that it would be unconstitutional

---

102. § 163-278.14A(a)(2) (2007).
103. *NCRL III*, 525 F.3d at 290.
104. FEC v. Wis. Right to Life, Inc. *(WRTL II)*, 551 U.S. 449 (2007).
105. *Id.* at 455–56.
106. *Id.* at 458–59.
107. *Id.* at 460.
108. *Id.* at 469–70.
109. *Id.* at 470. The Court determined that the ads were issue ads, not express advocacy or its functional equivalent, because they "focus[ed] on a legislative issue, t[ook] a position on the issue, exhort[ed] the public to adopt that position, and urge[d] the public to contact public officials with respect to the matter" but "d[id] not mention an election, candidacy, political party, or challenger" or "take a position on a candidate's character, qualifications, or fitness for office." *Id.*
110. *Id.* at 473–74. The Court indicated it would be permissible for courts to consider, for instance, whether the ad "describes a legislative issue" currently being or likely to soon be considered by the legislature. *Id.* at 474 (quoting Wis. Right to Life, Inc. v. FEC *(WRTL I)*, 466 F. Supp. 2d 195, 207 (D.D.C. 2006)). However, the Court indicated that, when

107 So did the court basically assume that any definition not precisely matching would be unconsitutional?

108 But why shouldn't there be a broader inquiry?

690   CAMPBELL LAW REVIEW   [Vol. 40:2

for legislatures to define the functional equivalent of express advocacy using such factors. Rather, courts asked to determine whether an ad constituted the functional equivalent of express advocacy should avoid imposing such factors because consideration of such factors was unnecessary in light of the regulation's very clear definition.[111]

The Fourth Circuit relied on the *WRTL II* decision and articulated a new two-pronged test for determining whether a communication was the "functional equivalent of express advocacy," notwithstanding the legislature's own definition. The court held that the state may regulate communications as the functional equivalent of express advocacy only if such communications: (1) "qualify as an 'electioneering communication,' defined by the Bipartisan Campaign Reform Act of 2002 ('BCRA') as a 'broadcast, cable, or satellite communication' that refers to a 'clearly identified candidate' within sixty days of a general election or thirty days of a primary election," [112] and (2) are "only . . . susceptible of no reasonable interpretation other than as an appeal to vote for or against a specific candidate."[113]

The court applied its newly articulated test and struck North Carolina's definition as vague and overbroad on its face because it relied on contextual factors and did not exactly match the definition laid out in the federal regulations.[114]

This interpretation—that a statutory functional equivalent test must not contain subjective factors—is at odds with other courts that have upheld the use of contextual factors in similar statutory tests, and in some cases even supplied them.[115] For instance, the Vermont Supreme Court upheld that state's expansive definition of electioneering communications by supplying a narrowing construction that allowed consideration of

---

considering an as-applied challenge, the inquiry should not revolve around other contextual factors such as the amount of money spent on the production of an ad, the number of times the ad was aired, or specific dates on which it was aired because such inquiry would lead to more protracted litigation. *Id.* at 473–74.

111. *Id.*

112. *NCRL III*, 525 F.3d 274, 282 (4th Cir. 2008) (internal citation omitted) (citing *WRTL II*, 551 U.S. at 474 n.7). The court interpreted the footnote as "stating that a communication must meet the 'brightline requirements' of the [federal regulation's] definition of 'electioneering communication' to be regulable as the 'functional equivalent of express advocacy.'" *Id.* (quoting *WRTL II*, 551 U.S. at 474 n.7).

113. *Id.* (quoting *WRTL II*, 551 U.S. at 469–70).

114. *Id.* at 284–85.

115. Vt. Right to Life Comm. v. Sorrell, 758 F.3d 118, 135, 139 (2d Cir. 2014) (adopting the narrowing construction supplied by the Vermont Supreme Court and upholding the definition against vagueness and overbreadth challenges).

---

109   Should they really be exclusive?

110   Did the court explain where this test came from?

111   Are there any courts that are consistent? Is Vermont the only example?

2018]   PATCH BY PATCH   691

contextual factors almost identical to those struck down in *NCRL III*.[116]
The Vermont court held that "the objective observer should look to
multiple factors: for example, the timing . . . , the images used . . . , the tone
. . . , the audience to which the advertisement is targeted, and the
prominence of the issue(s) discussed."[117] If the conclusion of the objective
observer is "that the purpose of an advertisement is to influence voters to
vote yes or no on a candidate," the communication is constitutionally
regulable as the functional equivalent of express advocacy.[118] The Seventh
Circuit Court of Appeals similarly upheld a provision of Illinois's
campaign finance regulations specifically *because* it was limited by the
same five criteria: medium, cost, timing, distribution, and content.[119]

The dissent in *NCRL III* rightly noted that the language of *WRTL II*
was not intended to create a bright-line test to which all such regulations
must conform.[120] Rather, it affirmed the application of a regulation that set
out sufficiently precise boundaries to achieve the government's interest
without burdening speech that did not need to be regulated to achieve that
interest.[121] The *WRTL II* Court did not articulate a constitutional standard
beyond which the government dare not regulate. Rather, it reaffirmed that
the government's definition was sufficiently precise to withstand strict
scrutiny when applied to express advocacy or its functional equivalent.[122]
The court then applied the definition to determine that the plaintiff's ads
were neither express advocacy nor its functional equivalent and that the
regulation had been improperly applied to those "issue" ads.[123] The result
was that the application of the law was found unconstitutional, not that the
law itself was unconstitutional.[124] And the Court certainly did not go so far
as to say that the federal regulation was the *only* constitutional means of
regulating ads that are the functional equivalent of express advocacy.

Application of this new bright-line standard in the Fourth Circuit was
unwieldy for the district courts. Only three years later in a similar

---

116. State v. Green Mountain Future, 86 A.3d 981, 998 (Vt. 2013).
117. *Id.*
118. *Id.*
119. Ctr. for Individual Freedom v. Madigan, 697 F.3d 464, 485 (7th Cir. 2012); *see also* Yamada v. Snipes, 786 F.3d 1182 (9th Cir. 2015) (holding that failure to include a temporal limit or exclude print media did not render a statute unconstitutionally overbroad).
120. *NCRL III*, 525 F.3d 274, 323 (4th Cir. 2008) (Michael, J., dissenting).
121. *Id.* at 316 (Michael, J., dissenting) ("The majority clearly err[ed] by mandating the elements of [the federal law], which [was] simply an *example* of a clear and sufficiently tailored statute, as an essential part of any campaign regulation.").
122. *WRTL II*, 551 U.S. 449, 465 (2007).
123. *Id.* at 481.
124. *Id.*

112 There are other courts consistent with the Vermont ruling. Why is this the better approach?

113 In other words,, the NC court erroneously assumed that there was only one constitutional way of regulating ads?

challenge, the Fourth Circuit abandoned the test it had articulated in *NCRL III*, holding that a state may regulate any communication that "is susceptible of no reasonable interpretation other than as an appeal to vote for or against a specific candidate."[125]

The court also overturned a district court decision the following year where that court had applied exactly the test articulated in *NCRL III*.[126] But the damage to North Carolina's campaign finance regulations had already been done. Using the *WRTL II* decision as a bright-line test steered the court away from a proper constitutional analysis and struck what was likely a perfectly legitimate regulation of the functional equivalent of express advocacy.

D. *Erroneously Applying* Buckley*'s "Major Purpose" Language as a Test*

The court also erred when it applied the language of *Buckley v. Valeo*[127] to North Carolina's "major purpose" test. NCRL asserted that the definition of "political committee" was unconstitutionally overbroad because it subjected organizations to regulation even when express advocacy was among several "major purposes" rather than the *sole* major purpose.[128] NCRL argued that *Buckley* permitted only "the regulation of entities that have *the* major purpose of supporting or opposing a candidate."[129]

The court agreed and interpreted *Buckley* as mandating that campaign finance laws could reach "only entities 'under the control of a candidate or *the* major purpose of which is the nomination or election of a candidate.'"[130] But this interpretation was in error. The *Buckley* Court

---

125. Real Truth About Abortion, Inc. v. FEC, 681 F.3d 544, 551 (4th Cir. 2012) (quoting *WRTL II*, 551 U.S. at 470) (reversing a lower court decision that applied the *NCRL III* test to hold an FEC regulation unconstitutionally vague and overbroad).

126. Ctr. for Individual Freedom, Inc. v. Tennant, 706 F.3d 270, 281 (4th Cir. 2013) (reversing the Southern District of West Virginia, which held West Virginia's definition of express advocacy was unconstitutionally overbroad because it failed the *NCRL III* test, and instead applying the "appeal to vote" test). The district court in *Tennant* held that, under the "appeal to vote" test, a statute would come "within the confines of the BCRA's 'electioneering communication' definition" and "survive vagueness challenges only when [it] reach[ed] communications that (1) are disseminated via cable, broadcast, or satellite; (2) refer to a clearly identified candidate; (3) are disseminated within certain time periods before an election; and (4) are directed at the relevant electorate." *Id.* at 280.

127. Buckley v. Valeo, 424 U.S. 1 (1976) (per curiam).

128. *NCRL III*, 525 F.3d 282, 287–88 (4th Cir. 2008).

129. *Id.* at 287.

130. *Id.*

---

114 So many acronyms can get confusing. Need to map out the rationale to ensure accurate understanding of which cases support which arguments.

only narrowed the scope of the federal regulation before it.[131] It did not hold that the Constitution erected a boundary there. Rather, it held that the federal law's definition of "political committee" only needed to encompass those "major purpose" organizations to fulfill the purposes of the law.[132] ————— 115

When Vermont Right to Life Committee attempted to make the same argument in a challenge to Vermont's campaign finance law, it was soundly rejected by the Second Circuit, which stated: "When the *Buckley* Court construed the relevant federal statute to reach only groups having 'the major purpose' of electing a candidate, it was drawing a statutory line. ————— 116
It was not holding that the Constitution forbade any regulations from going further."[133] Much like its application of a bright-line test to the definition of express advocacy, the application of *Buckley* as a bright-line test allowed the court to skip over the significant and meaningful constitutional analysis it should have undertaken.

E. Failure to Distinguish Fourteenth Amendment Vagueness

Finally, the court failed to analyze the separate vagueness issues raised under the First and Fourteenth Amendments, instead lumping them together in one "overbreadth and vagueness" analysis.[134] When a statute is challenged for overbreadth under the First Amendment and for vagueness under both the First and Fourteenth Amendments, the three doctrines are sometimes applied together to determine whether protected speech is "chilled"; that is, whether an average person, faced with a potentially sweeping, difficult-to-interpret statute, which *may* be applied against him,

---

131. *Buckley*, 424 U.S. at 79–80.

132. *Id.*

133. Vt. Right to Life Comm. v. Sorrell, 758 F.3d 118, 136 (2d Cir. 2014) (internal citation omitted). The Fourth and Tenth Circuits are the only two circuit courts to decide otherwise in the wake of *McConnell*, perhaps because the sweeping decision, issued by a fractured Supreme Court, fundamentally changed the understanding of the *Buckley* holding. *Compare* Yamada v. Snipes, 786 F.3d 1182, 1200 (9th Cir. 2015) (upholding a Hawaiian statute that applied to any organization with "the purpose" of influencing an election), Ctr. for Individual Freedom v. Madigan, 697 F.3d 464, 487–88 (7th Cir. 2012) (declining to strike Illinois statute which did not include "the major purpose" test), *and* Nat'l Org. for Marriage v. McKee, 649 F.3d 34, 59 (1st Cir. 2011) (upholding a statute which regulated "non-major purpose" organizations which spent or received more than $5,000 per year for the purpose of influencing an election), *with* N.M. Youth Organized v. Herrera, 611 F.3d 669, 677–78 (10th Cir. 2010) (invalidating New Mexico's disclosure law because it regulated beyond the bounds of the "major purpose" test).

134. *NCRL III*, 525 F.3d at 283–84 (holding contextual factors were "clearly 'susceptible' to multiple interpretations" and "provide[d] neither fair warning to speakers . . . nor sufficient direction to regulators as to what constitute[d] political speech").

---

115 Need to read *Buckley*. 116 Was the court just being lazy, or was it making a political statement?

694   CAMPBELL LAW REVIEW   [Vol. 40:2

might simply choose not to speak.[135] But the combined analysis, as undertaken by the *NCRL* court, leads to confusion. It is difficult to determine which doctrine was really at the heart of the statute's constitutional infirmity.

North Carolina's definition of express advocacy was an attempt to avoid invalidation under the Fourteenth Amendment's vagueness doctrine. The statute employed the phrase "to support or oppose the nomination or election" to delineate when a thing of value is a "contribution" or "expenditure" within the ambit of the statute.[136] It could simply have left the statute at that, allowing the reader to interpret what "to support or oppose" might mean, but it went further, providing a definition of evidence that would indicate an expenditure was indeed made to support or oppose a candidate. It did so by incorporating a modified version of *Buckley*'s magic-words test and employing an alternative, context-based test.[137]

The Supreme Court, faced with interpreting a similar definition in *McConnell v. FEC*, held that words such as "support," "oppose," "promote," and "attack" are sufficiently clear, are not vague, and need no further explication for the statute to be valid.[138] It is difficult to reconcile the Fourth Circuit's assertion that the legislature's extra step of providing clarifying language somehow made the phrase "to support or oppose" more vague than the phrases considered by the Supreme Court in *McConnell*. Perhaps it is because the court decided, without articulating, that those words were vague under the First Amendment, not the Fourteenth. The court decided not that the words themselves were ambiguous and capable of multiple understandings or definitions but that they allowed for a regulator to exercise an impermissible level of discretion in determining when the statute should be applied and when it should not.[139]

---

135. *Madigan*, 697 F.3d at 479 (citing Erznoznik v. City of Jacksonville, 422 U.S. 205, 216 (1975)) (reasoning that even in the context of a First Amendment challenge, "the potential chilling effect on protected expression must be both 'real and substantial' to invalidate a statute as void for vagueness in a facial challenge").

136. N.C. GEN. STAT. §§ 163A-1411, -1429 (2017); *see supra* discussion accompanying notes 39–41.

137. § 163-278.14A (2007) (amended and transferred to § 163A-1429 (2017)).

138. McConnell v. FEC, 540 U.S. 93, 170 n.64 (2003), *overruled in part on other grounds by* Citizens United v. FEC, 558 U.S. 310 (2010). Other districts interpreting similar provisions following *McConnell* have upheld statutes against vagueness challenges. *See Yamada*, 786 F.3d at 1193–94; *Vt. Right to Life Comm.*, 758 F.3d at 128–30; Ctr. for Individual Freedom v. Tennant, 706 F.3d 270, 286–87 (4th Cir. 2013); *Madigan*, 697 F.3d at 485–86; *McKee*, 649 F.3d at 64.

139. *NCRL III*, 525 F.3d at 283.

---

117 Need to verify this purported purpose is supported by the legislative record.

118 Logical conclusion—how can clarifying language make something more vague?

2018]   PATCH BY PATCH   695

F. The Need to Abandon the Precedent

At the time of the NCRL challenge, North Carolina's statute had a clear definition used to distinguish entities engaged in electoral advocacy from entities engaged in issue advocacy.[140] The statute employed a two-prong test that captured entities engaged in express advocacy as well as those who might resort to the functional equivalent of express advocacy to — 119 skirt the law.[141] In its review of the statute, the Fourth Circuit failed to follow a proper constitutional analysis.[142] It did not articulate the standard of scrutiny.[143] It improperly adopted the federal government's definition of "electioneering communication" as a judicial test.[144] It misinterpreted the *Buckley* Court's narrowing construction as creating another bright-line "major purpose" test to which all statutes should conform.[145] Had the court properly identified the burden, applied the correct standard of scrutiny, and balanced the burden on protected political speech against the government's interest in regulating campaign finance, it might well have found that the statute was, in fact, constitutional on its face.

This flawed analysis left tremendous confusion in its wake. District courts bound by the precedent were forced to apply the bright-line BCRA test, as well as the "major purpose" test.[146] And, even though the Fourth Circuit reversed those decisions, it did so without overruling *NCRL III*. As a result, the decision remains binding precedent for future challenges to North Carolina's campaign finance regulations. But, stare decisis does not — 120 require that the court continue to blindly follow improperly reasoned precedent. Just as a row of stitches must sometimes be ripped out to create a proper seam, the Fourth Circuit's *NCRL III* decision should be ripped from the circuit's jurisprudence and replaced with a proper constitutional analysis.

---

140. § 163-278.14A (2007) (amended and transferred to § 163A-1429 (2017)).
141. *Id.*
142. See discussion of Judge Michael's dissent at *supra* note 96.
143. *NCRL III*, 525 F.3d at 310–11 (Michael, J., dissenting).
144. *Id.* at 315.
145. *Id.*
146. Real Truth About Obama, Inc. v. FEC, 796 F. Supp. 2d 736 (E.D. Va. 2011), *aff'd sub nom.* Real Truth About Abortion, Inc. v. FEC, 681 F.3d 544 (4th Cir. 2012); Ctr. for Individual Freedom, Inc. v. Ireland, 613 F. Supp. 2d 777 (S.D. W. Va. 2009), *aff'd in part, rev'd in part sub nom.* Ctr. for Individual Freedom, Inc. v. Tennant, 706 F. 3d 270 (4th Cir. 2013).

---

119 How did the court get it so wrong?   120 Until it is overruled, what should other courts do?

696   CAMPBELL LAW REVIEW   [Vol. 40:2

III. FRAMEWORK FOR A COMPLETE CONSTITUTIONAL REVIEW

Future challenges to North Carolina's statutes are inevitable. Even if the legislature doesn't act to update the outdated statutes and outmoded regulations, the statutory scheme remains susceptible to a constitutional challenge. The Supreme Court's decision in *Citizens United* left unresolved the question of whether a statute that discriminates on the basis of the speaker's identity (for instance, by prohibiting contributions to candidates by for-profit corporations) would survive challenges under the First or Fourteenth Amendments.[147] This Part will provide a suggested framework for the court to use in the event it is asked to evaluate one or more components of North Carolina's statutory scheme in the future, rather than employing the tests articulated in *NCRL III*.[148]

A. Selecting the Appropriate Constitutional Balancing Test

The court must begin by identifying the type of burden placed on speech in order to apply the appropriate level of review in its analysis. Campaign finance regulations typically break into three familiar categories: (1) those that directly limit speech and expressive conduct by imposing limits on expenditures;[149] (2) those that regulate expressive association and

---

147. Citizens United v. FEC, 558 U.S. 310, 364–65 (2010) (holding "[t]he First Amendment does not permit Congress to . . . suppress political speech on the basis of the speaker's corporate identity"); *see also, e.g.*, Minn. Citizens Concerned for Life, Inc. v. Swanson, 692 F.3d 864, 879 n.12 (8th Cir. 2012) (noting "*Citizens United*'s outright rejection of the government's anti-distortion rationale, as well as the Court's admonition 'that the State cannot exact as the price of [state-conferred corporate] advantages the forfeiture of First Amendment rights'" (alteration in original) (internal citation omitted) (quoting *Citizens United*, 558 U.S. at 351)).

148. While it is beyond the scope of this Comment to fully discuss justiciability concerns, it is worth noting differences recognized in campaign finance challenges. For instance, a plaintiff who can show it has self-censored its speech may have standing even though a statute has not been enforced against it. *See, e.g.*, ACLU of Ill. v. Alvarez, 679 F.3d 583, 590–91 (7th Cir. 2012) (holding that a "plaintiff must show 'an intention to engage in a course of conduct arguably affected with a constitutional interest, but proscribed by a statute, and . . . a credible threat of prosecution thereunder'" (quoting Babbitt v. United Farm Workers Nat'l Union, 442 U.S. 289, 298 (1979))). Even when a plaintiff has engaged in some activity allowed by the statute, it may bring a challenge for actions it did not take for fear of prosecution. *See* Nat'l Org. for Marriage v. McKee, 649 F.3d 34, 50 (1st Cir. 2011) (rejecting the government's argument that "a 'plaintiff who engages in some conduct that is clearly proscribed cannot complain of the vagueness of the law as applied to the conduct of others'" (quoting Holder v. Humanitarian Law Project, 561 U.S. 1, 18–19 (2010))).

149. *See, e.g.*, *WRTL II*, 551 U.S. 449, 479 (2007) (applying strict scrutiny to a statute that regulated expenditure by non-profit corporations).

---

121 Unclear how author justifies ignoring valid precedent.

conduct by placing limits on campaign contributions;[150] and (3) those that compel the disclosure of information.[151] Regulations limiting expenditures must survive strict scrutiny,[152] those limiting contributions must survive "heightened" scrutiny,[153] and those requiring disclosures must survive a lesser "exacting" scrutiny.[154] When a statute's definition is used to impose several types of burdens, like North Carolina's political committee definition, the court should review the definition separately in the context of each application. —————122

Having identified the type of regulation at issue, the court must next determine that the government interest advanced by the regulation is sufficiently important to justify the burden on speech. The Supreme Court has held that preventing quid pro quo corruption or its appearance and preventing circumvention of regulations are the only sufficiently important government interests that would justify the imposition of contribution or expenditure limits.[155] The Court has characterized this interest as primarily being the prevention of quid pro quo bribery, wherein a donation is made to —————123 a candidate with the expectation that favorable government action will flow to the donor after the candidate is elected.[156] The Court has also recognized the government's interest in providing information to the electorate and in

---

150. McCutcheon v. FEC, 134 S. Ct. 1434, 1445 (2014) (declining to "revisit *Buckley*'s distinction between contributions and expenditures and the corollary distinction in the applicable standards of review").

151. *McKee*, 649 F.3d at 55 (applying exacting scrutiny to a statute which required disclosure). The court in *McKee* stated, "Since *Buckley*, the Supreme Court has distinguished . . . between laws that restrict 'the amount of money a person or group can spend on political communication' and laws that simply require disclosure . . . ." *Id.* (quoting Buckley v. Valeo, 424 U.S. 1, 19 (1976) (per curiam)).

152. *WRTL II*, 551 U.S. at 464; McConnell v. FEC, 540 U.S. 93, 205 (2003), *overruled in part on other grounds by Citizens United*, 558 U.S. 310; FEC v. Mass. Citizens for Life, Inc., 479 U.S. 238, 252 (1986); *Buckley*, 424 U.S. at 44–45.

153. *McConnell*, 540 U.S. at 144.

154. *McKee*, 649 F.3d at 55–56.

155. *McCutcheon*, 134 S. Ct. at 1441–42. At various times, the Court has also recognized that contribution limits might be justified by other governmental interests. *See, e.g.*, Nixon v. Shrink Mo. Gov't PAC, 528 U.S. 377, 401 (2000) (Breyer, J., concurring) (noting the government's strong interest in democratizing the influence of money in elections); Austin v. Mich. State Chamber of Commerce, 494 U.S. 652, 660 (1990) (identifying for the first time that the government has an interest in preventing "the corrosive and distorting effects" of aggregated wealth flowing into campaigns), *overruled by Citizens United*, 558 U.S. at 365; Burroughs v. United States, 290 U.S. 534, 545 (1934) (recognizing the government's interest in safeguarding the electoral process). The Court soundly rejected these other goals in *McCutcheon* and held "[a]ny regulation must instead target what we have called 'quid pro quo' corruption or its appearance." *McCutcheon*, 134 S. Ct. at 1441.

156. *Id.*

---

122 Why? What authority supports separate review?

123 It is important to step back and look at the original purpose of these statutes. What are we trying to accomplish? This test looks like it can help us accomplish our purposes.

698   CAMPBELL LAW REVIEW   [Vol. 40:2

gathering information to facilitate enforcement, and circuits around the country have nearly uniformly used this interest as sufficient justification to uphold disclosure and disclaimer requirements.[157]

After determining the government's purpose and its interest in achieving that purpose, the court must determine whether the law at issue actually accomplishes that purpose and whether it was drawn precisely enough to protect speech the government does not need to regulate to achieve that purpose. The critical inquiry is whether the statute or regulation has been drawn closely enough to achieve the government's stated purpose without unduly burdening the ability of the public to freely associate, pool resources, amplify individuals' voices, and engage meaningfully in the political process.

1. Strict Scrutiny Applied to Expenditure Limits

Regulations that limit expenditures must survive strict scrutiny.[158] The government must show that the statute or regulation is narrowly tailored to achieve the government's interest in preventing corruption.[159] While direct limitations have not been allowed since *Buckley*, the law may impose indirect limits to prevent circumvention of the law, for instance by treating coordinated expenditures as contributions and thereby subjecting them to limitations.[160] The Supreme Court has upheld such regulations as a

---

157. *Citizens United*, 558 U.S. at 369 (recognizing that (1) "the public has an interest in knowing who is speaking about a candidate shortly before an election" and (2) providing this information to the public is a sufficiently important government interest); *Buckley*, 424 U.S. at 66–67 (recognizing that disclosure laws further the government's sufficiently important interests in deterring actual corruption, avoiding the appearance of corruption, and "provid[ing] the electorate with information 'as to where political campaign money comes from and how it is spent'" (quoting H.R. REP. No. 92-564, at 4 (1971))); *see also McConnell*, 540 U.S. at 196; First Nat'l Bank of Boston v. Bellotti, 435 U.S. 765, 791–92 (1978).

158. Colo. Republican Fed. Campaign Comm. v. FEC, 518 U.S. 604 (1996) (holding that a law imposing expenditure limits on political parties could not survive strict scrutiny); FEC v. Nat'l Conservative PAC, 470 U.S. 480 (1985) (declaring expenditure limit on PACs unconstitutional).

159. *WRTL II*, 551 U.S. 449, 464 (2007).

160. *Compare McConnell*, 540 U.S. at 205 ("[R]ecent cases have recognized that certain restrictions on corporate electoral involvement permissibly hedge against 'circumvention of [valid] contribution limits.'" (second alteration in original) (quoting FEC v. Beaumont, 539 U.S. 146, 155 (2003)), *with WRTL II*, 551 U.S. at 479 (declining to recognize the anti-circumvention interest to justify application of a statute prohibiting a non-profit from airing issue ads). The Court in *WRTL II* acknowledged that there is a limit to how far the anti-circumvention interest can be extended. *Id.* (stating that "such a prophylaxis-upon-prophylaxis approach to regulating expression is not consistent with strict scrutiny").

---

124 Throughout this comment, the author has relied almost exclusively on primary sources. The constitutional analysis framework is strong and does not necessarily need to be supported by secondary source.

valid means of preventing circumvention.[161] It has, however, struck such regulations when they were applied to independent expenditures that did not pose the same risk of corruption.[162]

2. Heightened Scrutiny Applied to Contribution Limits

Regulations that impose contribution limits must survive heightened scrutiny, which requires that the statute be "closely drawn" to match the government's interest in "preventing corruption and the appearance of corruption."[163] Limitations on donations to candidates and parties can prevent quid pro quo corruption by limiting the amount of financial interest connecting a donor and candidate.[164] The further removed the candidate and donor are the more likely the government will need to rely on its interest in preventing the appearance of corruption—that is, preventing the public's *perception* that a quid pro quo arrangement has occurred.[165]

Whether such limitations survive heightened scrutiny will frequently depend on the identities of the contributor and recipient. The limitation will be most effective—and the regulation more closely drawn—when it prevents large financial contributions directly to a candidate from any source. Limitations applied to political parties rather than candidates are somewhat less effective because they are an intermediary between the donor and candidate.[166] Political parties use their resources to support a wide array of candidates, usually from diverse regions within a state and in different branches of government. Donations to the political parties are necessarily less likely to have the same kind of corrupting influence as donations made directly to a candidate.

The same logic leads to the conclusion that limitations on contributions to Super PACs are less likely to prevent quid pro quo

---

161. FEC v. Colo. Republican Fed. Campaign Comm., 533 U.S. 431, 465 (2001) (holding coordinated expenditures may be limited to minimize circumvention of contribution limits).

162. *Citizens United*, 558 U.S. at 357 (concluding "independent expenditures, including those made by corporations, do not give rise to corruption or the appearance of corruption").

163. *McConnell*, 540 U.S. at 173 (applying heightened scrutiny to regulation that limited campaign contributions); *Beaumont*, 539 U.S. at 162 (requiring that regulations limiting contributions be "closely drawn to match a sufficiently important interest" (internal quotations and citations omitted)); *see also* Nixon v. Shrink Mo. Gov't PAC, 528 U.S. 377, 386–88 (2000).

164. *McConnell*, 540 U.S. at 182 (holding that a ban on "soft-money" contributions was closely drawn to prevent corruption or the appearance of corruption).

165. *Id.* at 136.

166. McCutcheon v. FEC, 134 S. Ct. 1434, 1452 (2014) (reasoning that when money flows through independent actors, such as political parties, the risk of quid pro quo corruption is lower).

---

125 Need to explore the appearance of corruption as a valid governmental interest. Why is it important?

corruption, and thus less likely to survive the heightened scrutiny standard. When expenditures are not coordinated with the campaign, they have less value to the candidate, and the principals in the Super PAC are less likely to be accorded special favors by the candidate once elected (at least in theory).[167] Additionally, quid pro quo corruption requires prior subjective agreement, which cannot legally occur between a Super PAC and a candidate because, by definition, the Super PAC is prohibited from telling the candidate that it plans to assist the campaign.[168]

However, prior subjective agreement is not the only way that corruption or the appearance of corruption might occur. Let us return to our earlier example and imagine that John Hancock would like to support Ben in his run for state senate. He could contribute (i) $5,200 to Ben in both the primary and general election, (ii) an unlimited amount to the state party, (iii) $5,200 to the Senate caucus of Ben's party in both the primary and general election, and (iv) $5,200 to other candidates in Ben's party who don't have competitive races and can themselves contribute the maximum amount to Ben. This allows him to legally direct far more than the maximum allowable $10,400 to the candidate and makes it even more difficult to follow the flow of the money from the donor to the candidate.

Imagine then that Ben, who is fully aware of all of these legal donations, learns that Hancock has established a Super PAC. Does it really matter that they don't collaborate on the exact mailers to be sent by the PAC to potential voters? Ben knows that the Super PAC is supporting him. If the contribution limit is intended to prevent corruption by ensuring that an individual is not able to contribute a "corruptible" amount of money to Ben, does this system really accomplish the government's goal?

The court must carefully connect the limitation imposed to the government's interest in preventing not only outright corruption but also in preventing the appearance of corruption or the circumvention of the law. To the extent that a donor is able to easily circumvent the regulation by spending unlimited funds on behalf of a particular candidate, the government's interest may be undermined, thereby rendering the regulation underinclusive.

---

167. FEC v. Nat'l Conservative PAC, 470 U.S. 480, 497–98 (1985). In discussing the potential for corruption, the Court stated:

> The fact that candidates and elected officials may alter or reaffirm their own positions on issues in response to political messages paid for by the PACs can hardly be called corruption, for one of the essential features of democracy is the presentation to the electorate of varying points of view.

Id. at 498.

168. *See supra* Section I.B.

126   It seems like the system is not accomplishing the goal. Is this a problem that can be solved by the courts? Seems like this is a legislative problem.

3. Exacting Scrutiny Applied to Disclosure Laws

Regulations requiring disclosure must survive exacting scrutiny.[169] Providing information to the electorate is a "sufficiently important" governmental interest to justify the imposition of disclosure laws, as is its interest in preventing circumvention of the law by gathering information to enable enforcement.[170] While the law need not be narrowly tailored or even closely drawn, the government must show that it bears a substantial relation to those interests.[171]

It is not enough to simply say that the public has an interest in knowing the information. The government must show that the public has an interest in receiving the particular information it compels to be disclosed.[172] The court should also consider whether the government has shown that the information it gathers is actually made available to the public in a meaningful way and in a timely fashion to enable the public to evaluate the expenditures of money for campaign purposes prior to an election. The regulation can only bear a "substantial relation" to the government's interest if it is actually providing relevant information to voters prior to the election or using the disclosed information to enforce existing regulations and prevent circumvention.[173] While regulations in this context rarely fail due to overbreadth or vagueness, it is possible that a court could find that a regulation does not actually further the government's interest because it fails to capture enough relevant information, or because the government fails to make that information available to the public, or because the government fails to make meaningful use of the information once it has been disclosed.

B. First Amendment Overbreadth Analysis

After determining that the regulation is a justifiable means of furthering the state's interest, the court must determine whether the actual application of the statute is overbroad—that is, whether it has the potential

---

169. *See supra* note 97 and accompanying text; *see also* Buckley v. Valeo, 424 U.S. 1, 64 (1978) (stating that disclosure laws must survive exacting scrutiny).

170. *Buckley*, 424 U.S. at 66.

171. *Id.* at 64.

172. *Id.* (stating that there must "be a 'relevant correlation' or 'substantial relation'" between the governmental interest and the information required to be disclosed" (first quoting Bates v. City of Little Rock, 361 U.S. 516, 525 (1960); then quoting Gibson v. Fla. Legislative Comm., 372 U.S. 539, 546 (1963))).

173. *Id.* at 66–68.

---

127 Seems like this standard gets awfully close to potentially violating the 1st Amendment by regulating content.

128 Because not everyone can afford to speak, only certain voices/perspectives can ever be heard.

702   CAMPBELL LAW REVIEW   [Vol. 40:2

to sweep within its ambit too much protected speech.[174] The overbreadth doctrine is focused not on whether the statute is capable of achieving the government's interest, but rather on whether the government could employ narrower means to do so and thereby impose a lesser burden on protected speech. The Supreme Court has held that overbreadth is a "strong medicine" to be applied with hesitation and has consequently required that a statute must be *substantially* overbroad to justify being invalidated for overbreadth.[175]

Substantial overbreadth occurs when a statute poses a realistic danger of burdening "a substantial amount of constitutionally protected speech."[176] This analysis requires the court to conceive of every type of speech which may be regulated by the law and then analyze (1) how regulation of that speech is related to the government's stated interest, and (2) whether the burden of the regulation imposed might be so severe that it keeps the public from engaging in political discourse.[177]

The amount of protected speech that may be swept within the ambit of the statute without rendering it unconstitutionally overbroad is correlated to the severity of the burden imposed. When the state imposes expenditure limits, the statute must be narrowly tailored to avoid regulating protected speech at all, if possible. On the other hand, when the state seeks only to compel disclosure of information about speech rather than limiting the ability to speak, the law may burden a significant amount of protected speech and remain constitutional, because the burden imposed is so much less severe. It may be helpful to think of the regulation as a dart and protected speech as the concentric circles on the dart board. When the law requires disclosure, the government may win if its dart lands anywhere on the board, but as the burden on speech becomes more severe, the

---

174. Iowa Right to Life Comm. v. Tooker, 717 F.3d 576, 590 (8th Cir. 2013) (discussing extensively the disagreement among circuits as to whether "exacting scrutiny" requires narrow tailoring).

175. New York v. Ferber, 458 U.S. 747, 769 (1982). "[T]he overbreadth doctrine is 'strong medicine' and [we] have employed it with hesitation, and then 'only as a last resort.' We have, in consequence, insisted that the overbreadth involved be 'substantial' before the statute involved will be invalidated on its face." *Id.* (citation omitted) (quoting Broadrick v. Oklahoma, 413 U.S. 601, 613 (1973)).

176. City of Houston v. Hill, 482 U.S. 451, 466–67 (1987).

177. *See, e.g., id.* (holding a city ordinance unconstitutional because it did not allow "the 'breathing space' that 'First Amendment freedoms need to survive'" (quoting NAACP v. Button, 371 U.S. 415, 433 (1963))); *see also* ERWIN CHIMERINSKY, CONSTITUTIONAL LAW § 11.2 (5th ed. 2015). Relying on *City of Houston v. Hill*, Professor Chimerinsky notes "that substantial overbreadth might be demonstrated by showing a significant number of situations where a law could be applied to prohibit constitutionally protected speech." *Id.*

---

129 Should corporations have the right to political speech at all? It seems like individual voices are effectively silenced under this construct, and the construct is necessary to control potential corruption by corporations.

government must aim closer for the center. When it imposes expenditure limits, it only wins if it hits the bullseye.

C. First Amendment Vagueness Analysis

Even if the court finds that the law is adequately tailored to accomplish its purpose, it may still violate the First Amendment by allowing the government to discriminate on the basis of viewpoint.[178] The question for the court in reviewing a statute for vagueness under the First Amendment is whether the statute relies on standards that allow a regulator to justify a different application of the law to similar speakers or messages.[179] A law which relies on wholly subjective standards may leave room for discriminatory enforcement, resulting in viewpoint discrimination. The court must determine whether the law sets out ——————130 sufficiently precise guidance to ensure that decisions about enforcement will not be based on the viewpoint of the speaker. This review is based largely on the level of discretion given to the regulator, but also has in view the effect that such a subjective standard might have on the speaker who, unable to determine whether a regulator might enforce the law against him after he speaks, decides not to speak at all. This is particularly worrisome where a law regulating speech imposes criminal penalties, as is the case with North Carolina's campaign finance laws.

D. Fourteenth Amendment Vagueness Analysis

Because criminal penalties may increase the chilling effect on protected speech, courts frequently choose to combine the vagueness analysis under the First Amendment with the due process analysis under the Fourteenth Amendment, but this is not particularly helpful. In the ——————131 context of the First Amendment, the vagueness inquiry seeks to ensure that speakers are not forced to guess at the *application* and *enforcement* of a statute by a regulator.[180] In the context of the Fourteenth Amendment, the

---

178. *See* Grayned v. City of Rockford, 408 U.S. 104, 108 (1972) (stating that in order to avoid arbitrary and discriminatory enforcement, "laws must provide explicit standards for those who apply them")

179. *Id.*; *see also* Thomas v. Chi. Park Dist., 534 U.S. 316 (2002). Although the court in *Thomas* was considering a regulation that authorized issuance of permits for use of a public park, its reasoning is also applicable here. The Court held that "[w]here the licensing official enjoys unduly broad discretion in determining whether to grant or deny a permit, there is a risk that he will favor or disfavor speech based on its content." *Id.* at 323. Therefore, the Court required that a "regulation contain adequate standards to guide the official's decision." *Id.*

180. *See, e.g.*, Nat'l Org. for Marriage v. McKee, 649 F.3d 34, 62 (1st Cir. 2011) (stating that "the doctrine seeks to . . . prevent 'arbitrary and discriminatory enforcement' of laws by

130 The criminal penalties cannot be applied equally to individuals and corporations, either.

131 Why is this approach not helpful? What is the alternative?

vagueness inquiry seeks to ensure that the *meaning of the words* used in the statute are not susceptible of multiple interpretations, that is, that they give adequate notice to individuals of what behaviors are punishable.[181] Laws are impermissibly vague if they fail to "give [a] person of ordinary intelligence a reasonable opportunity to know what is prohibited."[182] If the law employs words with clear meaning, it will not violate the Fourteenth Amendment's due process as a result of vagueness.

132 ─

CONCLUSION

The result of the current campaign finance regime in North Carolina is that those with access to knowledgeable attorneys and accountants have a great deal more freedom to engage in political speech than those who do not. Even worse, the regulatory scheme is so fragmented and ineffectual that it no longer serves the government's interests in regulating campaign finance.   Circumvention, obfuscation, and erroneous reporting are common.[183] It is hard to imagine that this complex system of categorizing speech and speakers is accomplishing its purposes without drastically chilling political speech, which is why it is even more critical that the court be very precise in its analysis of the legislature's attempts to regulate campaign finance.

133 ─

The public's trust in our electoral system is eroding, and the legislature should act to update the laws and give them new teeth, and it should do so soon. When it does, and when the court is inevitably asked to once again evaluate the campaign finance scheme, the court should be as deliberate as possible, following a methodical framework to lay out its

requiring that they 'provide explicit standards for those who apply them'" (quoting *Grayned*, 408 U.S. at 108)); United States v. Hussein, 351 F.3d 9, 14 (1st Cir. 2003) (stating that a "statute is susceptible to [a vagueness] attack if it . . . prohibits or requires the performance of an act in terms so uncertain that persons of average intelligence would have no choice but to guess at its meaning").

181. *Grayned*, 408 U.S. at 108 (stating that a statute or regulation "is void for vagueness if its prohibitions are not clearly defined").

182. *Id.* For a thorough discussion of the two types of vagueness challenges, see Ctr. for Individual Freedom, Inc. v. Tennant, 849 F. Supp. 2d 659, 671–72 (S.D. W. Va. 2011); Holder v. Humanitarian Law Project, 561 U.S. 1, 18–21 (2010).

183. *See* Craig Jarvis, *Watchdog Group Calls on Sen. Hise to Recuse Himself over Campaign Finance Accusations*, NEWS & OBSERVER (May 9, 2017, 7:18 PM), https://perma.cc/8ZAR-2DAE; Nick Ochsner, *FBI to Probe Top House Republicans After WBTV Investigation*, CHARLOTTE OBSERVER (Dec. 31, 2015, 4:49 PM), https://perma.cc/43XE-VLF7; Travis Fain, *Berger's Campaign Audited, Forfeits $5,500*, WRAL (Aug. 16, 2017), https://perma.cc/3V8R-MEP4; Jim Morrill, *Charlotte Democratic Lawmaker's Unreported Campaign Contributions Prompt State Review*, CHARLOTTE OBSERVER (Nov. 16, 2017, 11:30 AM), https://perma.cc/5L5X-CKCK.

---

132 What is the significance and consequence?

133 Should the court declare the statutory scheme unconstitutional? Does the court really have the power to fix this problem?

decision so that it may be properly applied by the legislature when it once again responds with statutory revisions. Those statutory revisions are sorely needed, whether as a result of judicial action, or on the legislature's own initiative. The current scheme—rather than rooting out corruption and influence—appears to have the opposite effect: those with the most money are able to manipulate the law to get their message out to the public and their interests in front of elected officials, while those without such resources are silenced by the fear of prosecution lest they run afoul of this complex system of regulation and be subjected to criminal penalties. It is the difference between being given a megaphone and being given a kazoo.

*Anna V. Stearns**

—134

* J.D. 2018, Campbell University School of Law. The author would like to thank Professors Elizabeth Berenguer and Richard Bowser, who have given freely of their time, intellect, and wisdom to help develop this Comment, as well as Jordan Spanner, Ally Mashburn, Chris Moore, and the rest of the *Campbell Law Review* staff for their helpful comments, feedback, and support in preparing this Comment for publication.

134 Unclear how the courts could revise the statutes. At most, they can force the legislature to do that by declaring the statutory scheme unconstitutional.

Part III: Sample Outlines of Scholarly Writing

Part III provides outlines of different scholarly works to demonstrate the organizational paradigms and analytical frameworks explained in Chapters 5 and 6. For articles that have a table of contents, the table has been reproduced as the outline. For any articles that did not have a table of contents, I have created an outline of the organizational paradigm. Since a student comment has already been provided in full in Part II of this Appendix, I have not included an outline for a student comment. These samples include select articles demonstrating different organizational paradigms and analytical frameworks, a student note, and a dissertation for your reference.

1. Student Note: Lucy Jewel, *Something Seems Fishy—The Application of the Fourth Amendment to Coast Guard Searches of Vessels:* United States v. Boynes, 23 Tul. Mar. L.J. 553, 566 (1999).
   - I.   Introduction of facts of *United States v. Boynes*
   - **135** —— II. General explanation of Fourth Amendment in context of maritime law
   - III. Critical analysis of *Boynes* in light of Fourth Amendment maritime jurisprudence
   - IV. Conclusion

2. Article using Comparative Paradigm: James Q. Whitman, *Consumerism Versus Producerism: A Study in Comparative Law*, 117 Yale L.J. 340 (2007).
   - I.   Introduction
   - **136** —— II. Beyond the Civil Law/Common Law Dichotomy: Comparative Law as Social Science
   - III. Consumerism Versus Producerism: A Brief History of a Distinction
   - **137** —— IV. Refining the Distinction
   - V. Atlantic Conflicts: Antitrust and Retail Pricing
   - VI. Regulating Retail: Hours, Merchandise, Square Footage
   - **138** —— VII. Consumerism, Producerism, and the Culture of Rights
   - **139** ——VIII. Consumerism and Producerism Across the Landscape of the Law
   - **140** —— IX. Conclusion

3. Article using Problem/Solution Paradigm: Teri A. McMurtry-Chubb, *Burn This Bitch*
   - **141** —— *Down: Mike Brown, Emmett Till, and the Gendered Politics of Black Parenthood*, 17 Nev. L.J. 619, 650 (2017).
   - **142** —— I.   Introduction: "Black Parenthood as Lethal"

---

135 This Note follows the traditional paradigm of introduction of the case, explanation of law generally, critique of the particular case, and conclusion.

136 This section offers a critique of the traditional comparativist approach and framework.

137 These sections describe the background of the relevant dichotomy.

138 These sections describe the salient features that govern producerism and consumerism.

139 This section analyzes the interaction of consumerism and producerism.

140 On the whole, we see explanation of A (producerism) and B (consumerism) and then analysis of how these lenses interact with the landscape of the law.

141 The author relies on a framework utilizing critical gender and critical race theories.

142 The introduction provides salient examples to support the author's ultimate thesis.

4. Dissertation using Historical Paradigm: Judge Bradley Letts, *The Cherokee Tribal Court: Its Origins and Its Place in the American Judicial System*

I. INTRODUCTION

II. BRIDGERS' ARTICLE

    a. In 1979, Ben published *An Historical Analysis of the Legal Status of the North Carolina Cherokees.* It is currently the only authoritative source on Cherokee——146 and North Carolina state law. This dissertation is an update to that article.

III. CHEROKEE SINCE 1979

    a. *"Most people think casino gambling will be what alcohol was to the Indians of___147 past generations. I have seen these Indians, and you have more Indian blood than they have."* Donald Trump

    b. Francis X. Clines, *The Pequots,* N.Y. Times, February 27, 1994

    c. *Background & Legal History of the Eastern Band of Cherokee Indians*

    d. *Changes Since 1979*

    e. *Government to Government Relations with the Cherokee Tribe*

    f. *Indian Gaming*

    g. *Harrah's Cherokee Casino & Resort*

    h. *Economic Development in Cherokee*

IV. THE CHEROKEE TRIBAL COURT & ITS PLACE IN THE AMERICAN JUSTICE SYSTEM ——148

    a. *CFR Court*

    b. *CFR Court in Cherokee*

    c. *The Establishment of the Cherokee Tribal Court*

    d. *The Doctrine of Tribal Court Exhaustion*

    e. *Transfer of Venue to Tribal Court*

    f. *Application of Tribal Law in North Carolina State Court*

    g. *Certified Questions of Law from the Cherokee Court to the Cherokee Tribal Council*

    h. *The Legal Doctrines of Full Faith & Credit and Comity*

    i. *Contempt Powers in the Cherokee Tribal Court*

---

143 The author exposes the problems inherent in black parenthood in America.

144 The author emphasizes and analyzes how two specific problems were confronted, one by Emmett Till's mother, the other by Mike Brown's father.

145 In the conclusion, the author calls for the destruction of "the falsehood of patriarchy as a savior for Black families and communities" and for recognition of "the role [that] white supremacy [has played] in creating instability in Black communities." She offers the solution of recognizing "Black fathers['] . . . right to participate in their children's lives and [for protection] from a system of white supremacy that would render Black fatherhood unnecessary and obsolete."

146 This dissertation is an update to an article written in 1979. It relies in large part on a historical framework. The author begins by situating the dissertation in the existing discourse community.

147 The author provides a historical background of changes in the law since the last article was written in 1979. This part seems to be more descriptive than analytical.

148 This section of the dissertation seems to take somewhat of a descriptive approach, describing the tribal legal system and its intersection with North Carolina law.

V. CIVIL JURISDICTIONAL DEVELOPMENTS IN CHEROKEE
149————— a. *Sovereign Immunity of the EBCI*
  b. *Civil Jurisdiction on the Lands of the Eastern Band of Cherokee Indians*
  c. *Control of the Land and Skies by the Cherokee Tribe*
    i. *Land*
    ii. *Skies*
  d. *Guns*
  e. *Hunting & Fishing*
  f. *Intellectual Property in Indian Country*
  g. *Alcohol*
  h. *Employment Law in Cherokee*
  i. *Sex Discrimination in Indian Country*
  j. *Health Care on Cherokee Lands and in Facilities Operated by the Cherokee Tribe*
  k. *Taxation on the Eastern Cherokee Lands*
  l. *Membership & Voting on the Cherokee Reservation*
  m. *Protection of Indian Arts & Crafts*
  n. *Tribal Control of Environmental Regulations*
  o. *Protection of Graves & Cherokee Cultural Artifacts*
VI. DOMESTIC & FAMILY RELATIONS JURISDICTIONAL DEVELOPMENTS
  a. *Child Custody Actions*
  b. *Indian Child Welfare Act in the Cherokee Tribal Court*
  c. *DSS Court*
  d. *Uniform Child Custody & Jurisdiction Act ("UCCJEA")*
  e. *Parental Kidnapping Prevention Act ("PKPA")*
  f. *Child Support in the Tribal Court*
  g. *Guardianships*
  h. *Marriage in Cherokee*
  i. *Divorce in the Tribal Court*
  j. *Juvenile Delinquency*
  k. *Education*
  l. *Probate*
VII. CRIMINAL JURISDICTIONAL DEVELOPMENTS IN CHEROKEE
  a. *History of Criminal Law in Cherokee, North Carolina*
  b. *Who Is an Indian?: Definition of Indian and Indian Tribe for Purposes of Criminal Jurisdiction*
  c. *Criminal Jurisdiction in Indian Country & on the Qualla Boundary*
  d. *Criminal Jurisdiction over Non-Indians*
  e. *Oliphant v. Suquamish Indian Tribe decision & the "Duro Fix"*
  f. *A Civil Solution for Regulating Conduct of Non-Indians on Cherokee Lands*

---

149 These sections provide a comprehensive analysis of current tribal jurisprudence and its relationship to North Carolina law. Some portions of this analysis look through a comparative analytical lens while others take an interdisciplinary approach. Legal realism through a tribal rhetorical lens frames the analysis as well. Notice the breadth of a dissertation is much broader than an article. This particular dissertation is effectively a treatise.

APPENDIX **X**

Citations for
Scholarly Writing

THE BLUEBOOK

The Bluebook is divided into three major sections:

1. light blue pages for practitioners
2. white pages for scholarly articles (and more details for practitioners)
3. tables for particular jurisdictions, abbreviations, and other similar categories

For a scholarly article, you should rely exclusively on the white pages.

Consult the outside back cover for quick reference to the rules; consult the inside front cover for a quick reference for law review footnotes. In the twentieth edition, use

- Rule 10 for citation rules for cases
- Rules 11-14 for citation rules for constitutions and legislative materials
- Rules 15-18 for citation rules to periodicals and other secondary services
- Rules 20-21 for citation rules for foreign and international materials

Small Caps: One of the conventions of scholarly writing is the use of small caps. You might have noticed that in the samples throughout the *Bluebook*, certain citations include small caps. For example, the citation to the U.S. Constitution requires certain letters to be in small caps and others to be in lowercase. Certain titles of other publications also require the use of small caps.

How to create small caps: In Word, click the small arrow in the Font Ribbon to bring up the Font Box. Click the small caps option to turn on small caps.

Put citations in footnotes, not text.

Use a shorthand for citations in early drafts.

- Stopping to put every citation into correct format as you write interrupts the flow of the writing process.
- Using short cites like "*id.*" or "*supra*" or "*infra*" correctly in early drafts will inevitably lead to confusion during the editing process as citations are "orphaned" when you move text.

- Finalizing footnotes should occur during the last editing phase of the article.
- *Id., supra,* and *infra* are shorthand citations that eliminate the need to retype the entire citation either in long form or short form. You should not use any of these shorthands until you are in a final editing stage of your project.

OTHER HELPFUL HINTS

If you decide to use one of the "helpers" described below, remember that you are ultimately responsible for ensuring your citations conform to whatever style is required by your publisher. Often, the automatic generators produce a correct citation, but there is always a chance the citation is not 100 percent correct. Use samples and automatic generators as a guide to get you started with correct citation format, but confirm citations are correct by consulting the governing style manual itself. The editors for your journal will also review the citations to ensure they conform with their style sheets.

I. ALWD Guide to Legal Citation

While citation formats in the *ALWD Guide* are substantially similar to those created following *Bluebook* rules, the *Guide* itself is more user-friendly. The *Guide* begins with introductory material explaining the purposes and uses of citation and important information on how to use the *Guide*. It then moves on to citation basics, specific rules for different sources, specific rules for online sources, guidance for incorporating citations into documents, and instructions for properly quoting. If the *Bluebook* is daunting to you, consider referencing the *ALWD Guide* instead. You may find the *ALWD Guide* makes it easier for you to understand how to build and place citations in your article.

II. HEINOnline

Conveniently, every article you pull from HEINOnline includes a cover page with sample citations for the most common citation formats. Here is an example of the citation options on the cover page for the Megale article annotated in Appendix IX.

III. Zotero

Zotero has a collection of citation databases through which you can choose to have the program format your citations in whatever format your publisher requires. To select your preference, click on Edit, Preferences, Cite and then select your preferred citation style. If your preferred style does not appear in the list, you can click on "get additional styles" to download a different one.

To generate a citation, you can click on "copy citation" under the Edit tab or use the citation feature integrated into your word processor.

Revising, Editing, and Proofreading

Once you have turned your outline into a draft paper, you can use this appendix to guide you through the revising, editing, and proofreading phases of the project.

REMINDERS FOR WRITING A GOOD ARTICLE

- Choose a topic
- Conduct a preemption check
- Research
- Purposefully read authorities
- Create a research summary
- Create an annotated outline
- Choose an organizational paradigm
- Choose an analytical framework
- Hook the reader with a persuasive introduction
- Provide sufficient background
- Use parallel constructions
    - Be consistent in the order of thoughts throughout paragraphs, sentences, phrases, series, etc.
- Move from general to specific
    - Lead with strongest points
    - Deal with most important issues first
    - Accommodate your order to the law
- Limit the topic
- Focus on strengths, but avoid excessive zeal
- Deal with weaknesses

Ask yourself:

- What am I trying to say?
- What words best express it?
- What image can make this clear?
- Is this image fresh enough to have an effect?
- Could I express this more concisely?
- Have I said anything that is avoidably ugly?

Checklist (follow these steps in order/each stage may take weeks and multiple passes to complete):

Stage 1: Identify the organizational paradigm and analytical framework.

A. What is the question?
B. Does this organization scheme advance the goal of answering the question?
C. Does the analytical framework provide a systematic method for studying the question?
D. Ask yourself:
    1. Does the central point emerge quickly and clearly?
    2. Is the logic explicit and sound (in other words, have you best expressed what you are trying to say and do you have support for what you are saying)?
    3. Have counterarguments been rebutted?
    4. Do the arguments flow from one to the next?
E. Is the tone relaxed but definitive? Some other advice at this stage:
    1. Do not make nitpicky refinements, but feel free to make broad edits for obvious errors in spelling, punctuation, and headings.
    2. Read the document as a whole.

Stage 2: Revise the document to improve usage and style.

A. Identify whether you have misused any of these common words or phrases:
    1. Hold (courts only)
    2. Reason (courts only)
    3. Argue (parties only)
    4. Find (juries or courts only)
    5. Contend (parties only)
    6. Claim (parties only)
    7. Allege (parties only)
    8. Whether (alternatives)
    9. If (conditions)
    10. Since (relationship in time)
    11. Because (causal relationships)
    12. Due to (a debt owed)
    13. There is (get rid of it!)
    14. There are (get rid of it!)

15. It is (get rid of it!)
16. -ion (Is the word that ends in -ion a nominalization? If so, choose a stronger noun, preferably an actor instead of a thing, and convert nominalization back to a verb.)
17. Which (use for alternative information)
18. That (use to set off necessary information)

B. Eliminate legalisms.
C. Eliminate prepositional phrases that prop up wordy constructions.
D. Correct any obvious faults in word choice, grammar, or punctuation.
E. Read through at the paragraph and sentence level.
1. Underline the subject of each sentence once, verbs twice.
2. Ensure subjects and verbs agree and that there is a subject and verb for each sentence.
3. Is the subject the focus of the sentence?
4. Is the verb accurate?
5. Are the subject and verb too separated in the sentence?
F. Correct punctuation.
1. For items in a series, use a comma before the last "and"
2. Include commas and periods inside quotations marks; semicolons and colons outside quotation marks.
3. Semicolons separate two independent clauses.
4. Commas need a conjunction if separating two independent clauses.
G. Check for commonly misspelled words.
1. Trail/Trial
2. Judgement/Judgment
3. Statue/Statute
4. Form/From
5. Tortuous/Tortious
6. Principle/Principal
H. Avoid the first person.
I. Avoid contractions.

Stage 3: Refine to improve readability.

A. Eliminate the wall of words.
1. A good rule of thumb is for each page to have at least two paragraph breaks.
2. Can long paragraphs be broken down?
3. Can short paragraphs be combined?
B. Underline the topic sentence of each paragraph.
C. Ensure each sentence communicates one main idea.
D. Ensure sentences flow together with accurate transitions.
E. Cut each sentence by 25 percent.
1. Collapse sentences into clauses, clauses into phrases, and phrases into single words.
2. Replace long words with shorter ones.
3. Replace fancy words with simpler ones.
4. Eliminate "which" and "that" to the extent possible.

Stage 4: Polishing.

A. Read the document aloud — make notations but do not stop to fix anything.
   1. Can a point be clarified through example or analogy?
   2. Is clear who is doing what to whom?
   3. Do ideas flow smoothly?
   4. Is there a sense of momentum carrying the reader on?
   5. Have you quoted only where necessary?
   6. Are quotes incorporated into the narrative?
   7. Are there any choppy sentences?
   8. Are there any confusing sentences or paragraphs?
   9. Circle any typos.
B. Fix choppy places by adding in transitions.
C. Simplify the writing to better communicate ideas.
D. Correct typos.
E. Finalize footnotes.
   1. Use a full citation the first time you cite a source.
   2. Use *infra* and *supra* when appropriate.
   3. Use short citations after you have fully cited the source.
   4. Use *id.* appropriately.
   5. Use small caps appropriately.
   6. Underline or italicize citations appropriately. (See Appendix III.)
   7. Include text in footnotes to provide the reader with necessary background information that is not necessary in text.

COMMONLY USED TRANSITIONS[1]

Transitions

For Contrast:

however	nevertheless	but
on the other hand	conversely	still yet
by (in) contrast	notwithstanding	instead
on the contrary	nonetheless	though
contrary to _____	alternatively	although
unlike _____	even so	even though
despite _____	rather	

---

1. An early version of this chart of common transitions was provided to me in Spring or Fall 2000 by my law school professor David Walter, now director of legal writing at Florida International University in Miami, Florida.

For Comparison:

similarly	analogously	in like manner
likewise	in the same way	for the same reason

For Cause and Effect:

therefore	accordingly	hence
consequently	thus	since
as a result	because	so
for		

For Addition:

also	moreover	besides
further	too	and
in addition	additionally	furthermore

For Examples:

for example	to illustrate	specifically
for instance	namely	that is

For Emphasis:

in fact	certainly	still
above all	indeed	clearly

For Evaluation:

more important	surprisingly	unquestionably
unfortunately	allegedly	fortunately
arguably		

For Restatement:

in other words	more simply	to put it differently
that is	simply put	

For Concession:

granted	of course	to be sure

For Resumption After a Concession:

still	nonetheless	all the same
nevertheless	even so	

For Time:

subsequently	later	earlier
recently	eventually	afterwards
meanwhile	shortly thereafter	until now
initially	simultaneously	since
formerly	at the time	by the time

For Place:

adjacent to	here	nearby
next to	beyond	opposite to

For Sequence:

first, second, third	next	then
former, latter	final	later
in the first place	finally	primary, secondary

For Conclusion:

in summary	in brief	thus
in sum	in short	therefore
to sum up	to conclude	consequently
finally	in conclusion	to (in) review

INDEX